Decades Behind Bars

Decades Behind Bars

A 20-Year Conversation with Men in America's Prisons

GAYE D. HOLMAN

McFarland & Company, Inc., Publishers

Jefferson, North Carolina

ISBN (print) 978-1-4766-6923-6
ISBN (ebook) 978-1-4766-2848-6

LIBRARY OF CONGRESS CATALOGUING DATA ARE AVAILABLE

British Library cataloguing data are available

Front cover image © 2017 iStock

Printed in the United States of America

*McFarland & Company, Inc., Publishers
Box 611, Jefferson, North Carolina 28640
www.mcfarlandpub.com*

Acknowledgments

I owe much to many in the writing of this book. My completion of the manuscript is due in large part to the consistent support and encouragement of my three talented, diverse friends who are members of my valued writing group. They kept me on task, held me up when I was drowning in doubt and plied me with laughter. Susan Lindsey's professional editing skills add immeasurably to the book's clarity. Her patience, organization, and extraordinary knowledge of both words and computers saved me from overwhelming embarrassment and frustration. Katie Bush, one of the readers of the final draft, helped me forge a better narrative with her keen insights and probing questions. She helped balance my perspective with her well-timed humor. Bobbie Bryant served as a worthy model with her constant energy, dedication, and thoughtfulness, and she inspired me by completing three books of her own.

I also owe a great deal of appreciation to both Larry Chandler and Dr. Glenn Johnson who kindly agreed to read and respond to my final manuscript. Larry Chandler, a long-time correctional employee and administrator, kept me straight on the nuances of Corrections and added to my own knowledge, insights, and writing in many valuable ways. Glenn Johnson suffered through innumerable early drafts and, with insightful questions, ensured that this book had meaning to someone unfamiliar with the correctional process. His encouragement has been most appreciated.

I would also like to thank my son Matt Holman, who on his busiest days took time out to give me feedback on my latest chapter, and my son Dan Holman, who warmly encouraged me to move ahead with the project.

I am extraordinarily appreciative of the many people who generously shared their time, knowledge, and experiences with me. Their input helped this be a more balanced, objective work. Those include Dr. Amy Smith, Keith Hardison, Phil Bramblett, Betsi Cunningham, Russell Cunningham, and Paige McGuire.

I also feel deep gratitude to the many others who prefer to stay anonymous in this political atmosphere. They deserve public thanks as well, but they know who they are and I hope they realize how valuable their help has been.

Lastly, there is no way I can express the depth of my appreciation to the imprisoned men who spent hours on this project—talking with me and writing lengthy letters and essays over a period of years. They dug into painful memories that opened new emotional wounds and shared the private thoughts and experiences that haunt their solitary moments. They have made serious mistakes in their lives, but their efforts with this project demonstrate that everyone has something valuable to give to others. My appreciation of their efforts is sincere and deep.

Table of Contents

Preface

For two decades, I walked through steel gates, into sally ports, and across prison yards into a world unfamiliar to most people, a world that was home to thousands of convicted felons. I was educating inmates, and in a few years, I became coordinator of my community college's prison program, which gave me free access to all of the area prisons. I taught sociology in three male facilities and a women's prison, and helped establish college programs for men and women in five community-custody facilities. I worked with the wardens and deputy wardens and their bosses in the central office.[1]

In 1994, after ten years of working in Kentucky prisons, I received a sabbatical from my school and permission from the Department of Corrections to conduct a study among the male inmates at two medium-security facilities in the Louisville area. Fifty men worked with me, discussing in writing and personal interviews every aspect of their complicated lives. My idea was to bring their voices alive, to explain the prison experience and the things that brought them there by using their own words. The men opened themselves to me, digging into emotions that some said they had never spoken of before.

I produced a manuscript, used it for various projects, and filed it away.

I am no longer working in the prisons, but I am involved in reentry efforts, helping released men get a new start in the community. Recently, I came across a man who was in my first prison class. We reminisced about the various men we knew, and I started wondering about them. I scoured our state's inmate website, seeing if I could find people I remembered. I found some of them still in prison, their appearance greatly changed from my memories. Many had hair thinned or gone. Some had gained weight. All had aged considerably. Few looked really well. I had kept up with some of the other, more recent students after their paroles or release. They had called me over the years as they were freed, and gave me occasional updates about their lives. I hadn't forgotten the men, but I had forgotten that earlier study.

One day it came to me like a lightning bolt. I had a wealth of data and information—information of a depth I had not seen elsewhere. It was now exactly twenty years later. Twenty years after fifty men had openly shared their hopes for their lives, things they feared, things they would work for. Where were are they today? I wondered.

I approached the Kentucky Department of Corrections, and jumped through the hoops of forms, description of the proposed procedure, and multiple layers of approval. I received permission to conduct a follow-up study. They kindly agreed to update the whereabouts of the men in my original study. To my great surprise, of the original fifty, fifteen were still in prison. Nine had been released and were on parole, still under the control of a parole officer. DOC could help me contact those men. The others had served out their sentences and I would be on my own to find them. I knew that two of them were dead.

I found I was reluctant to insert myself into the lives of those who I hoped had moved on since their time in prison. My interest kept turning to those who were still incarcerated so many years later, and I decided to focus on them. The original project was to talk about prison and what imprisonment means to a man. Now, I wondered, what does it mean to a man to be locked away most of his life? The original subjects were all college students at the time—which means most were among the brightest and most motivated inmates. Their discussions years ago had been insightful. What would they say now?

In addition to the remaining men in the original study, I added two more men to the list—men who had been in prison in 1994 and with whom I had kept in touch, but who were not part of the first study. A third man was added whom I got to know through reentry efforts just as he was returned to prison. He too had been in prison in 1994 and most years since. One of the original group was released before I could make contact with him.

After rereading all their writings from twenty years ago, I wrote each of the seventeen men a personal letter. I explained what I was doing and sent him a form to sign giving his permission to be part of the study. I asked questions that arose from what he said so many years ago. I also sent a long list of generic questions to each man. And then I waited to see if I would hear from anyone.

The letters started arriving. For both sides, it was like hearing from old friends.

The former students remembered things about me and our classes that surprised me and that I had forgotten. One man said I was the first person he had heard from in three years; another shared he had advanced Huntington's disease, his writing scrawled almost illegibly across the pages. The first letters often shared news of the death of parents; little was said about other personal relationships that I knew they had at an earlier time. They agreed to help with my new study.

I was worried about the cost of postage and paper in an environment where money is important and most often scarce. They said not to worry about it. They were glad to cover it. I heard from all of the men, and a fascinating correspondence began.

Today there is little available to help the public understand the nuances of imprisonment. But it is important that everyone knows more than the statistics behind the broken system. We need to know, at a very personal level, what it means to incarcerate someone for most of his life.

This book expands the public conversation about incarceration. Here the men speak firsthand about their experiences and their personal changes over the years—for better or worse. This book has a solid academic foundation, but it is a book for the masses. It is a book for anyone who has seen a shackled, expressionless man on TV and wondered what he was thinking or what brought him to that point. It gives us an honest and sometimes surprising look into the lives of men who have caused serious harm, who have lost everything, but who still fight to be seen by themselves and others as meaningful individuals.

Through the words of the inmates—from both the 1994 study and my more recent correspondence—readers will learn what daily life in prison is like. They will hear what imprisonment means to an individual. The readers will gain an understanding of both the positive and negative influences that the long-term prison experience brings to inmates and all involved with them. They will learn what forces save some men and what forces destroy others. Perhaps the readers will understand what it really means to lock up a man for decades.

The men in this study are housed in state correctional facilities, which are run by state authorities for those convicted of a state felony of more than one year. Inmates convicted of federal crimes serve their time in federal institutions.

While all the inmates have spent time in jail, most of their incarceration has been in prisons. Jails are used to incarcerate those waiting for trial or transfer and those with misdemeanors or felonies with less than a year's sentence. Jails operate differently from prisons and are not included in this book's discussion.

Private prisons are run by for-profit corporations and contract with local, state, and federal facilities. The debate on the use of private prisons has been long and heated.

The individuals in this study are representative of our nation's incarcerated. The difficulties they face, the effects of their incarceration on their families and friends, and the horrendous costs to our society, monetary and otherwise, are universal. The words from these men in Kentucky could have been spoken by any prisoner who has spent decades behind bars.

I have kept the identities of most of the inmates in this study anonymous by changing their names. Although some insisted I could use their real names, I know of their vulnerabilities while incarcerated. I would not want their trust in me used against them in the future.

The same is true of most of the staff and administration who are identified only by their positions. I conducted my interviews with them mostly off-site, over meals or coffee. Correctional employees are a tight brotherhood with intricate social networks. In order to talk openly, many required anonymity.

This book is limited to male inmates. In working with both male and female offenders, I have observed that the lives of these two incarcerated groups are surprisingly different. The women have a powerful message as well, but the two experiences cannot appropriately be covered together. At another time and place, the women's experiences can be studied, but within the covers of this book, we are entering the walls of male institutions.

Each reader will bring his or her own experiences to the conversational table. Each will come with a different personal agenda. Some readers may have been victims of crime and are hurting. Others may have incarcerated family members or friends and will be distressed. Some may be involved in law enforcement or have family members who work in the justice system and see things from that perspective.

To enter the criminal justice system is to enter a subculture unfamiliar to many. A glossary is included at the end of the book to help the reader understand the vocabulary that is common in everyday prison life. A list of issues to consider is included at the end of each chapter to stimulate thought and further conversations. Notes and a bibliography are offered if the reader becomes interested in learning more about the innumerable related areas.

I've tried to present this material objectively. I lay responsibility on the readers to examine the feelings that wash through them upon reading about these men and to reconcile those emotions with their preconceived thoughts. As the author, I am motivated by the hope that in this process, new conversations will be started and new questions voiced.

Introduction

The first time I walked across the prison yard alone and unescorted, there wasn't a soul in sight. It was "count," a time when the eleven hundred medium-security male inmates were frozen in place, their heads being carefully counted and often re-counted. I remember feeling apprehension, but it was more the first-day-of-class jitters than worry about my surroundings. That was soon to change.

The officer started yelling at me the minute I entered the school doors.

"You're late," he barked.

I withered as he fussed and complained about the difficulties I had caused.

"I can't leave 'em in a room by themselves," he continued. "Can't have 'em bunched up like this either."

The inmates, crowded uncomfortably on wooden benches and standing shoulder to shoulder in the hallway, watched with amusement as I stammered about miscommunicated starting times and offered apologies.

The officer's anger soon turned to stony silence as he pivoted and led the parade of teacher and students up a stark tile-walled stairway, around several corners. On the way, one inmate whispered to me, "Don't let him bother you." We stopped at a room where green plants lined the windowsills and trailed their leaves from the top of the bookshelves.

"Find your seats and sit down," the officer barked at the men. "And don't put up with nothin' from them," he said to me before disappearing to take care of other duties.

Still shaken from the experience with the officer, I looked at my new students who were watching carefully to figure out what would happen in this encounter. They were like all new students—eager, apprehensive, waiting—but I knew they were all convicted men. I had been told they had killed, raped, abused. In those days, they were all still dressed in their own clothing rather than in khaki uniforms, so they looked like any all-male class. Some looked curious. Others were amused. Most had sympathetic, welcoming expressions as if they knew the emotions that flowed through me. An exception sat in the far back corner. A hulking young blond with a set jaw glared at me. I recognized his face from weeks of news stories—he had shot a cop in the head in a high-profile undercover drug deal gone bad.

Off to a rough start, I decided to come clean. I told them I had just returned to Louisville. This was the first class I had taught for the college. It was the first time I had taught an all-male class. It was the first time I had taught in a prison. I admitted the incident with the officer had me a bit shaken, and I apologized that they had to wait and be put in a difficult situation. I said I would help them with sociology; they would have to help me learn how to operate within the prison. It was the right tone. Only later did I learn why.

The students were happy being assigned to "the plant room."

"It's pretty," someone with a country twang said.

I was happy too—a sociologist having the opportunity to get to know firsthand about prisons. We were back on the right path. But as we started this journey together—twenty-two male felons and a forty-four-year-old, five-foot-tall woman barely topping a hundred pounds—I had no idea where my road with them, and the hundreds who came afterward, was going to lead. They were to change the direction of my life and the way I perceived the world around me.

During the first ten years, I came to know the prisoners personally. I slowly passed their subtle tests, establishing the delicate line between authority and respect. I was in a unique position. I was not an employee of the Department of Corrections (DOC), but had free access within the institution. I followed the rules to a T, but it was clear that I refused to get into the area of discipline and write-ups, as I wanted to stay free from the identification with Corrections. I didn't have to follow the rigid chain of command that shackles new ideas and problem-solving. I was free to knock on administrators' doors.

And after I aged a bit, even the officers relaxed a little. In the early days, they did not approve of women working on the yard in male institutions and seemed convinced that romance, or worse, was the inevitable outcome.

I was often amused as I realized that, in some ways, I gradually became invisible to the people who worked there. Knowing that I wasn't part of the DOC chain of command, employees talked freely among themselves and interacted with prisoners in a way that I don't believe they would have if they thought I could be involved in write-ups or disciplinary actions against them. I saw and heard things that helped balance what I heard from the prisoners. It gave me a clearer perspective on the reality of things that happen behind bars.

Trust and respect are key concepts within the prison population. Both have to be carefully established and always adhered to. I learned not to ask or push too much, but by developing a sensitive "internal antennae" system, I came to detect things to question or rethink.

The appreciation the men felt towards many of the outsiders coming in to work with special programs went a long way in eventually getting to know them. When they felt respected, the men began to lower their defensive façades and share more of themselves. But volunteers had a challenge not to get overly involved, to not forget the areas of gray that surround the sharing of any anecdotes. Volunteers were often used for sympathy and became foils in inmate manipulations.

Over the years, I sorted through the confusing maze of establishing trust mixed with mutual respect, understanding, appropriate skepticism, and a greater tolerance of ambiguity.

To understand prison, the men who reside there, and the people who keep them there, one has to like the color gray. In a system where everything is painted with the extremes of black and white, good and evil, trusted and untrusted, the reality is between the two, in the gray area of understanding. Over the years, within the confines of the razor wire-topped fences, I have seen some of the most hardened convicts do the kindest of acts. And I've seen those trusted with their care and rehabilitation resort to nothing short of cruelty. It remained a constant struggle to deal appropriately with flawed individuals (both officers and inmates), acknowledging their strengths while being aware of their shortcomings.

Over time, I learned about the men's families, their lives, and their crimes. I learned how prisons worked. It was a fascinating, if troubling, journey that I took with these men. As a free, law-abiding citizen, I struggled to reconcile the men I knew with the legacy of fright and hurt that they left behind them with their acts of violence, deceit, or thoughtless mistakes. I shared society's emotional reaction of hot anger when a friend was kidnapped and raped. I felt it when my car was vandalized and things stolen.

As I came to know these criminals personally, I faced the fact that I could not dismiss them as uncaring, useless animals. They were men and women—human beings who hurt, cried, laughed, loved, and hated. Most of them had been victims themselves. Many of them agonized over what they had done. They looked for answers to how they could have hurt so many people, destroyed so many lives. Some struggled to change. Some were convinced the change to a better life would be easy, that once they were free, life would be fine. Others, more realistic, knew what was in store for them and were frightened of the future. Some had given up hope that they or their lives would ever be different. Some planned future crimes. But even those who said things would never work out for them in the legal world still struggled internally to develop personal codes to make their lives worthwhile, or at least sensible.

The United States has well over two million people locked up in our jails and state and federal prisons. We have the dubious distinction of imprisoning a larger percentage of our citizenry than any other nation in the world—well ahead of Cuba, Russia, and China. And although the United States has only 5 percent of the world's population, our prisons hold one-fourth of the entire world's incarcerated.[1]

Increasingly, there is a long-term population within our nation's prisons that needs attention. Since 1984, the number of prisoners serving life sentences has quadrupled. Today, one in nine inmates is serving a life sentence. A third of those inmates serving life will never have a chance at a parole hearing. Many others will be considered for parole but refused release. And not all men with life sentences committed violent offenses, nor were all of them adults when they committed their crimes.[2] There currently are more than twenty-five hundred children in the United States with life without parole sentences.[3] Their incarcerations will cost us billions before they die of old age. These extraordinary figures don't include the offenders who do not have literal life sentences, but whose penalties far exceed their life expectancies.

Our state and federal budgets are being strangled by the costs of imprisonment. Correctional spending is the third-largest budgetary item in most states, falling behind only health and education. Our appetite for punishment costs taxpayers eighty billion dollars a year.[4] As the costs rise, correctional needs suck away new possibilities to improve education, health care, and infrastructure for society as a whole.

The public has little awareness of what it takes to effectively run a prison, even with the most bare-bones budget. They have little understanding beyond what they see and hear on TV about what prisons are really like. They are conflicted about what prisons should accomplish.

With economics as the driving force, a controversial but positive move has started to reduce the populations housed in the nation's jails and prisons. Young drug offenders are given second and third chances and placed in community treatment programs. Some offenders with lesser crimes are brought up for early parole consideration. Hopes rise throughout the institutions, but inmates who have lived long years behind bars are finding their expectations of early freedom dashed.

Our society does not openly discuss why we are sending people to prison at increasing rates even though the crime rate is dropping in most states. "Out of sight, out of mind" describes society's attitude about incarceration. As a whole, we are not interested in what happens to offenders once they leave society and disappear behind the razor wire. Prisoners become invisible to us as individuals. Many people say that is okay, but they do not consider the monetary or social costs that must be paid for the care of the wayward. When we lock up people in the United States, we want them behind bars for a long time. But it is not the best practice for any of us. We have to consider the larger implications of our policies.

The thought of votes in the ballot boxes keep politicians and even justices afraid to make decisions they know need to be made. They worry that if a high-profile felon reoffends, the blame will fall on their shoulders.

Much-needed discussions are beginning to take shape, thanks to the stark figures produced by national think tanks such as the Pew Research Center, the Sentencing Project, and the Brookings Institution. In the past few years, books and articles have been produced that look at the troubling statistics and explore the inequalities of the correctional system, the self-perpetuating prison industrial complex, and the conflicting laws and sentencing processes of our land. The disparities at all levels are troubling.

We desperately need to have these discussions, but there is still something missing. The conversations fail to address important elements of the dilemma. There is a disconnect between the mood of the public and the intellectualization of the problem.

"What is the purpose of incarceration?" we should be asking. Is it for rehabilitation, retribution, deterrence, or incapacity? Those four goals are not always compatible. If rehabilitation is complete, how many more years of a man's life should be given for retribution? Or is deterrence as a lesson for general society the desired goal? There is much to talk about, and the average citizen needs to be involved in the conversation.

I am different for having spent years with these men as they struggled with their lives. They have placed deep trust in me and have taken much time and energy to help me with this project. They hope, as I do, that the sharing of their experiences will contribute to public conversations about imprisonment or, at the least, cause the readers to think. As one man, now in his thirty-fourth year of confinement, said, "I'm glad to help. I'd like to think that my life had some meaning beyond some lines on a rap sheet."

Issues to Think About

1. What experiences and emotions do you bring to the reading of this book? Have you been the victim of crime? Has a family member been incarcerated? Involved with law enforcement? How do you think those experiences will affect your reading of this book?
2. Did any of the statistics in the introduction surprise you?
3. Why do you think the United States locks up a larger percentage of its population than any other country in the world?
4. What do you think the purpose of incarceration should be: rehabilitation, retribution, punishment, or deterrence?

One

"I'm weary all the time"
An Introduction to the Men

How to speak of the journey since 1996? I'll tell you, a lot of turbulent water has passed under this old bridge since then. I'll be fifty-seven in May and I feel a hundred…. I'm weary all the time.

—*Michael*

As the letters arrived from prisons around the state, I scanned each envelope with anticipation. Familiar names on the return addresses flooded my mind with memories. Each envelope was stamped on the back with a variation of the standard prison warning: "Prison mail uncensored. Not responsible for content." One institutional stamp informed me that, in the future, the inmate's dorm number must be included on the correspondence or he wouldn't receive my mail. The long arm of orders, regulations, and warnings reached out to pull me back into the correctional mindset.

I soon learned that the opened envelopes were a door to deeply hidden pain and sometimes I breathed deeply as I started to read. It was a joy to hear from each of the men, but the straightforward way they shared their experiences tore at my heart. The unembellished sharing of facts reflected deeply held feelings. They were more insightful, more introspective because of the years they had spent locked up, thinking.

As our letters flowed between the prisons and my mailbox, I saw the ways the ensuing years had changed these men. Most letters reflected their younger selves—just more extreme. Some had become more bitter. Anger had become deeper. Others had become more wary, the emotional walls around them thicker. But a few men had become surprisingly mellow. They had found direction and purpose in their lives. A few were becoming unhinged.

I puzzled about their changed personalities.

Michael

Each of Michael's letters was filled with surprising honesty and candor. I have known this man since he was ten years old and our paths kept crossing over the years. I was his caseworker at McDowell Hall when he lived at Kentucky Children's Home. KCH was a nurturing state institution for emotionally disturbed children. The troubled children were not considered delinquent, but were emotionally scarred and out of control at home or school. Michael has few specific memories of those years except for a tall fence surrounding the place. His memory is wrong. There were no fences, except around the swimming pool, but in his mind, he has been in prison all his life.

From KCH, he was moved to the Youth Reception Center when his actions crossed the line into delinquency. I saw him again years later at Kentucky State Reformatory and then some time later at another correctional facility. He was out for a few years, but always returned with a charge related to aggression or violence.

Michael is now fifty-seven years old. He has grayed and grown a short stubbly beard and a light mustache. He is lean and short, only five feet four inches tall. The keen intelligence and humor evidenced in his letters are there in personal contacts, but his insecurities, emotional instability, and underlying anger are more obvious and boil just below the surface. DOC says his risk assessment rating is "very high."

Michael is always friendly when we meet. Each time we find each other, we talk over old times. But I never got to really know him as an adult until we began to exchange letters for this project. His letters are all open and candid.

> Well, where to start? To state for the record, I don't think you're asking all that much of me, so it's not like I'm making a grave sacrifice. You are my only contact with the outside world, and the personal feelings I share with you can't do any more damage by you knowing them, than the events that caused them. Retrospection can be painful and sometimes a learning experience. In for a dime, in for a dollar. Sometimes pain is the only proof I have I'm still alive.

His sense of humor remains intact.

> If you think you need to expand on your earlier work to help others and more people, then by all means—Hook me up to the gerbil wheel. ☺ I would be glad to help.... With all that said, it's a pleasant surprise to hear from you. I am chagrined that you found me in prison again, where unfortunately, I seem to spend all my life.
>
> How to speak of the journey since 1996? I'll tell you, a lot of turbulent water has passed under this old bridge since then. I'll be fifty-seven in May and I feel a hundred.... I'm weary all the time.

As we wrote, Michael caught me up on his family. I sensed his isolation.

Aunt Bea, did I tell you about her? She's dying of heart failure, haven't heard from her sister in a while, so I don't know if she has passed or not. She was like a second momma. So other than you, Ms. Holman, there is no outside world right now.

Well, some would say that I've done so much time that prison is my home, but I've never felt that way. In truth, I've always been in prison, and when I get out, it only means my cell got bigger with a bigger yard. I've always been doing time. So yes, I am a very sad man. And yes, in the past I tried to kill myself twice. And while I do not consider suicide as an option, I do cry out to God to take me out of this life where I have no use. I don't feel that way all the time, but it is a pervasive feeling.

There is a new seriousness, a new thoughtfulness to Michael. "I'm not the most stable person you'll ever meet," he said years ago, and that may still be true. But he seems tired of his troubled life. He wants something different, but doesn't know how to get there.

Michael's journey is not over. After the research was done, before this book was completed, Michael was released from prison and placed in a halfway house. He refused his medication, couldn't handle healthy relationships, and ran away with only three months left in his sentence.

Wayne

Wayne will soon be released after spending thirty-one years behind bars. In the prison setting, he was always very quiet and private around me, but ready with a gentle smile and polite nod when we passed on the walkway. We occasionally talked about his family, but nothing deep and never a lengthy conversation. It is only through letters that I've gotten to know him as a person.

I often wondered how Wayne managed to survive within prison as he is slight—five feet six inches and 113 pounds. He showed no signs of aggression or anger. He didn't talk much to anyone. Yet he seemed to get along fine and had the respect of the other men. He explained in letters that when he was first arrested and in the county jail, the older men noticed his privacy and liked it. They talked with him and taught him about the "convict code" and how to survive without problems in his upcoming prison stay. He took care of himself and overlooked things that were going on around him. He minded his own business and it served him well.

For men with long sentences or life sentences, you go through a wide range of emotions at one time or another whether you want to admit it or not. When you first get sentenced to a lot of years or life, you're shocked, angry, in disbelief.... You wonder how will I do this much time. Then it's up to you. You have to mentally prepare yourself. As the old convicts use to say, you had to hook up your wagon and do it, or let the time do you. I mean you have to prepare yourself. What are you going to do once you get to prison? In order to do that much time, you more or less block out the outside world.

At one time or another, every one of us has gotten angry and felt like there is no hope, but for some unknown reason, we all keep going. When I got served-out in 1996 after doing thirteen years, that is when I really felt like giving up, that I was never getting out. The worst thing that I had to do was make the call home and tell them that I would not be home for another twenty-something years.

After the shock of getting served-out wore off, I was determined not to let them win. I was either going to die standing on my feet or I was going to walk out the door one day a free man. Like a lot of men doing long sentences, you just do one day at a time. Never looking forward or behind you.

I had asked in my original letter what they missed most. Wayne addressed that, too.

What I miss most? You really try not to think about it when you've done or have to do a large amount of time. Thinking about the outside world while you're in prison makes doing time hard and slow, at least for me. But it's probably the small things that everybody takes for granted: home-cooked meals, sitting under a tree, or looking at the stars, and being with family.

Wayne will be a free man in a few months, having served out his long sentence with some time subtracted for good behavior. He is forty-eight years old. He has caring parents who moved to the Louisville area after his crime and who have visited him every week for the past thirty-one years.

As my serve-out date gets closer, it seems surreal being locked up all this time. It's like being in limbo. Everything changes around you, but inside your little bubble, everything basically stays the same. Anyone who has done a large amount of time who tells you they aren't nervous or a little afraid of getting out is lying to you and themselves.

Without my parents' love and support over the past thirty-one years, I would have been another casualty of the prison system…. They have been taking care of me my whole life. It is time I was there to take care of them for a change.

I suspect Wayne will have more adjustments than he and his family anticipate as he asserts his role as an independent adult after so many years.

It will be a struggle, but I think Wayne will be fine.

Stuart

The most alarming letter arrived with my name and address scrawled across the face of the envelope at an angle, the penmanship large, uneven, and shaky. It was from Stuart. Something was clearly wrong and different. His letter was written on notebook paper, his cursive handwriting weaving large and uneven across the lines.

Nice to hear from you…. I would love to help. I have one small problem to share. In 1999, I was diagnosed with Huntington's. It's a nervous disorder like Parkinson's.

They shake and jerk; muscles and mind shrinking. I can't swallow. I got it from Mom in a gene.... My writing is terrible, my memory is good, emotions unstable.

After exchanging a number of obviously painfully written letters, I received permission to go see him. It was good to spend time with him, but the changes were startling. Stuart, his body shrunken from earlier years, had difficulty standing—his movements were stumbling and uncertain. His arms flayed continually and spittle flew from his mouth as he struggled to form his words. He had become bald, his face covered with a thin gray beard. His mind was intact, but I struggled to follow his words. I did not see evidence of anguish or frustration. Instead, he seemed at peace.

Stuart has received a lengthy deferment, ensuring that he will never leave the institution alive. An appeal was turned down based on the results of a psychiatric evaluation that concluded that he should stay where he is as he would sexually offend again. When he told me that, he did not argue against the decision.

Recently, after spending almost a year in segregation because of behavior that probably stemmed from his progressive disease, prison officials saw that he would be more properly placed in the health care facility. There he has a small room to himself and staff and inmates to help care for him. He waits patiently for the day he believes the Rapture will come and he will be with Jesus.

"I look forward to it," he says with excitement.

We talked about Chicken Hill, the cemetery on a green rise tucked in the heart of the prison property. He is content.

Cam

Cam was a student who always drew our teachers' attention with his deep insights, skilled way with words and poetry, keen good looks, and magnetic personality. I followed him over the years with interest as he had attended high school with my sons, and as a mother, I identified with him and his parents.

Without effort, Cam attracted female staff and workers, often causing him trouble when his liaisons were discovered. One of our own teachers became too attached to him, causing a crisis for me as the coordinator, but that is another story. I thought he would be one of the first to write. But there was silence. I followed up with another letter. And then a third. He finally answered.

Gaye, Everything is fine between us and I am truly sorry for not responding before now and to have disappointed you. My intentions, of course, almost always good, don't always seem to pave the road beneath me at times. Especially as of late, they seem to be fleeting thoughts at best. Procrastinating doesn't help! Nor does existing in the Cess Pool of the DOC. I'm in a rut.... Nothing to be alarmed about because it isn't something I can't handle—if it were—I wouldn't admit it....

The last line says it all to me. "It isn't something I can't handle—if it were— I wouldn't admit it ..."

I hadn't set out to make him feel guilty. I just wanted him to know how valuable his input was that he had written and shared twenty years ago. His response let me know that the years had taken a toll. While Cam always shared his emotional depths in his schoolwork and writings, outwardly he was a young man in control. That response and the tone of the rest of his letter showed the same characteristics. But underneath the charm and humor was a man who wouldn't outwardly admit the pain, even while the anger and frustration rose subtly to the surface.

Another letter, arriving much later, talked about the emotional darkness that had overcome him during the long years he had been locked up. He said he was trying to climb out of the deep pit, but he didn't know if he could succeed. Later letters and things I heard about him indicated he was still struggling with himself and the administration.

Billy

Billy, the only African American in the original study still left in prison, is an angry man, but has been eager to help with the project. He speaks much of racial discrimination in the prison system, but his anger, which pops up often, seems more anchored in hurt and disappointment than in race.

His mother died just after we began the correspondence. I sent him a sympathy card and her obituary, which cemented our relationship. He answered every question I asked, even though my lists were meant to be of a pick-and-choose nature. Though short answers, they said a lot.

In his first letter, before his mother's death, Billy spoke of his family's closeness or non-closeness, and I felt his pain. What he didn't say spoke more clearly than what he did say. "Some of us are very close and some of us are distant. I'll give more input at a later date and time. It's hurtful to speak on now. So circle this question, Mrs. Holman, and we will discuss it later."

Later came sooner than expected with the death of his mother. In his sadness, he began to open up about friends and family.

I have no friends! Those who I considered a friend never wrote to me, never came to see me, and never sent me a single postal money order that could of helped me out tremendously. Not saying that any of them owed me anything because they didn't. It would have been the thought that counted, especially if you say that you are truly my friend to begin with. As far as family, I can only communicate with them through writing letters. And most of the time, they won't even respond back.

Why? Only they know why. I can't call because everyone has blocks on their phones, and don't want to accept a call from me.

Billy continued on, though, shifting from gentle nostalgia to anger with each letter he wrote. His inner conflict showed through. "I keep going through difficult times with *faith*, *willpower*, and *determination* to overcome and be a free man, and wanting to succeed in life at something worth living for other than being a confined, locked-up black African American male." But he admitted he is angry. "I am angry every day! Because of the choices I made in life that put me in the horrible place. And strain and heartache and pain I placed on my loved ones. I'm angry now just writing this because it's where I'm writing it—from 'Prison.'"

Grant

Grant is also an angry man, a bitter man, even though he doesn't realize it. I believe he sees himself as a gentle soul, and he was always a genuinely caring, quiet person—and helpful—but he was angry twenty years ago and he still is today. He has an outwardly subdued, soft-spoken demeanor. He does not get into trouble in the institution. But his conversations point to an internal burning anger. His many years in prison as a persistent felon have not been kind to him.

In his first letter, Grant tried to apologize for an incident that had occurred years ago in which he had lost his temper. He said that it was good that he learned from it. The attitude he mentioned does not speak well of his adjustment. "I learned a very valuable lesson. The lesson was that I'm not, nor will I ever be allowed to be a human anymore. To people like you, I suppose I'm to be pitied and to others, about 75 percent, I am to be disdained." He concluded: "Listen to me, Gaye, I have nothing but grateful respect for you. Prison is hard and I was simply pushed over the edge by the simple reminder of the truth that inmates (me) was at no time to be considered human, nor to be trusted. My fault for thinking too much."

He has taken all the suggested classes and received the degrees that were offered. He has held responsible jobs on the yard. His DOC risk assessment rating is low. But he has been denied parole six times in the twenty-four years he has been eligible for release. His sentence expires in 2043. He is sixty-six years old.

Duane

Duane was in some of my first classes back in the days when he was involved in the underworld of prison—gambling, drug dealing, stores. Even then, he was a likeable, interesting soul. He and another man anonymously left candy on my desk each week. When I discovered their identities, they brushed off their kindness by saying they had plenty of money, giving me a wink. Duane had grown up in prison, but even back then, he was trying to find a new way through his life. Now, it seems, he has changed completely. He is one who has mellowed and grown. "The thought of being incarcerated all of my adult life doesn't play a factor to me because you are aware I haven't spent thirty years in prison lying around. I have allowed myself to grow out of childhood into adulthood. I don't think as an eighteen-year-old boy, but instead I think as an adult."

Duane claimed his life was completely changed by a religious experience. He was known for years as a major player on the yard but was respected by all, and letters I received from others mentioned him often.

"Duane got religion," the men penned in disbelief. His life story will be recounted in a later chapter.

Bob

And then there was Bob, who was released after twenty-six years, soon after we reestablished contact. He produced a piece he entitled "Musings." It began:

> The fact that I have been in prison for a long time comes as no shock to many. I put myself in prison and accept total responsibility for my actions that got me there. Ah, what did you do, you might ask? If it matters that much, look me up and find out for yourself. I was certainly not a choirboy, and on paper, I look anything but a saint. But remember one thing: I'm not the same man/idiot-child I was all those years ago. As time marched on, post-incarceration, and as society changed, so did I. I grew older, grayer, balder and, in my humble opinion, wiser. An axiom: The person who does not learn from his/her incarceration and who continues to be caught up in "Groundhog Dayitis" is truly an idiot. (Forgive me, Lord, but a raca by any other name is still a raca!)[1] I was a fool for about five and a half years. I was an angry, litigious horse's butt. I escaped, had a transcendent experience (which is a whole other story) and finally extracted my head out of my hinter regions—something I'm still doing by the grace of God.

The letters kept coming. A few wrote once or twice and drifted away. Others wrote pages of helpful answers. The responses to my many questions were wildly diverse and, at times, confusing. Some men said a particular institution was the most unfair, cruel prison in the state. Others claimed the same facility was the safest and best. Some complained about the declining quality of the guards. Others said they got along fine with most of them. All decried in chorus about the quality of the young people coming to prison these days. Like older people on the outside, they fussed about the youngsters who had no respect for themselves or others. Most of them saw the majority of other inmates, both young and old, as disgusting, troublemaking, non-thinking animals. But the youngsters were the worst, they insisted.

As the correspondence became deeper, the issues for me became clearer. I had to understand what these diverse men had in common. I sensed there were common threads that ran between the angry and the mellow, between the adjusted and the malcontents. I began to ponder what was at the heart of the changes that I noticed, both good and bad. I began to understand the impact incarceration had on the lives and psyches of the men.

I was fascinated with how the men dealt with the reality that they may never leave prison. I saw how this closed society molded individuals and how outside forces reached within to save some. I saw things that gave men strength in prison, but which might not hold them up when they were released. I saw some things that I can't explain.

Like them, I feared for their futures but grasped their hopefulness.

Issues to Think About

1. As some of the men are introduced in this chapter, do any of them stand out to you? If so, why?
2. What are your thoughts as you are introduced to the men? Do you feel sympathy? Anger? Disgust? Why?
3. Do you have questions you hope will be answered in later chapters?

Two

"Gnaws at your heart like a worm"
The Emotional Impact of Incarceration

The worst thing about prison would have to be the feelings of loneliness, of not being really able to trust anyone, of needs unfulfilled, and of a bitterness that gnaws at your heart like a worm.

—John

Life in prison continues day by day in a timeless fashion, the sameness broken only by the regular flow of men moving in and out of the institution. Behind the rolls of razor wire, intertwined with the numbing daily routine, bubbles a unique and troubling culture. It is that culture—with its emotional isolation and tension—that the men mentioned first. They adjusted to the stark physical setting fairly soon, but the mental pressures took longer to reconcile.

In trying to unweave a complex tapestry or tale, it can be impossible to find the loose thread that is central to the piece. So it was as I stared at the tightly interwoven web that explained the emotions of those imprisoned. Their feelings were similar; the individuals were unique. My own reactions were woven within the tapestry, and were also difficult to extract or understand.

I chose to begin in the middle with Norman's thread. I chose to start there because he called me shortly before I wrote this chapter and he was much on my mind. Important parts of his life had crashed, and I didn't see how he could move ahead. It had been years since we sat together in the prison college office, debating politics and education. He was an important part of the 1994 study. He has been out of prison for some years now, but his story and the effect of prison on his life are important to know. This book is primarily about men still incarcerated after twenty years but, inside or out, the impact of incarceration never leaves the men alone. Norman's words from two decades ago were echoed by all the inmates who wrote to me more recently, and his past still reached out to grab him.

The first night of class was just over and the teacher called me as soon as he got home.

"Do you know who that is in my class? That's Norman Edwards.[1] Do you know how well known he is in the musical community? What is *he* doing in prison?"

The prison administrators were already buzzing about Norman's case. He had arrived there with a 190-year sentence for a crime committed twenty years before he was charged—non-violent oral sex with three teenagers who had remembered the events only after retrieving hidden memories as adults. The case was rife with local politics and personal vendettas, but Norman was tried, sentenced, and sent away to die in prison.

Norman was an educator with a master's degree and additional graduate work. He was cultured, held a position of prestige in his mostly rural community, and had a self-admitted arrogance that did not serve him well. For him, doing time seemed to be harder than for some of the men who were from a lower socioeconomic class. He felt different and separated from the others. He, and other men like him, chafed at their loss of entitlement. They suffered from a greater sense of isolation and loss and had trouble sharing in the same enthusiasms and interests on the yard that added a little brightness to the day for the other men.

Here is what Norman said twenty years ago. Things have not changed. There are a number of men like Norman on the yard today.

"They'll argue for hours about this or that team and who should have won the last game. Well, who cares?" groused Norman. He continued:

It is difficult to force the public at large to listen to complaints and concerns of us inmates. There is such a huge disparity of backgrounds, both intellectually and environmentally, in this institution. On the one hand, there is the inmate who came from such awful situations that this life here is the best he's ever had…. On the other hand, there is me and a few others like me who feel that each day here is pure horror. Conversation is of the lowest intellectual level imaginable; the language used by the majority of the people here is unrepeatable; the personal habits are abominable; and the separation from loved ones and friends turns the world into a lonely abyss, void of tenderness, affection, love, and caring. To me, this is a cold, unfriendly world, one which I detest….

I am used to being around people who are deep-feeling people, people who can express ideas and feelings both expressively and openly. Here, there is none of the closeness, the friendship, the warmth that friends and cohorts develop…. I don't trust many people here and literally can't stand to be around most. This is awful, I know…. I empathize with them…. I'm sorry for them in their plight…. But they are so different. Every aspect of this place is foreign to me.

I have always been a warm, compassionate, even passionate, loving person, but I can feel, almost on a daily basis, myself burying those qualities because this place is so devoid of those qualities. I miss going to the symphony, the art gallery, Actors Theatre, friends. I miss making music, playing my double bass, and conducting the orchestra. The guys here talk about missing smoking a joint and getting drunk and chasing some women in the bar. How am I supposed to get used to that garbage?

Inside I am filled with dismay to be spending valuable years of my life like this ... years when I could give so much to so many.

Another time, Norman became more philosophical and more agitated and disturbed. This time, his comments were directed toward the correctional system rather than against his fellow inmates.

I will always follow all its rules and make every effort to adjust to its sometimes-unreasonable demands, but I will never succumb to its values, its lack of regard for human life. And I will never participate in its philosophy of dehumanizing the human spirit. Meanwhile, the political system, with its inhumane agendas, continues to hide the truth from the public and continues to try to convince them that the current philosophy of the criminal system will solve the crime problem. How long can they be fooled???

I'm not really good at putting my feelings on paper, and that's another thing I miss ... long talks about intelligent subjects ... face to face. Anyway, I feel like this is very disorganized.... I have so many feelings about this situation.... I just know that this is wrong.... I don't know how to even begin to make people outside of here understand the torment and the pain. Instead of understanding, they want to make it worse. "Take those damned prisoners' TVs. Take away all privileges. Make 'em sorry for what they have done" ... if they only knew what the torment of just the separation feels like. I guess I'm too soft-hearted, but I'll never understand how people can be so full of hate.... I'll never comprehend man's inhumanity to man. Enough now ... my heart hurts....

Twelve years later, Norman left prison. His surprise parole happened when a significant group of his former students led the efforts to free him. One of our highest state officials, who was from the area and knew Norman and the situation, lent his influence to the effort.

Norman's life was forever changed. He had no money to get ahead when he was released. During his divorce, his wife received his retirement fund. A senior citizen when he left prison, he lived rent-free for years in a different county with an old musician friend, trading rent for help with the man's music business. Norman was in his mid-seventies when he called and not at all well. He was living on his meager Social Security income and money he picked up at local musical gigs on the weekends.

His call was to tell me his friend had just died. He had expected to be left the house or some funds as the man had no family. However, he was told by the attorney that it didn't happen; the friend was in debt, and when it was all paid, there would be nothing left. He had to move, had no money, and had to obey the strict residency requirements for sex offenders.[2] Finding rental housing, even with money, is nearly impossible in those cases. He didn't know what to do.

I took him to his friend's graveside funeral service. The physical change in Norman was shocking. He had aged greatly in the previous year. He was seriously overweight and his knees were shot; he walked with a cane, weaving dangerously as he tread on uneven ground. He had trouble standing up from the chair unassisted. His face was covered with red psoriasis. His breath came in short, rapid gasps. I wondered if he had long to live. I wondered what he would do when he had no place to stay. He may have been free, but his years in prison never lessened their hold on him.

The men in prison are lumped together in a basic security risk classification. That classification has as much to do with the men's abilities to get along with others as it does with their crimes. At the time of the original study, the men were all in medium-security facilities that were double-bunked, indicating that they were able to function fairly well overall. Their crimes ran from murder to serial rape to forgery and robbery.

Being involved in fights or rule-breaking activities can cause a reclassification and a move. In the years since I first knew them, several of the men in this study have been moved to a dreaded maximum-security facility and back again. A few have remained in maximum security. Only one of the men is in a more comfortable minimum-security setting today, a place mostly open to those with non-violent crimes.

Within the broad security categories, there is little separation by age, crime, education, sexual orientation, intelligence, or social class. But those statuses often influence how the men see and experience their incarceration. There are many different kinds of people thrown together in close living situations in prison. People who could find nothing in common on the streets are put together—sometimes even as "cellies" (roommates). All they seem to share in common is the fact that they have broken laws.

Jack explained:

> For the first few days after arriving in the prison was what I have described as a form of culture shock. Everything is new—the rules (written and unwritten), the buildings, and the individuals. All of this is very different to what one encounters in the outside world. Out there, you can for the most part choose who you want to be associated with, where you would like to go, etc. In the prison environment, all of that freedom of choice is taken away from you. You may end up celling with a convicted murderer or working with a rapist. There's just no way to tell what a person has done by looking at them, so therefore, stereotypes are out the window. A rapist doesn't look a certain way, nor does a murderer have a particular shifting of his eyes.

Jack continued his discussion of prison. At the time he wrote this, he was in his early thirties with a joking demeanor, making light of many things, but alternating the humor with a serious, sometimes brooding, mood.

I do not think there is any certain type of person who comes to prison. There are stereotypes, which I think have mostly been created by the media and television. You have people from almost all walks of life, all faiths, and all ethnic backgrounds....

There are people who have great talents: music, visual arts, and intellectual. These are not the people you will see portrayed on the six o'clock news. They are not out trying to "shank" someone else, they are not trying to escape, nor are they killing guards. A prisoner is trying to do his time as quickly, and usually, as quietly as possible.

I am not typical, and neither are any of the thousands of others incarcerated in the United States. Each has his story and they vary as much as the individuals themselves.

You will find that in a prison setting there are those who are very angry, others who are very docile, and some who are ambivalent to their surroundings.

So, am I typical? Not by any means. Are the others typical? Not on your life. Each person is unique; this goes for being in prison, too.

The individual life experiences that men bring to prison have some influence on what hurts them the worst in their incarcerations. Norman, heard from earlier, was from a higher socioeconomic level. That higher social level may have helped him get out of prison early, but it made his stay more tortuous.

Ken was from a lower socioeconomic background. From the time he was eleven years old, Ken was forced to survive by his own body and wits on the streets of one of the nation's meanest cities. He was in and out of juvenile facilities as he got older. An extremely bright man, he was not surprised when he arrived in prison.

When I was a child, I knew where I was going and I didn't care. My mother and father and his father before him was all in prison. I knew where I was going....

Before learning—basically I was illiterate—I thought it [prison] wasn't so bad. I was raised in places like this. I was just away in a different place. I thought "What's so bad about it? Big deal." It took me away from a dump.... Then through education and loneliness—being away from my family—I saw it's a terrible thing—it is.

These people from the streets [inner cities], they don't really understand what life is about. Most of us don't know about life. We are stuck. We go from one low-class neighborhood to another. We only see the black area of the country and think that is what life is.

When I was first locked up, I started the GED program, but couldn't handle the work and had to start with the literacy program. I went jail to jail, state to state, and worked my way up to the college program here. Reading opened up doors. I learned what life can be like.... The broader your world becomes, the more you realize how much you missed.

Jones is another man who came to prison straight from the rough streets. He brought his experience with him, and prison had become his home.

Jones was sent to an orphanage when he was four, and he has lived in juvenile facilities and prisons ever since. By 1994, he had been incarcerated for the previous twenty-four years except for three unsuccessful years on the street. He made the emotional adjustments necessary to survive in the prison environment. He was a rowdy jokester, always laughing, making light of things. But he was also deeply involved in many of the illegal activities that penetrated the yard. Only a few people knew the depth of his thoughts and the sincerity of his own special moral code. His private comments are important.

> About prison—it's a good school, but it's not something I'd advise. You have to be strong to survive. You learn to deal with different situations there. It will make a man out of you or eat your mind away and make you weak. You have to make up your own mind.
>
> I've been evil before. I haven't always been like this [joking and cheerful]. It's part of my survival. I play things out through the humor. When I'm making people laugh, they can't feel bitter. I make myself laugh, and when I laugh, I can't be bitter.

Jones found a way to survive emotionally over the years by hiding his real emotions from others and from himself at times. While he found a way to help others through humor, he was especially isolated from himself.

It was hard for the men to put their feelings into words, because the experience was so unique, so troubling, so confusing for them, that they hardly understood it themselves. Tom explained:

> What is it like being in prison? When you get down to it, this is not a very easy question to answer. It is also something that is very different for each person. We all have our own private, and in many cases, subconscious, torments which are seldom if ever revealed to anyone—least of all to ourselves. We suffer the pain without being able to see where it is really coming from.
>
> People are always complaining about things such as the food, medical care, and the treatment received from guards and staff. However, the things that really hurt, cut the deepest into our hearts, and cause the most damage and change to ourselves are never spoken of—never actively acknowledged. For me, the worst part of being in prison is how the situation has separated me from the people who I hold the closest to my heart: my friends, my lover, and most of all, myself.
>
> Prison separates you from those close to you, not only physically, but spiritually, piece by piece over time from their lives, feelings, thoughts, and emotions.

The emotional isolation within the prison setting seems to be orchestrated to some extent by prison rules, which understandably are primarily concerned with security. Men are not allowed to share items, borrow from one another, do favors for one another, or spend too much time together. Of course, these things do happen, but the men risk being in trouble for even acts of kindness. One man gave a pair of old tennis shoes to an inmate who had no outside financial sources. He received a write-up for the action. The giving of items can mean there are less-obvious, perhaps illegal, trade-offs involved.

Showing kindness is seen as a weakness, and weakness is a danger in prison. If inmates confide in someone, they may turn out to be a "rat." If they trust someone, that person may use that trust to place them in their debt. To survive, the men hide their feelings. They do not let each other know what they think or feel. I've even heard of men who haven't told anyone they made parole, being afraid someone jealous would retaliate in a way that they'd be forced to fight and ruin the parole before they could leave the institution. If they have made enemies or owe money, the time between the parole hearing and release is a very tense time. The inability to trust anyone isolates the men further from each other—and from themselves. It underlines the discussion elsewhere in this book about why treatment programs that require sharing feelings are often not effective in prisons.

There is still more to incarceration that is hard to explain. Things happen at a different pace in prison. A warden told me that his job was to make every day as uneventful as possible. "All a warden has to do to survive is create nice, dull, boring days. No assaults, no deaths, no escapes. Just routine days."

The men constantly refer to the staggering sameness of activities in prison that is hard for free people to understand. Small things are blown out of proportion because there is nothing to look forward to. John wrote: "To say prison life is easy is a gross error. Prison life is ordered. It offers the same thing every day with very little change occurring.... So to say prison life is easy is wrong. It is simply the same every day."

Stuart, the man who is now dying of Huntington's, wrote this about prison life when he was healthy twenty years ago.

> Prison is so cold and hard emotionally that I keep an emotional fence around my heart. Answers, responses, looks, dress, are mostly repetitive, mundane, lifeless, predictable, never giving or taking warmth for fear of overlapping into the morass of problems which permeate this prison.
>
> It's the boredom of the place that's worse. People have no idea what this type of boredom means—the terrible depth of it. They have never lost everything there is to do. Everything is much slower in here. I'll plan a half a day around a shower or a phone call—sometimes even weeks around the phone call.
>
> It's a whole different world in here. You can make adjustments to the physical things. We are pretty adaptable creatures. You adjust and take whatever is given you. But it is the mental pressure. It's at a more animal level. It pressures you into becoming an institutionalized person.

Over and over, I heard about the emotional anguish and frustration when I talked to men about their incarceration, especially in the first decade of their imprisonment.

Some of the anguish is internal—they suffer from a constant awareness that it is their own actions that have caused harm to others, to their families, and to themselves. There is no way to take back anything or undo the harm they've caused. That realization eats at many of the men and makes them prisoners of their own minds—a much worse punishment than being locked up, they say.

> The full impact of what I had done smacked me squarely in the face about two weeks after I was arrested and sitting in a dirty, dreary jail cell. Words cannot describe the full range of emotions that ran through me … the flood of tears, the regrets and recriminations, and the hopeless wish to take it back. I had become the very sort of person I was taught to despise, hate, and avoid: a criminal, and not just a garden-variety criminal, but a murderer.—Bob

> I pray these memories will someday subside, but until they do, I guess I'll just continue to deal with them. Sometimes they seem as if it happened yesterday. I sit here in prison suffering the consequences of my actions that took place that night. Someday, my debt to society will hopefully be paid, but nothing can bring him back now. Sometimes I can't help but think that I'll be dealing with that tragic night for the rest of my life. Society will probably never realize how in my mind I pay every day.—Leslie

> My incarceration has caused some of my family members to lie about my whereabouts…. They have to live with the fact that being incarcerated leaves a certain stigmatism that remains forever on the family name…. As for my children, they are the ones that suffer the most, in my opinion. They have to live for the next thirteen and a half years without a father being there whenever they need me…. Those effects (of being incarcerated) could possibly change the course of people in a negative way, and I am the one responsible for that. That is the one thing that I can never forgive myself for—all the unintended consequences of my criminal activity.—Ken

> When I was sentenced, no matter what they did to me, I was glad it was finally over for me and my family. I figured no matter what they did, it cannot compare with having to live with what I've done for the rest of my life. The pain of what happened has got easier over the past eleven years. I've never talked about what happened on that day to anyone and I never will. I've never been much on sharing my feelings or my problems with anyone. Everyone has their demons to live with and this is mine.—Wayne

Twenty years later, the emotional content of their anguish had changed. Like with Wayne mentioned above, the pain of what had happened seemed to have softened. Now the emphasis was introspection about their wasted lives. They pondered over what they could have accomplished in the years they had been locked up. There no longer was the intense anguish they seemed to be dealing with earlier. It had been replaced with a deep sadness of what might have been. They talked of years wasted, talents unused, of loss that could never be fixed. Deaths of parents weighed heavily. Al said: "My life has been a waste. A total waste. I know what I could have done, great things. I missed doing things with my kids. I've learned things here, but I can't use them."

There is a group of inmates not well represented here. With some exceptions, the group in my original study was composed of men in their early thirties and older, many of whom had been in prison awhile. They had been sobered by their experiences, and their age gave them introspection into their situation. They trusted me. Missing are contemplations from the youngest inmates. However, the responding older men often spoke of their thoughts (or failure to think) when they were young.

Twenty years ago, I found it was hard to get the youth to sit down and talk seriously. Only a few—about five—were included in the original study. Some others talked with me, but not "on record." My best understanding of this group came from my personal observations, their angry, outwardly directed comments, and from the older men who were not too long out of their shoes.

There was every indication that these young drug-using and drug-dealing people were scared, troubled, and unhappy, but they tried hard to conceal those feelings from themselves and others. Outwardly, they gave the impression of swaggering young toughs who did not mind being locked up. But they were naïve in many ways and they were often used by the older inmates. Jack wrote:

> There is also a lot of pain involved in seeing real young people come into the system. I don't think half of them take this time seriously enough. They're young and so when they enter the prison system, it's like a learning experience for them ... for some, the experience is more than I believe they should ever have. These are the smaller, less-educated men (young boys) that have these type of negative encounters while being in here. And there is this unwritten rule that states everyone is man for himself. Which means you can't say, "Hey watch this guy. He might try to trick you into doing something stupid." That would be bringing trouble to your doorstep, and that's something everyone tries to avoid ... most everyone that is. So the young ones have to learn for themselves.

Many of these young men, although coming from poverty, seemed to have plenty of money to make their time more comfortable in prison. Perhaps it was money left over from their drug trafficking or other crimes, or sent by their girlfriends or relatives. Often mothers and grandmothers of the young ones would scrape together their sparse funds to send to the incarcerated youths so they could have the things they needed to make life more comfortable in prison. Or perhaps they were continuing their lucrative lives of crime in the new prison setting.

Outwardly, life did not seem too bad for this group. "If you come from nothing and you go to nothing, what difference does it make?" Ken reminded me.

In many ways, prison offered a structure for them that they should have had on the street. Some of the inner city guys were meeting up with their old friends. But, if they wanted out of the cycle, their friends could make it even harder to work toward a new life.

As a group, the young men didn't seem to feel too much guilt about their crimes because they felt they had no alternatives and everyone in their community was doing it. Most started their crimes when they were juveniles. As one explained:

> You get holes in your shoes, but nobody can buy you new ones. So you find some cardboard in the dumpster and fix them. Then the cardboard wears through, and still you can't get new ones. You know this guy who will give you a couple hundred for runnin' a deal for him, and pretty soon, you have all the money you need. Hell, I had a car before I was old enough to get a license.

Another man said his mother continually warned him about his drug-dealing companions. But when he started helping with the rent and putting steaks on the table, she stopped asking questions and said no more.

The youth I talked with privately said they would prefer another life, but they did what they thought they had to in order to survive on the streets. They knew they were going back to the same life when they were released, so they spent their time in prison talking about how they could beat the system next time. In their hearts, they wished for a different life, but had no vision of how to get there. As a group, they were volatile, angry, impulsive, and inwardly hurt.

Some of the young took advantage of education and vocational programs, but they had to take some ribbing from their peers to participate seriously. Education gave them focus and stability, but those who did not participate returned again and again to prison until they were forced to take stock of their lives. But by then, it was often too late, and they were stuck with lengthy persistent felony convictions. Prison became a deadly serious matter.

If the still-incarcerated men are to be believed—and the administrators say they are—the current wave of youngsters (sometimes called Generation Z) is different from many of those coming into prison twenty years ago. The new group of youngsters are said to be more out of control, more self-centered, and lacking any sense of personal responsibility. They have no respect for the old convict code and won't play by the code's informal but effective rules.

Everyone blames the intense new drug culture for the change. The older men were into drugs and alcohol when they committed their crimes and admit it affected their long-term health and even mental processes. They see the youngsters today as a new breed and even more destroyed by drugs and the culture surrounding it. They are unpredictable, unbalanced, volatile, and causing lots of trouble in the institutions. They say the young ones have no respect—no respect for themselves, others, or any rules.

Michael, who has spent his entire life in and out of prison, truly knows about the anger of youth. He wrote about the ones he lives with today in the institution.

> These young wild kids are worse than me and my kind. These kids are rotten and selfish to the bone. They have no moral compass. It's all about them in *everything*. When they show their true colors, everybody else's needs, wants, desires, or concerns are of no substance. And they will lie, knock you down, tromp your toes, push you—beat you down. They do whatever to get their way. The trend for today is rude and obnoxious, with me, me, me.

I saw a lot of anger, especially among the young, but it is not limited to that age group. Prisons are filled with angry men. They were angry when they murdered, raped, or used drugs. The anger goes back for years, and they carry it with them burning inside. It pours out with every encounter and gets worse during the first years of incarceration. But the men have to learn to contain their anger, or they will spend countless days returning again and again to "the hole"—the part of prison where life can truly be hell.

After a while, the men learn to keep their behaviors somewhat in line, but conversations with some of them warn of a building pressure that is frightening to contemplate. Bill said:

> To be quite honest, there is no way a human being could be subjected to this treatment for years and not change. I have my days when I fanaticize [sic] of getting revenge on those who deliberately tried to torture me and my family emotionally, physically, and psychologically. At times, the mistreatment so enrages me that I have had thoughts of killing.... You know there is no real purpose in what they are putting you through other than the fact they know they have the power to do so. Some of these officers are barely out of high school (I'm old enough to be their father). My thoughts become especially vicious when the mistreatment is directed towards my family. I wouldn't want a neighbor who had endured years of abuse in a prison.

Other men shared their hidden angry feelings. Lee said:

> I've learned I'm just a number and a paycheck to these people. I learned that because I broke one of the laws of this society, I do not deserve to be treated with human dignity or compassion. I still feel hate, mistrust, and anger inside myself. My attitude is changed so much that I am emotionally confused at times.

Chuck, a man who admits he carries great anger inside himself, said, "Prison is a breeding house of further crime. By nature, prison is a cruel, lonely, and abusive place—it tears at the souls of men.... Many felons develop a hatred for society and will resort to any means to stay free (some more horrible than others)."

He tells of talking with another inmate about the crime that brought him here. "I asked him if he were given the opportunity to go back, would he change anything about his crime—he said yes. He said that if he could go back, there wouldn't be any witnesses left to testify against him."

One of the things that came as a surprise as I shifted through hundreds of sheets of interviews, letters, and essays from the men is the number of times they equate themselves and their incarceration with animals. I have heard the reference over and over again, and I believe it gets to the heart of what the men are saying about prison. They are fighting for their humanity. But they believe that society sees them as subhuman—on the level of animals. They want to see themselves as more in spite of the crimes they have committed. They keep insisting that being treated like animals will indeed make them into subhuman creatures.

It is as if we understand animals better than men.

> I'll try to simplify this. If you take a dog, lock him up, and treat him harshly, don't try to teach him anything, after a period of time, you will release a mean dog. But if you take this dog while you've got him locked up (the first time) and teach him, chances are that when you release him, he will be a benefit to himself and others.—Max

> Most people change over a period of time with help, or sometimes without help. That stuff about once a criminal always a criminal doesn't apply to all men and women in prison. There are good people in prison who, under the influence of drugs, alcohol, or something, turned bad or made a mistake. Some would like another chance and need all the help they can get including "love." Even a dog deserves a second chance.—Robbie

> Hell, even the family pet could possibly turn into "Cujo" if he were constantly poked, kicked, and mistreated.—Bill

> Instead of helping prisoners they only house them like cattle.—Al

> The treatment we receive from the officers here is poor. They talk to us with little or no respect. We suffer from verbal, mental, and, if the opportunity presents itself, even physical abuse. We're treated as if we're animals instead of human beings. The living conditions are like that of an animal's cage. If we are placed in cages like animals, treated like animals, live like animals, then we have no other choice than to act like animals.—Doug

A now-famous 1971 study from Stanford University simulated prison life and has become classic in the literature. That study, by Phillip Zimbardo, concluded that the very nature of prisons, the way they are organized, produces problems. In situations in which one group of people (the officers) has total control over another group of people (the inmates), social and psychological problems inevitably arise among both groups. Many of those in control tend to become brutal and sadistic, while the inmates become inwardly directed, lose their self-awareness, become depressed, and show signs of extreme stress. In fact, the reactions of the voluntary student subjects in Zimbardo's study were so disturbing that the experiment had to be discontinued after a short time.[3]

Few of the men I have talked with would say that prison is all bad. They would say it is mostly negative and harmful to them, but there are bright spots as well.

Les was a gentle speaking man who committed a violent crime. He actively pursued every treatment and educational program available to him and tried hard to stay out of trouble. He was eventually released and I don't know what his life is like today. But I suspect he is okay. There are optimal times for release, and hopefully he got out soon enough that the value of the experience remained positive. He wrote:

> I came to prison scared and alone. I feel prison saved my life because it has given me the time and tools to reevaluate my life…. If I had not come to prison, I am sure I would be dead. Honestly, I think prison saved my life. I'm learning the things I should have learned as a child. I'm starting to get some self-esteem and I'm learning a lot about myself. You probably won't believe this, but I'm really not that bad of a guy.

Cam was one of the few youthful offenders twenty years ago who was introspective enough at the time to contribute to this particular discussion, although he would do it only through writing. This is the man, still imprisoned, that we heard from in the previous chapter. He is bitter and struggling today and I saw the beginnings of that anger in his early writings. But back then, he had feelings of optimism. I wonder what would have happened if he had been released years ago; my guess is his spirit would still be alive. In 1994, he wrote:

> I was headed down a dead-end street, cruising a thousand miles an hour to meet Death himself. I had no respect for life in general. On the edge is where I stood. The old saying, "Sex, drugs, and rock 'n' roll" was my motto, my shield…. Being incarcerated for one, has literally saved my life. It has given me a better perspective and outlook of life, not just my life, life in general! Although I'm a very sad man now, my spirit is finally alive….
>
> But being incarcerated has showed the pits of the system. I've been jailed for four years and in that short amount of time, I've become very prejudice of authority. I try not to be, but it is inevitable. They've made me mean, angry, sad, and prejudice. How can I care for someone who treats me like I'm the filth under their nails?

Now, twenty years later, he has received two ten-year "flops" or setbacks and his next parole hearing is not until 2022. He seems to be losing his way, but he is still struggling to hold onto himself. Recently he wrote:

> What I am about to share with you I've only recently confided to my cell mate (no one else) and I don't know why I share it now. Perhaps I trust you: I have allowed myself to be practically swallowed by some monstrous pit. At first, I thought it was just some rut that we many find ourselves in, but seem to recover after a week or two.
>
> After the realization that it has been almost two years, I decided enough is enough! I believe it began soon after my second ten-year deferment and almost

simultaneous divorce, when I started constructing the walls to close myself in— where it is safe and I don't have to feel the pain. Inevitably, this only accomplishes one thing: making me a shell of a man and *that is not who I am.* [Emphasis is in the original; his printed words were retraced a number of times.]

I am sooo much more, as we all know. To wrap this sad tale, I now use the uncaring, negative, self-absorbed parts that reside in us all as stepping-stones and rungs of a ladder. But I'm not completely sure if I have emerged unscathed. We'll see.

Shak was another of the few youthful offenders willing to talk back in 1994. A bright African American male, he struggled constantly with his anger. He tried hard to find new avenues for himself through education, but he was still volatile. He wrote about both in the piece below. I noted at the time that I wondered which force would win in the end.

The prison system is a breeding ground for hostility. It has caused me to become very bitter and anti-social. The way we are treated here angers me a lot. Sometimes I feel like I want to get out and get revenge on the people who mistreated me. It makes me want to retaliate. I now have a vendetta against authority figures of all sorts. The only thing that keeps me from acting foolishly is the other way incarceration has affected me.

The second way is I have gained a certain amount of patience and understanding. I understand that the behavior of the officials stems from ignorance. I now feel that my incarceration has also been a motivator for me.

Today, Shak is a free man, but still on parole. I know nothing of his personal situation, but records show he has been in the community for the past eleven years and the men tell me he is doing okay. He will be on parole until 2023.

It is a constant struggle to stay objective in listening to the constant string of complaints and feelings of angst that pour out of so many. But it is important to hear these words and still try to understand the impossible task facing Corrections. They are mandated to house thousands of men and women who have little in common other than that they broke the law and have been banished to prison for years. These inmates bring with them every dysfunction and sadness society can dish up. They bring hurt, despair, mental illness, and burning white anger with them. They reach prison through a justice system that is rife with inequality and unfairness. They see what money can buy—including freedom—and they chafe because they have none.

These inmates bring trouble with them. The mentally ill and unbalanced, and those with out-of-control anger keep things tense. Their antisocial activities continue within the walls. There are those who regularly stuff bags down the plumbing to overflow toilets, who start fires in the ventilation system, who will fight anyone at the drop of a hat.

Almost all inmates, even those following the rules, have some way to protect themselves. Homemade weapons are found with every shakedown— the potential for violence in a community on edge is very real.

Those who guard the inmates also bring their own sets of problems into the institution. They do not join Corrections for big wages. Officers' families are often on food stamps. The starting salary for an officer in our state is about twenty-one thousand dollars. One has to ask why they work in Corrections. Can they not find better paying employment? Do they have a need to control others? Do they have a sadistic side? Or are they looking for a career in criminal justice? The officers are almost as varied as the inmates. Twenty years ago, I'm told, many officers joined Corrections because it was a good job. It offered a steady income, friends worked there, and there was a good retirement and benefit package. Today most of the benefits and retirement advantages are gone. Because of staffing shortages, twelve-hour shifts have become a requirement. Recruitment of officers is a serious challenge. Everyone—inmates, staff, administrators—mentions that the quality of the new hires is dropping. There are exceptions, of course.

Corrections has a challenge to control a potentially dangerous population with often minimally educated, poorly paid personnel, some with questionable motives. I believe the problems start in the training sessions. There the new officers are taught to fear the inmates. They are told all inmates are out to trick them, to find ways to break the rules, to harm them. Seldom are gray areas discussed. For years, I resisted having our college teachers go through the correctional training session for volunteers. I put them through my own orientation of caution, warnings of the importance of following rules, of advice on how to appropriately conduct themselves. The few semesters I lost my fight and the teachers had to go through DOC orientation, I lost teachers before classes began. Corrections scared them to death. Or, even worse, they reacted to the extreme warnings with frustration after meeting the men and finding their students to be polite, bright, and eager learners. In their heads, DOC became wrong, the men victims, and the teachers became vulnerable in their naiveté.

One evening, I took students from my downtown community class into the prison to meet with their prison counterparts. The officer, unhappy with the extra duty and with the students seeing the prisoners in a positive light, had some of the students frozen to immobility by telling them before we went in that all the men in the class were either baby rapers or sex offenders who were looking them over "real good."

Everyone would be better off not to deal in stereotypes. The man who reached for his gun and shot his wife and lover when he came home and found them in bed may not be a compulsive liar. The young kid who, as a teenager, killed his mother when she was sexually abusing him is not a thief.

Nor are most officers sadistic bullies. Honestly, most officers do their jobs well. They handle their areas calmly and patiently and seldom run into problems. The only shortcoming is that they don't stop the bad apples in their ranks. They cover for them. They subtly punish those who report infractions of fellow officers. And that inappropriately tight brotherhood causes trouble for all.

Volatile men with seething internal anguish and sometimes sadistic and inconsistent guards mix in a dysfunctional system like a chemistry experiment. Most of the time, things are quiet and numbingly routine. But then there is an explosion. The potential is always there.

Issues to Think About

1. Do the personal accounts in this chapter match the images or stereotypes you have of inmates?
2. What do you believe would be the hardest part of being incarcerated?
3. The author found a change in the way men talked about their emotional reaction to imprisonment over the twenty-year period. How did the emotional content change? Why do you think that happened?
4. Troubled young people are causing increasing challenges both in our communities and within the prisons. Should that population (ages eighteen to twenty-four) be handled the same as the older men? What are your thoughts about this population?

THREE

In the Belly of the Beast
Entering Prison

By nature, prison is a cruel, lonely, and abusive place—it tears at the souls of men.

—Chuck

Thirty-three years ago, Leslie arrived in prison scared, distressed, and anxious. He rode in the blue Corrections bus that rolled down the long lane to a stone fortress looming at the end. They pulled into the sally port, and heavy gates clanged closed behind them. Shackled with thick chains, he and the other new inmates were herded into the bowels of the stone basement, and his incarceration began. Leslie remembered:

The scene was much like a horror scene you would only find in movies. Men, beat down with humiliation … degraded. A certain darkness loomed over the area where we were immediately taken once we unboarded the big Corrections bus. Old hospital gurneys rested in place, parked against crumbling concrete walls that had entire chunks missing. The aged storehouse for men, still used daily, seemed to have a certain ancient feel to it. The rooms and hallways were crude. Wires were hanging down and there were dimly lit fixtures that seemed to be decades old. There were no frills whatsoever, just very large steel doors with no windows filling the hall. Each door opened by staff took much effort where the building had settled over the years.

Men had horror written across their faces as we were taken from the bus, unshackled and loosed only long enough to be ushered into a very large room that had numerous missing panes from the windows. First we were fingerprinted and had our mug shots taken.

We were then accosted by a lieutenant yelling, "Strip all the way down, boys and girls, and I don't want to see one f***ing cigarette or jumpsuit in this room. Place all of the jumpsuits in this barrel in the corner of the room. We'll be back to get you five at a time."

As he closed the door and locked it, the airflow was recirculated. It was a dreary, cold, dark December afternoon. Snow was blowing in through the windows that were busted, and the temperature changed drastically in only a few minutes.

Stripped naked, most of the men sat on the benches with blank stares upon their faces, fear and dread plagued every moment of time. I recall hanging my head in depression, in shame and in self-loathing, thinking to myself, "You fool. You've done this to yourself." Trying hard to hold back tears, I could hear others around me quietly sobbing. It is not a time to confront, looking a man in the face or seeking out who it was who had broken. For that could get you hurt. I left it alone, seeking my own consolation.

The men who were taken first were not returned, so stories of where they went or what they were being subject to was mere conjecture.

Finally, my time arrived. I, along with four others, were escorted naked down the hall to an old bathroom/shower area. It was filthy and the stench of old wet uniforms filled the air. Mildew and mold took up residency in the corners, under toilets. Finally, I had reached the bay where I would stand. An inmate who was hired to work "intake" approached me with electric clippers and quickly buzzed off all facial hair. I was then told to stand with legs spread and arms extended and turn as directed. This procedure is called "delousing." The officer will use a spray bottle for the body hair areas. Then it is just a standard shower.

The fear of the unknown was somehow more than the confronted task at hand. Each of us was given a clean uniform and escorted to a place where we would be rationed three small towels, three washcloths, three pairs of socks, four razors, shaving cream, and four uniforms.

Then we were escorted across the yard to the "fish dorm." Dorm 10. Dorm 10 sat where the first nursing facility was later built.

The Correctional Facility

To really understand the prison experience, one must understand how prisons look, sound, smell, and operate. "Correctional facility" is the politically correct term these days. But the people who live behind the razor wire know they are in prison.

Prisons are as different from one another as the people who live and work in them. Wardens shift between prisons every few years, so invariably there are changes in procedures and programming. But at the heart of things, each facility has its own personality and set of unwritten rules. While all are supposed to operate under the same rules within the correctional philosophy of "firm, fair, consistent," the reality is that some are more humane and treatment oriented than others; some more firm, more fair, and more consistent than others. New wardens have trouble breaking the unspoken ways that things have operated for years.

Just as the diverse inmates share things in common, there are key things all prisons have in common. It is the commonality that is important for the public to understand.

All the male prisons I've been in smell alike. Today, most (not all) prisons are constantly cleaned, floors mopped, stripped and waxed with anesthetic-scented fluids. The scent mingles with a musky masculine odor that comes from a thousand or more men living in tight spaces. If you close your eyes, there is a subtle bouquet of metal, cleanliness, male perspiration, aggression, frustration, tension. After a short while, you don't pay attention to the smell as it enters your nose and pores.

Prisons sound alike, too. Hollowed voices echo around the stark concrete-block rooms with nothing padded or soft to muffle the sound as it bounces from wall to wall. The click-clicking of a noisy fan often adds to the prison ambiance. Occasionally a classroom will have much welcomed industrial-grade carpeting, which helps. But in most cases, people have to struggle to talk or hear in rooms whenever several are gathered. Dorms, gyms, and chow halls operate at painful decibels.

Prisons do not look alike, but there are many physical features they have in common. In the beginning, it was the physical environment that shocked and oppressed me most—all brown and gray and black and white with no color, nothing to please the eye or soothe the brain. The clanging of gates, the constant wait to have doors unlocked and relocked, the starkness of the dorms, the cold ever-present view of rolled razor wire and evenly spaced guard towers constantly remind newcomers where they are. But after a few months, the details, like the smells and sounds, rolled into my subconscious as part of a pervasive fog.

The two prisons where the men in this study were housed in 1994 have changed little over time. The facilities are at opposite ends of the physical spectrum, but are similar to prisons found around the United States. The first is an imposing monument to ancient prison architecture. Built in the 1930s, the institution is distinguished by an administration building topped by a ten-story stone tower that hangs over the institution with power and authority.

Bob, a man who spent many years within the prison, once told me that his life hit bottom when he was driven down that long road, and he looked up at that frightening edifice. Twenty years later, the exterior appearance is less austere; two new additions at the front of the institution are topped with bright blue roofs. The cheerful color is for the public. It cannot be seen from inside. The imposing tower remains. An old inmate, now long deceased, told how he, as a youthful convict in the 1930s, helped quarry the stone and build the structure while they lived in tents surrounded by armed guards.

Internally, the facility looks old. There are continual problems with keeping up the aging buildings, and some are being razed and replaced with structures that are more modern. But the place has a more open feel, and while older and more raggedy, many of the men and staff seem to like it better than the contrasting modern facility nearby. The older buildings left standing have skilled brick and tile work inside and out that give some feeling of variety and humanness.

The administration allows flowers to be planted around the school and there are some large grassy areas between the separated buildings. While I was there, they removed several nice larger trees, saying they blocked a clear view from the guard towers. A few small trees remain around the chapel. Overall, however, the general appearance is drab.

Our teachers are often startled at night walking out through the deserted central part of the institution. Skunks wander across the grounds in the dark, heading to the centrally located and very smelly dumpster. The men feed the skunks on the sly, so they are quite tame and unafraid. I never smelled their distinctive spray. A number of feral cats also roam the grounds. The men feed them as well and enjoy their presence and, according to one of the officers, the cats will never let anyone but the khaki-clothed inmates near them. The warden kindly allows them to remain, although they had to be rounded up and taken out to be neutered. A caring officer makes sure they are fed regularly and hopes a cat program will eventually be allowed in the institution.

I am sure he is long gone now, but I used to watch a pathetic old inmate stand for hours staring at the huge rusting air conditioning unit outside the chow hall near the same area where the skunks are often seen. He used to work with machines, I was told, and when allowed to stand and look at the unit, he remained calm and quiet. This was in the days before the nursing facility had been built. With some startling exceptions, this institution has had flexibility and a heart.

Prisons are monotonous in their routines, but occasionally the sameness is broken by interesting unplanned occurrences. The ten-story tower is a big attraction for birds. As dusk settles around the surrounding rural area, the skies fill with swooping flocks of starlings, circling with an ever-increasing cacophony of sound and birdcalls. At night, they settle on the tower and the rooftops, safe until the next morning. I enjoyed watching and hearing them.

Then one day, the maintenance department had to go onto the roof for repairs. Some unsuspecting soul removed the trapdoor and several feet of bird droppings showered on his head and blew into the spaces below. The EPA closed down the tower; offices were moved. In short, it was a mess as the tower was decontaminated from the disease- and germ-laden bird droppings and airborne dangers.

After that, we got much enjoyment watching the fight between the birds and the administration. Periodic loud noises and recordings from the tower roof would set the birds off in a mass of flapping wings, only to return shortly. After a while, the noises lost their effectiveness and another sound or method would be tried. It was a circus of enjoyment in a place where anything novel is welcomed.

Then there was the time when the school was painted. Actually, painting continues non-stop in an aging facility. Accreditation boards are always greeted with freshly waxed floors and new paint jobs everywhere. But this particular time, the official in charge decided to save money and ordered the inmate painters to mix all the leftover paint in the institution. They poured in industrial metal paint along with latex and acrylic. The result was a dark purplish-brown concoction that smelled as bad as it looked. When it was applied to the walls in the school, people started dropping like flies. My coworker and I had to leave early with splitting headaches. The painters were throwing up. Teachers were dizzy. They opened doors and turned on fans to improve circulation. This went on for several weeks. Finally, the school was closed down. Rumor was that some of the men forced to be in the school had their families call the EPA who visited and demanded it be closed. When it reopened, everything was freshly painted, the unforgettable odor was gone, and we moved on, waiting for something else to break the monotony.

In contrast, the newer nearby institution is a modernistic, low-slung, solid white concrete facility that, at first glance, looks more like a hospital than a prison. Visitors, after being impressed in the administrative area with cathedral ceilings, skylights, and huge plants, grimace once they enter the heart of the facility. Two long rows of white buildings with an uneven concrete walkway stretching wall to wall between them form an incredible wind tunnel in the winter and reflective oven in the summer. The undrained concrete walkway collects water during heavy rainstorms, leaving no choice for people entering the yard but to wade right through up to their ankles and live with wet shoes the remainder of the day.

The solid concrete slabs of the walkway crack and rise with weather and aging, causing people to stumble or fall frequently, especially in icy weather. One volunteer in a wheelchair was dumped unceremoniously into a heap as the chair hit the edge of a broken block. I have lost many boxes of books from handcarts being pushed along the uneven surface.

The central grassed area is sealed off with high chain-link fences, and the men walk from their identical white concrete dormitories lined in a row, to the identical white concrete buildings that house their work areas and school. There is not a tree anywhere. In recent years, a small flower garden and an outdoor mural have been allowed. There are some small garden areas around the dorms cared for by the inmates. There is a small fenced-in playground and area for family visits.

Both institutions have ball fields and recreational spaces with walking tracks that are set back from the central areas.

Over the years, there was one pleasant colorful change in the two institutions. The visual pleasure was the work of a large, good-natured middle-aged inmate from Switzerland. Bruno spoke with a heavy accent and claimed he had never painted before coming to prison. He began painting miniature pictures in his cell and news of his talent spread. He was asked if he could paint a mural on the wall at the school. The picture of the peaceful Swiss Alps led to a second painting of an outdoor lake, and eventually a string of five-by-eight-foot murals stretched down the hall.

Recently, I was in the nursing care facility at another institution, and there were Bruno's murals decorating the walls that had previously been drab tan. He had been transferred; his paint and his talent moved with him. He is now long gone, but his remembered visions of his beloved homeland remained, carefully taken care of, feeding the spirits of those left behind.

Only a few weeks after penning this description, I received a letter from one of the men, Doug. Usually a happy optimistic soul, he was angry. He mentioned Bruno's paintings.

> Unfortunately, the warden had them painted over (because they're evil). Oh, my bad! The reason given was "to protect and further legitimate state and penal interests." I promise, they have some talking points and catchphrases that make me want to scream! Really though, what could it hurt to have paintings on the walls—other than make it nicer?

I am puzzled by one observation. Over the years, the men in question have served time in prisons all over the United States. But never, not once, has one of them mentioned the physical differences between the places, other than whether they were double-bunked or assigned to dayrooms, or had a room to themselves. To them, the physical environment is not what counts. But I think the physical setting has a lot to do with the attitudes and perceptions of the staff and inmates. Others are beginning to agree and write about it.[1]

Security

State vans or buses carrying new inmates arrive almost daily, pulling into an enclosed area marked "Receiving and Delivery." The vehicles roll in and giant gates clang shut behind them, encapsulating the human contents within the institution. Once inside, the men learn that their lives have changed.

Today, all new inmates are run through a central facility that is more modern than the institution that Leslie entered years ago. The first-time fears, the humiliating procedures, occur in a cleaner environment. After orientation and classification, the new inmates are shipped around the state where they face a variety of situations. The exact procedure and locations for intake differ between institutions and states, but the procedures are similar. The feelings of fear and humiliation are present no matter where the prison is.

The men are fingerprinted. Their inmate number is placed on a board and held in front of their usually expressionless faces as the camera blinks. The captured image will be embossed and always worn clipped to their khaki uniforms.

Everyone else, staff and visitor alike, goes through a different security point to enter the institutions. It is much like security at the airport, removing coats, placing smaller items on a conveyer belt for X-ray. Other belongings are physically searched and if individuals set off the X-ray machine as they pass through, an officer runs a wand over them. Depending on who is around watching at the time, clearance of regular workers varies greatly. More often than not, a regular staff member is waved through with a precursory touching of a lunch bag and no one views the X-rays if an item is put on the belt. Other times, though, if administration is around or if an officer is new to the position, the search can be irritatingly thorough.

Visitors enter the belly of most institutions the same way—through a series of ominously clanging sliding gates. They might be huge, black iron-barred gates or thick metal-and-glass doors, but the effect is the same. A series of three to four gates and checkpoints separate the outside world from the world of the inmates. In the sally ports, visitors wait for the gate to open, then they walk in and wait for it to close before the one leading to the next area is opened. Occasionally, an employee will stand in front of an unlocked door, waiting unconsciously for it to open. Even employees can become institutionalized.

There are similar sally ports for vehicles delivering goods to the institutions. Each vehicle is checked and searched as it enters. A mirror on a pole is placed underneath to check for clinging inmates or contraband as the truck enters and leaves the institution. Like everything else, security depends on the officers. I have seen drivers and their trucks passed in without inspection after gifts of several gallons of orange juice and chocolate milk were presented to the guards. In contrast, sometimes they have practically taken my car apart when I delivered books. Most of the time, though, the procedure is sensible, routine, and appropriate. Escapes from the institutions themselves are rare but do occur in a variety of innovative ways.

The most shocking escape attempt that occurred while I was working there ended in unspeakable tragedy. Two young unthinking inmates jumped into an open garbage dumpster and waited to be transported to freedom. As planned, the dumpster was emptied into the garbage truck, but the men had never noticed that it was policy to compact the trash before it left the institution. They were both killed, their broken bodies later found in the dump.

Escapes are infrequent and difficult. The main security issue is the never ending contraband that finds its way into the institutions.

Life on the Yard

For the inmates to proceed beyond the outer set of gates, they must be handcuffed and shackled. But within most prisons, they are free to walk around. They cannot stop and congregate and must stay on the walkways, but at times when the yard is open, there is free interchange among the men and a feeling of organized freedom. Some institutions have more controlled movement, and the inmates need passes to move from one area to another. Guards are ever-present in the towers. Everyone wears ID badges. All staff members have walkie-talkies. The men never forget where they are. But life does go on.

Everywhere there are lines. Twenty years ago, Sam wrote:

> You're standing in lines for everything that you get here. Standing sometimes in very long, very slow moving, very unfriendly lines for as long as three hours to only be disappointed when you finally reach the front. There are lines to spend the little money one makes as a janitor. There are lines to receive your medicine. Lines for medical attention. No matter what the weather—rain, sleet, snow, or hail—the lines be there. I never thought I would be standing in so many smoke-filled, tobacco-chewing, loud-talking lines in my life.

The lines are still there, with added short lines at a kiosk where the inmates order their canteen items electronically. At many of the institutions, the major lining-up areas have been covered to protect inmates from the rain, and the smoke and tobacco have been eliminated. Some of the wait times have been shortened. But none of those changes were accomplished without related problems arising.

The public thinks that inmates spend their time lying around playing cards. For the most part, that is not true. Those who are trying to make a new life for themselves are as busy as those of us on the outside. After being at a facility awhile and developing a good reputation, a man can work himself into Correctional Industries, where the men put in a full day at constructive jobs: running printing machines, making license plates and uniforms, and building furniture for governmental agencies. They might attend school at nights and try to fit in homework, exercise, and leisure.

There are, of course, those who don't want to do anything, and they are the ones who cause the most trouble. In most states, there are incentives, both negative and positive, to force the inmates into some type of job. But as the institutions hold twice as many men as they were designed for, many jobs are busywork. Administrators are held back by regulations and laws that forbid the use of physical force to make the men work.

The men are creative in how to make their poorly paid positions more lucrative. Pay varies between states and even between institutions. A typical wage for many jobs is eighty-five cents a day (eighteen dollars a month), but there is a way to make that amount unofficially increase by charging extra to do the job right. For example, if inmates want a decent haircut, they pay the inmate barber in stamps or canteen supplies. If they want their clothes neatly folded or ironed rather than stuffed wrinkled in a bag, they pay extra under the table. The fee used to be paid in cigarettes, but when smoking was banned, the underground currency changed to stamps and food. It costs six stamps to have trousers shortened—three stamps per leg.

Dormitories: Cell Blocks with a Nicer Name

At the end of the workday, some of the men talk about it being "time to go home." Others resist that term and loudly declare the institution will never be home, no matter how many years they spend there. The dormitory is where they live, and the dormitory areas affected me the most when I first saw them. I couldn't grasp what the men were trying to say until I visited them myself. The dormitories are just cell blocks with a nicer name.

My first visit some years ago to one of the newer dorms started with a surprise. I felt comfortable as we walked into the central area where the control booth is located and where the open two-story halls lead off like an octopus's arms. I was standing, looking around, as my escort chatted with the dorm officer. I noticed a man glaring angrily at me. I focused my attention on him and realized he was urinating. The bathroom area in this "state-of-the-art" dorm had no walls; only a partial waist-high barrier separated the tile restroom from the central area. The facilities were designed that way for security measures, but the men say they are degrading.

> The living environment provides no privacy whatsoever. You're taking a shower with more than yourself. I am saying there is always someone observing you as you try to take a shower. There will be sometimes as many as sixteen inmates in the shower with you. It is the same when "paying your respects" in the restroom. I would have never imagined sitting side by side with someone taking a crap.—Sam

> We are being watched or monitored in every aspect of our daily lives here. They monitor and tape-record our phone conversations. They listen into our rooms via an intercom system. But I guess the worst part is the bathroom system.—John

In the men's prisons, female officers work the dormitories alongside their male counterparts. Over the years, I heard complaints time and again from the men about how the female guards carefully look them over as they view them in the shower or other areas where they are naked. The situations vary by institution. The administration says the women behave professionally, and affirmative action laws open all areas of assignments to women. The men are incensed and say many problems come from having the females in the dorm areas in the evening. Norman wrote: "I consider having to shower and go to the bathroom with female guards standing and watching very degrading and a form of harassment. I am basically a very private person and abhor the idea of open bathrooms, but this is made even more stressful by being subjected to the watchful eye of women guards."

Cal, always angry, doesn't have much patience with the complaining. "What gets me is why would anyone expect privacy in prison? If the men (term used loosely) have a problem, they need to grow up."

In the men's most recent responses, they did not complain as much about the facilities as they did twenty years ago. Some dividers have been built for the toilets, and some of the issues of female officers resolved through legislation. My sense is that after more than twenty years in a prison environment, the men are used to the indignities. But crowding still presents a problem at most institutions around the country. Wayne explains:

> This prison was built in the early eighties to house around five hundred inmates. The dorms were single cell (one man to a cell).... Each floor has its own bathroom consisting of one shower stall with one shower head, two toilets, three sinks, one urinal. But when they double-bunked all the cells in 1989, it went to twenty-eight to thirty men using one bathroom. They doubled the population, but not much of anything else.
>
> Each room, or cell, in the newer dorms accommodates two men. The cell is ten by six and a half feet. The rooms are nine feet high. There is a three-by-three-foot shatterproof window in a steel frame in each room. On the side of the wall, the base of the bed is made of concrete block topped with a three-inch poured concrete slab six feet long and thirty inches wide. When the dorms were double-bunked, a steel bed frame was bolted to the concrete bed that allows about a thirty-six-inch head clearance for the lower bunk.
>
> Along the back of the room, there is a concrete block table with a three-inch concrete slab about twenty-five inches wide, which stretches wall to wall. And there is a built-in non-moveable stool. On the wall across from the beds, there is a small shelf bolted to the wall large enough to hold shampoo bottles, soap dishes, and other things they refer to as "hygiene." Next to the shelf are two stand-up lockers about five feet tall and two feet wide. Between them is a shelf with a wooden rod underneath for hanging clothes.
>
> That leaves a space six feet long and thirty inches wide for two men to walk around in. Room decorations are not allowed. Nothing can be hung on the walls. No decorative coverings on the table or floors. There are limited amounts of state-provided clothes and bedding allowed in each room and a limit on personal items such as books. If they have the money to buy them, each man is allowed a small TV, radio, headphones, gym shoes of prescribed color and style. Each is allowed to purchase a ten-quart cooler to keep purchased food chilled.

This tiny barren space was home to Wayne for thirty-two years. He left a short time ago and moved home with his parents. I wonder how he is adjusting to living in a regular bedroom all by himself. Another man, in for fourteen years, told me he had to sleep on the floor his first few nights of freedom—the large soft bed in his home was too disturbing.

Amenities that used to be limited to the honor dorms now extend to all. There are two microwaves for each wing of the dorms and an ice machine. "Stingers"—electrical coils that can be placed in a cup of coffee or water to heat it—are no longer allowed; in fact, one man said the young ones don't even know what stingers are.

I have mentioned the problem of overcrowding. Some men don't live in the small cells that are considered prime locations. People new to the institution or who have lost their privileges and room, are bunked close together in the dayroom, which was originally intended to be the public area of each wing. The noise, the lack of privacy, the crowding, makes the dayroom assignment especially onerous. So many people in such tight spaces—it is no wonder that both the men and officers chafe whenever there is a lockdown and a restriction of movement. It can be a tense time.

I have not been privy to one part of the everyday prison experience and that is the dormitories at night. The atmosphere in the school and workplaces is markedly different from that in most of the dorms. The honor dorms are calmer and more civilized than the regular dorms, but men act differently among one another than they do with people they respect—or pretend they respect.

Men constantly remind me that what I see in people is not what they see. In the dorms, the air is blue with uncontrolled and coarse conversations. At times, men masturbate while watching the female officers walking around. Men who pray loudly in the chapel run drugs on the yard. Inmates who share their deepest doubts with me are said to be hard-core, uncaring men elsewhere. The contradictions and contrasts have amazed me from the beginning.

The inmates see the aggression and hardness in others and try to fit in. They believe they are the only ones who carry anguish and pain with them daily. I have yet to sit and talk with one of the toughened convicts without finding a spot within them that hurts and yearns for something more. Tears welling in jaded, hardened eyes tell the true tale. Without question, the men and officers see the inmates differently than I do and have different experiences with them. The question is, which personality represents the "real" person and which will win in the end?

Issues to Think About

1. As you are introduced to life within prison walls, is there anything that is different than you previously thought?

2. Some of the inmates say that the behaviors and attitudes seen by the author are not true reflections of the incarcerated offenders—that most other inmates are unfeeling and uncaring. The author believes the men do not let each other see their more thoughtful, caring sides. What do you make of this contradiction?
3. Is there anything you find disturbing about the prison environment? Why? Should harshness be part of the punishment?

FOUR

On the Yard
Day-to-Day Life in Prison

No, I did not (and do not) follow every single rule posted. If I were to do so, I could never get out of bed! I guess it carried over into my earlier years of my incarceration. I never liked to be told what to do by someone I did not respect.

—Cam

Daily life in prison is not usually the stereotypical nightmare depicted on TV. It can be dangerous, and tension is always beneath the surface, but for the most part, well-run prisons move along in a slow boring fashion. It is the relative calmness—not the violence—that should be the most surprising. Most prisons today are overcrowded facilities, often originally designed for half the population they now house. Yet in most, men sleep, eat, work, and live in a somewhat orderly, predictable manner.

Times of extreme trouble and danger, or times filled with relative peace and educational opportunities, depend more on the administration and their policies than anything. Some of the TV reality shows take place in county jails or segregation areas where there is nothing constructive to do and men are at their worst. In a chorus, the men say life is more ordered and tolerable in prison than in jail. But that does not make daily life easy.

Violence

Most prisons are relatively calm. But that doesn't make them safe, and danger can rise and ebb. During the time I was in the two prisons central to the first study, there was a murder, at least two rapes of female staff members, several very serious physical attacks, innumerable fights, and two young men killed in an escape attempt. Serious issues were kept very quiet by the administration. Those violent incidents were not everyday occurrences like they were thirty years ago, but even in the best-run, calmest institutions, trouble is just a word or gesture away. A change of administration and policies can upset the applecart. At one previously safe and calm institution, both the men and the officers say trouble is brewing; both groups fear a riot is a real possibility.

In that institution, the hard-nosed military-trained warden orders in Correctional Emergency Response Teams (CERT) for situations that could be handled with less force. (CERT are specially selected and trained teams that come into the correctional facility to deal with dangerous and potentially violent situations. The teams are dressed in protective gear and carry special weapons and equipment.) Like the painting-over of the pleasant pictures, the warden eliminated perks that made life more tolerable. He painted yellow arrows on the sidewalks, indicating the flow of walking traffic. He continually picked away at the settled routine, upsetting even the most placid inmates and guards.[1]

In all prisons, the men speak of boredom. But they also speak of the constant, never-ending wariness and tension that lie just below the surface, affecting everything in their lives.

Count

The procedure known as "count" dictates the rhythm of the institution. It is necessary for security, and while irritating, I believe it helps keep the slow pace of the institution and keeps the men calm and under control. I also think it is one of the things that makes reentry into the community most difficult.

Every three to four hours, the institution is shut down. Most of the men are required to return to their cells or their workplace where they wait as they are literally counted. The exact procedure differs among institutions. Talking is frequently forbidden. It doesn't matter what is going on, how important something seems to be, it stops when it's time for count. The procedure is a source of derision and frustration as everything revolves around it—and it seems more often than not, the count never clears on the first try. Officers count the men in their area and report the number to a central location. The tally has to be exact before the men are released. A delay, of course, impacts anything else that is planned for the day.

While frustrating, it does slow down the pace of the place. Upon release from prison, perhaps the thing that bothers men the most is the frenetic speed of everyday life where things never stop moving. In prison, things are slow and predictable. I was frustrated whenever count rolled around when we were in the middle of something that seemed important, but over time,

I came to appreciate the chance to take a breath, to see that things can wait. But being used to the procedure doesn't translate well when men released from prison are expected to maintain the frenzy of everyday life.

Chow

Everyday life in prison is excruciatingly routine, and things we take for granted on the outside are big issues there. Eating, for example. The food service is like that depicted in prison movies on TV—banged-up divided plates with food slopped on them in a disgusting manner. The food is heavy on mayonnaise and grease and light on other flavoring.

The food service, like many things in Corrections, has been privatized in recent years, which had caused even more problems. The men continually complain they do not get enough food and grouse about the quality. Grievances are frequently filed over food issues. There was a prison riot some years ago in the state that seemed to be connected with complaints about food. The official report was there were other problems to blame, but the men still say informally that food was at the heart of it.

Leslie wrote:

> The chow hall—that's always a unique experience to say the least. Our chow hall is extremely overcrowded and noisy. There are people who come in yelling and screaming to a buddy. They will be in line standing right beside you screaming at the top of their lungs. That makes tempers very short.... The tables are so close together that it's inevitable that people bump into one another and spill stuff. It's a stressful situation, but compounded by the noise level, it's a major problem. Myself and my friends try to eat as fast as we can and get out. It also causes tension when the guards try to rush us even more. They cram all these people in the chow hall and wonder why there is nowhere for them to sit. It doesn't make sense. They watch us like we are trying to steal something. It's really aggravating and frustrating.
>
> Another thing in the chow hall that's annoying is the fact that they give us dirty utensils. There is food left on the trays and silverware. The cups are either dirty or have soap left in them. It's sickening. I don't want to eat off these things. I stand there and go through several trays until I find one that "looks" clean. Then you have the servers who give their buddies more than everyone else. It's petty, I know, but it gets very aggravating and stressful. I try not to let it bother me. I blank out as much of the noise, the crowding, and the guards from my mind that I can. I try to get in and out as fast as possible.

Twenty years ago, the chow hall was the place in the institution where you heard the most about racial tensions. Blacks and whites voluntarily used separate lines at one institution and sat at different tables. The giving of extra food often took on a racial tone in the telling. That has changed in recent years. Blacks and white mingle in line and at the tables. These days, the complaints about some getting more food than others are related to who has a server friend rather than what race one is.

In some places, the nationwide company responsible for prison food incorporates a food service training program for their inmate workers. The classes make some food available for the inmates to purchase that can be microwaved in the dorms to avoid the physical hassle of the chow hall.

To avoid the chow hall, inmates with money will often buy snacks and cold food from the canteen, which they can keep in their rooms in a small cooler. On special occasions, the men pool their food, cooking it in the microwave available to them. It is a change in recent years, but many men now eat their evening meal back at the dorm, paying for the food themselves. The institution is supportive of this change. The men buy from the canteen, which generates millions in profits each year, adding money to the correctional coffers and paying for things the public sometimes objects to.

Sex

HIV and hepatitis are common among a population that was sexually permissive and involved in intravenous drug use in the past. The prison administration is faced with a difficult dilemma, and their approaches to the problem fluctuate between the years and between administrations. Sexual activity has been strictly forbidden for as long as I've been around and brings strong penalties if violators are caught. But everyone knows there is no stopping it. Sexual activity in the prisons is quite widespread and often winked at by the officers, some of whom are involved themselves.

Although everyone knows the reality of the situation, no condoms are available to the men since the activity is illegal, so in all likelihood, disease is being spread daily. Implications in terms of future health care expenses for Corrections cannot be ignored.

The men's attitudes toward same-sex sexual activity within prisons is somewhat hard to understand. We discussed homosexuality in my sociology classes and I found it almost impossible to conduct an objective discussion on the subject, probably because of their internal emotional conflicts. The majority speak with extreme hostility about homosexuality.

Yet privately, the respondents estimate that 40 to 50 percent of the men have been involved at least once in homosexual activities in the prison. These reactions speak to the internal conflict that plagues them.

Tom does a good job of explaining what I have heard from others:

In prison, men are separated from their mates and intimate relationships, not only physically but emotionally.... This fact leads to two types of sexual relationships in prison....

The first type of sexual activity falls into a category that can be referred to as a long-term relationship. The two people involved form a monogamous relationship that, in most cases, lasts until one of the participants leaves prison or is transferred to another institution. These relationships tend to be very strong, and close emotional ties are formed. Sexual activity is indeed a part of these relationships; however, they are based more upon a human need for closeness and intimacy.

This type of emotional and sexual activity is more common in the institutions where the population is double-bunked.

An interesting significance about these relationships, as well as in all prison sexual relationships, is that they almost always occur between a heterosexual and a homosexual or bisexual.... Once the heterosexual inmate has left the prison setting, he reverts back to a heterosexual lifestyle.

The second type of sexual activity that occurs most often can be referred to as a one-night stand. This category includes, just as the name implies, one-time sexual encounters between inmates who are not cell mates.... In contrast to our other category, the sole purpose of these relationships is for the physical act of sex. The relationships tend to be short lived with only one or two encounters before the relationship terminates. If any emotional ties do develop between the participants, they are feelings of possession as the heterosexual partner feels as if he owns the attentions of the other.

The sexual activities of the heterosexual men confuse and disturb the inmates. John explained how heterosexuals become involved and how they rationalize the actions to themselves.

Many of the inmates here were homosexual before ever being locked up. Others were "turned out" either to pay off debts by trading sexual favors or because they were simply too weak and were intimidated into sex.... Many of the men who have "punks" are considered macho unless they are caught catching as well as pitching. Many of the inmates who engage in homosexual activity don't consider it that since they only receive gratification, but don't in turn reciprocate.

Rape at this institution is very rare although it has occurred.... However, with the number of punks available, there is no reason to take something most will be able to find willing partners for, or at the most charged a couple of packs of cigarettes for. Prostitution, as with any other vice, occurs, and is readily available for anyone wanting sex.

In the double-bunked rooms, sexual activity can occur with relative privacy. In some institutions, men are strictly forbidden to enter each other's rooms or "break the plane of the door." Yet sex still occurs. John continued:

Each day at three, six, and nine o'clock, the wings to the dorms are closed for the purpose of counting the inmates. After the count is conducted, the wings remain closed for approximately thirty minutes and this is one of the best opportunities for homosexual activities to take place.... In my particular wing, there is a steady parade of men visiting this one particular room. Everybody knows about it, talks about it, and I wonder how the guards could not know. Nevertheless, it goes on and on.

The guards probably do know about it, but for whatever reason, they have decided to look the other way. It's not hurting anybody, so why cause trouble for them, one officer intimated to me.

Being Gay in Prison

The percentage of homosexual men in prison is probably the same as in the general community. Life is difficult for the gay inmate although jokes may make it seem otherwise. Mel, an openly gay man, explained:

> Some might think being a gay man in prison would be like a kid in a candy store, and I guess for someone looking for meaningless, detached sexual encounters, it might be. For someone looking for a meaningful relationship, it feels like I'm dying of thirst in a desert.
>
> The language on the yard is excessively homophobic. One cannot walk around without hearing "dick sucker" this or "fag" that, convicts hurling gay epithets at one another in reference to someone being weak, detestable, the lowest form of life. Where many people refrain from using the "N-word" because it is deemed intolerant or politically incorrect, convicts have no qualms about using gay epithets. Even though I intellectually know they aren't specifically speaking of me in the moment, or are even aware that I am overhearing their conversations, it's difficult at times to keep from feeling personally attacked.
>
> The junior high mentality of many convicts and their attitudes about sexuality and masculinity brings up much of my junior high insecurities: feeling left out, judged, torn between my attraction to them and my fear of being found out. I'm not secretive about my sexuality, but it's not something I broadcast either.

The homosexuals, like the heterosexuals, may seek out physical relief, but what both groups really yearn for are caring, loving, supportive relationships. The men don't just look in their own ranks for those relationships. During the years I was in the institutions, officers, teachers, staff, nurses, counselors, volunteers, and even administrators were ignobly escorted off the grounds and fired for their activities with inmates. These more often involved emotional attachments and, at times, have lasted over a long period, even after the staff person left the institution. A lot of gossip flies after each incident is discovered, but the men involved are often protective and caring towards the other person.

One man cryptically ended one of his letters to me by saying, "You will be shocked to know that I have two beautiful children, ages eight and twelve." He has been incarcerated without break for twenty-two years. He is a good looking, confident, virile man. I know of at least two relationships he had with staff in the past. These offspring were conceived with a staff member while he was incarcerated.

Another man told me he impregnated his girlfriend during an "open house" visit, which used to be a yearly event to allow families to visit the dormitories to see where their loved ones lived. I thought the open houses were a good idea and would be very helpful to the children to be able to see where their fathers lived. I had no idea. Those have been discontinued.

Others mentioned having sexual relationships with people from the community while living in minimum-security facilities where there is more freedom. Sexual activity is very much part of life in prison, and I suspect it will continue to be.

However, in the past few years, the policy involving sex between inmates and others has taken a startling turn due to the 2003 federal Prison Rape Elimination Act (PREA), put into effect in 2012. Initiated by the horrific statistics that indicated 13 percent of inmates had been raped while incarcerated, the law was enacted to deal with the inequities of power that are inherent within the institutions.[2] Institutions are required to prove their compliance to this zero-tolerance policy or be fined a percentage of federal grant money. Now, men are shown a film about PREA in their prison orientation and again when they are moved to their permanent facility. There are no consensual relationships, they are told.

Today, when a liaison is discovered between an inmate and staff member, the employee, male or female, is arrested and charged with a sexual offense, regardless of stated mutual consent. The staff members can be incarcerated themselves as a result, and will live with the conviction of a sexual offense. The administrators I have talked with are supportive of the legislation.

It's a good example of needed protection with teeth, but it is a zero-tolerance policy that has serious unintended consequences. Of all of the staff I know who were escorted out of the facilities, only one might have been involved in a coerced situation, and it involved female inmates looking for favors from a male administrator. Whether it will stop the romances remains to be seen. I'm told they have decreased, but not stopped.

Recreation

Many of the most vocal members of the public do not understand the need for recreation within prisons. They talk about country club prisons with nice recreational facilities but, at least in my state, there is nothing "country club" about the state correctional institutions. Each one does have a ball field, short walking track, weight equipment, and most have a gymnasium. If we locked men up in their cells with no exercise for twenty or more years, we would have sky-high medical bills and an institution better suited to be a mental hospital. Regular exercise and team sports keep the men healthy and acting in a socially approved manner. Recreation is a money saver and a much-needed physical and emotional outlet.

In many states, recreation is funded by the canteen money generated from the men themselves. Most prison canteens are run by private enterprises these days. The prices are jacked up well above the going price in the community and Corrections gets a hefty bite of the profits. In most places, canteen money covers additional services or items, especially for things that the public is reluctant to supply. Athletic equipment and cable TV, including a sports channel, are funded that way. Some states use canteen money to help fund the college classes.

The extent of organized recreation depends on the creativity and energy of the recreation director and the available funding. Sometimes visiting groups come in and play the prison teams. In some institutions, there are intramural competitions.

During national play-off times, things can get raucous in the dorms, with noise reaching levels that are excruciating for those few not interested in sports.

The recreational areas are frequently mentioned in contexts other than sports. The rec field is the one place where men can occasionally be by themselves. There are benches scattered around the edges of the walking track.

Daniel wrote many years ago of the day he turned twenty-one in prison. He wandered alone to the rec field and sat on a bench, thinking about his life. He was at the depths of depression, he said, and sitting there was what he remembered most about his birthday into official adulthood.

In the rec areas, where activities are less structured, troubles can also arise. One young man, new to the institution, defiantly ignored the informal prescribed procedures and rearranged the weight pile that some of the men had set up for the next day. He was beaten nearly to death for his arrogance. The rec field is also a place where drugs are hidden and exchange hands. But it is an area crucial to the control of the inmate population, giving young, strong men an appropriate physical outlet for their aggression and frustration.

Programs

This chapter could expand to a book in itself if correctional programming was fully discussed. All institutions have "programs." The programs are required to obtain the coveted accreditation for each facility and they also give the administration hope that there is a rehabilitative component to the time spent behind bars.[3]

Each institution has literacy classes, GED, and vocational education. The waiting list is long for vocational classes, and the skills learned there often translate well into later employment. Many states have brought back college programming in spite of the huge setback when Pell Grant funding was recalled. Numerous studies show that education is the most effective tool for reduced recidivism, and college programming is the most effective.[4] The men in this project mentioned education as the thing that helped them the most. In some cases, they said, it actually changed their lives.

There are far fewer educational programs in place today in Kentucky's institutions than there were when I began in 1988. It is mostly a financial issue and not usually a lack of caring on the part of administrators. On the other hand, top administrators sure make some puzzling decisions.

What has increased in number and complexity are other programs of a rehabilitative nature. Multiple classes with multiple acronyms abound—SAP, TIF, SOTP, MRT, New Beginnings, and Anger Management. The subject matter of each is useful, needed by many, often poorly presented, and derided by most of the inmates. However, completion of classes makes a good impression on the parole board, and the board even requires certain certificates for parole consideration. There are waiting lists for the classes and often a selection process, and they are the pride of DOC.

There are problems inherent in canned programs that are required for an already recalcitrant population. Many programs purchased from outside vendors are not community specific, nor does the presenter have any commitment to the curriculum. My personal observation (with no statistical backup) is that the most effective programs are the ones of a voluntary nature that affect rehabilitation through indirect methods. Most often, non-correctional individuals—who bring a new energy into the mix—are the ones who teach these programs.

At a local institution, Shakespeare Behind Bars is the most outstanding program and is featured in an award-winning documentary of the same name. Writing programs, drama groups, even yoga classes, help the men explore their inner turmoil in a circuitous way that allows them to embrace their issues without having to be forced to confront them. That type of program is not always welcomed by Corrections because of the realistic possibility of over-involvement from the community teachers and the extra efforts required by prison staff. The parole board doesn't seem to hold them in the same esteem.

Wes has been in and out of prisons for years. His rap sheet is long. His desire to live right is sincere, but he has trouble holding things together during his brief times of freedom. He knows he needs the programs, but he hates them. He is extraordinarily bright and personable. His insights show the dilemmas facing both the administration and the men in finding effective ways to make inmates see how they need to change. Here is Wes's take on programming:

> In my opinion, for any of the programs to work, we would have to first be honest and open. It is very difficult for us to be honest and open about ourselves. Most of us have done horrible things to our family, have been horrible parents, and have been horrible friends. We have mostly done things that we don't want to talk about, and we sure as heck don't want the whole yard talking about, which if we talk about it in a class, then it will be all over the yard tomorrow. I think that is the main obstacle—we have to deal with other inmates who we don't really trust, like, or can put much faith in.
>
> I look at AA [Alcoholics Anonymous] as a forced thing. They force me to go. I was never given a choice. In prison, you are "forced" to go, and by that I mean that they threaten to not give you good time or parole or let you live in the honor dorm, or something; they are always threatening you to make you go. That's why I dislike those meetings that "hold your meeting sheet" till the end of the meeting before you can get it back. Do they know that if they lay them out that everyone will pick them up and leave as soon as they stamp them? Of course they do. It's no secret that nobody wants to be there.
>
> There are several things that I have to do if I want to stay out. Accepting AA is a big one. I know that AA has got to be part of my life as long as I want to stay sober. My dislike for AA meetings is a problem. This is something that I will have to address as soon as I get out, and right now I have no idea what the answer is. I know just going to meetings and sitting there, full of resentment for being there, that is not only not going to help me, it will send me straight back to prison.

Wes was not in my original group twenty years ago, but he was in prison at that time. I got to know him when he was out for a short six-month period. He started attending my church and struck up a friendship with a couple of people on our reentry committee.

Then trouble struck. He had messed himself up again. He had illegal prescription pills in his room and a rubber stamp that he had been using and selling to avoid going to required programs. His disdain for required programs carried from the prison to the community. His made-up AA group was "Serenity Now," which comes from a humorous episode of *Seinfeld*. He was returned to prison.

We began a fascinating correspondence as he agreed to join my project. His letters were unrivaled in length and interest. He claimed to be a quiet man, but loved to write—and write he did and well. In written words, he was free to share his deeper thoughts. He discussed in detail his thinking process, which he was the first to admit was faulty. He searched for how to fix himself. He gave his opinion on all the questions I asked and, as he wove his answers, found the weaknesses in his own arguments.

Even though he was in a minimum-security prison with a good deal of freedom when he wrote, he was a good person to explain what others tried to say about the prison environment.

I do think it is important for you to understand more fully what I mean when I say a general statement like "I really do not like it here" or "I am counting down the weeks."

Now, this is where the worst of society ends up. For the most part, almost everybody here are drug addicts, thieves, liars. We are the people who wouldn't work, pay our taxes, pay our rent. We could not make it. We stole from our neighbors, lied, cheated, wouldn't clean up after ourselves. Now, these people, for the most part, have not changed. Most go along with the program to try and stay out of trouble and not get write-ups, but the majority doesn't even care about that.

We live in open wings, like an army barracks, so everybody just sits around all day watching everybody else, waiting for somebody to leave something lying out that they can steal. Stealing is rampant. They will steal your towel, your headphones, anything. Your pencil. So every day, you have to be on guard, worrying that some-one is going to steal something. Then you have packs of young aggressive blacks who go around and try and borrow stuff off white guys and if they won't let them have it, they start calling them racist and trying to get all the blacks to jump him. This is just a couple of examples, but stuff like this goes on every day, all day long. I know how to deal with all the craziness because I have lived with it for so many years, but I don't like it at all. If you get MSNBC, catch a few episodes of *Locked Up*. Those same people are here, too. Not literally, but those type of people.

I guess I try and look at the positive things about this place, but believe me, it is a very dangerous place. Guys pass AIDS here shooting up; there are all kinds of stuff going on. Every day in here is a nightmare to me. I try and make the best of it, but it's really messed up.

Wes has made parole again. He is unusually candid for a man who hates prison. He was asked where he sees himself in five years. He answered, "Since I first came to prison in 1986, I have never been able to stay free for longer than fifteen months. I can't see five years ahead. The fact is, I will either be back in prison or still on parole, so I'll just hope I'm still on parole, working every day."

The multiple programs he has been through have done no good and only make him more resentful. He is not that different from others. But he needs some help. I think his reluctance for treatment goes beyond his objec-tions to being forced to attend classes, but making him attend is only going to build a thicker wall of resistance.

I think if there is to be real change, all of the classes need to be made available at the beginning of a man's institutionalization or whenever he is psychologically ready for them, not just at the end. The teachers need to have expertise in the field and be experienced instructors. The classes need to be imaginative and engaging. I would put more money into private counseling sessions and less into what they are offering today. I'd pour money into edu-cational programming at all levels so that there would be few waiting lists. When a man becomes serious about change, tools to act on that new moti-vation need to be immediately available.

But I'm not in charge and no one is listening to the men.

Issues to Think About

1. Is there anything about everyday prison life that you hadn't thought about before?
2. What sort of programming, if any, do you think should be implemented in prison settings? Should prisons offer college classes?
3. If you were in charge, how would you handle the issue of sexuality in a population of inmates, the majority of whom are at an age when men are typically sexually active? Do you support the zero tolerance policy of the PREA?

FIVE

In the Lion's Mouth

Crime and Rule-Breaking
Within the Walls

When you have your head in the lion's mouth, you don't ring the dinner bell. Here your head is always in the lion's mouth and someone is always ringing the bell.

—*Norman*

It is hard to understand how men who are paying such a high price for breaking society's laws can turn around and do the same thing within the walls that hold them. In prison, there are more eyes watching, there is swift punishment and dreaded segregation. There is much to lose. But, there is also much to gain.

It needs to be said that serious crime in prison is not as dramatic and pervasive as TV drivel would have us believe. Both workers and inmates can live and work without the "underbelly" of the institution directly touching them daily. Everyone knows there are things going on—drug use, running stores, loan-sharking, gambling—but contact with these activities can normally be avoided. There are exceptions, of course, and the men have to be ever-aware not to get inadvertently involved.

For the many years I worked in the prison, my job frequently was affected by the students breaking rules, but I was carefully kept in the dark on the details. As coordinator of our college program, I was our school's contact with all of the prison students (about two hundred each semester). They were free to drop in and talk, and on my days in the institutions, there was a steady stream of men eager to chat with an outside face as well as deal with school issues. During those private conversations, I learned a lot by just keeping my ears and eyes open, and noticing things going on around me.

Obviously, many of the men attracted to the college program weren't as involved in the nefarious operations at the institution as others might be.

But, especially in the follow-up portion of this study, I found that some of the top dealers of trouble were solidly in our ranks. They were the leaders because they were the smartest. I also found that while I knew of the activities and the general details, in twenty years I had not learned exactly how things worked. Uncovering the details I lacked proved a challenge.

During the recent follow-up phase of the study, most of my communication came through letters, as I was no longer in the institutions at that point, and the men were scattered around the state and elsewhere. I wrote asking about the underground activities and specifically how they unfold. They wrote all around that question, but I got no direct answers. They were amazingly open with other requests, but most continued to ignore my inquiries about institutional rule-breaking. I finally realized what I had known, but hadn't thought of. All mail coming in or out of the institutions is subject to being opened and read, so the men still incarcerated weren't going to admit anything on paper. Most of the information came from men now released, but also from private interviews. One man with very little to lose bravely answered my questions, but directly addressed those who might be reading, calling these "theoretical" situations.

For myself, I tried to be a stickler for the rules, and the illegal activities within the institution seldom touched me directly. I was careful to make sure I was above reproach. Each day before entering the institution, I carefully locked my purse in the car trunk, stuffing needed items in my pockets or book bag, carefully making sure there was no contraband. I warned teachers to take pocketknives off their key chains and make sure cell phones were left in their cars.

In the institutions, after a while, we knew how to act and what the rules were and we didn't give it much thought. I never had problems with theft except learning to watch my pens like a hawk if I wanted something to write with by the end of the day. We knew not to leave anything valuable unattended, but that's true in the outside world as well. Once a teacher took off her watch during class, put it in her book bag, and later found it gone. The men in the class were incensed, apologetic to the teacher, and humiliated that one of their own would steal from someone who had come in to help them. As I remember, the watch showed up later, the men having taken the matter into their own hands. My question was, what good was that watch for an inmate? They couldn't wear a woman's watch. But they could trade it for other goods by using willing employees or contracted workers who regularly come into the institutions. Or they could sneak it to a visiting girlfriend as a gift.

Little issues can cause employees trouble. Fortunately, my mistakes were never caught, noticed, or cared about by the higher-ups. One semester we had a drawing class and, at the request of the teacher, I thoughtlessly added

India ink (a contraband item) to the students' special supplies. To my chagrin, all those bottles of ink disappeared within hours of my arrival at the institution. No doubt there were a number of tattooed arms, thanks to my ignorance. Another time, after much negotiation with the administration, I got special permission to bring in hand sanitizer for use at a graduation dinner. I promised to personally account for it, as sanitizer contains alcohol. That quickly disappeared too, although how anyone could be desperate enough to drink hand sanitizer I could never understand. All were little things, but these incidents reminded me that I was operating in a unique setting, even while dealing with trusted inmates.

Occasionally, I intentionally broke the rules when it came to my clerks. They did an enormous amount of work for me when I was not in the institution and they were only paid eighty cents a day for their efforts. During registration, with book handouts, etc., they were invaluable. They worked many extra hours without pay. As a reward, I brought them their favorite candy bar or some sweet item that they could not get through the canteen. I knew I shouldn't do it, that it showed disrespect for the rules. It presented a quandary, but I noticed all the other prison supervisors brought treats for their helpers, subtly leaving them on their desk with a nod. Most officers routinely turned their heads as long as the candy wasn't eaten in front of them.

One time, I deliberately broke a larger rule. The men in one of our programs secretly got together, each donating a certain number of cigarettes, which then served as illegal currency on the yard. My clerk gathered the cigarettes and paid an inmate in the woodworking shop to construct a clock for me as a thank-you. It was presented to me quietly, hidden in a brown sack. I didn't know what to do. I couldn't refuse something that heartfelt. I felt sure the warden would have approved it if he knew (his own desk was covered with craft items made by the men), but I couldn't ask because my clerk, the clock-maker, and ultimately the others, would have been in big trouble. So I sneaked it out. It is a treasured item in my home.

But even today, I'm troubled thinking of my well-meaning rule-bending. I subtly taught that rules (or laws) can be ignored if the intent seems right. That is not a good lesson to be taught to men in trouble for breaking laws. Compassion and rules often are not compatible and present a dilemma within the correctional setting.

There was one incident that I was inadvertently drawn into. I had a clerk whom I didn't trust. I could not state specific behaviors to ask for his removal, but I sensed his attitude was wrong. It wasn't long before he pulled me in as a cover for an illegal transaction with an officer. This inmate clerk's desk was located within the computer lab of the school. Something of great concern had happened with the computers, and security from the central office came and secured the room. No one—not even the teachers or school director—was allowed in the room for weeks.

My clerk was a nervous wreck. He walked the floors in concern. And then one day, he was calm and said he was going to be allowed to go back to the lab. I knew that was impossible and told him so. But sure enough, that afternoon, the officer on duty asked me if I'd like to go and get some books that we had stored there. The clerk followed us in, asking if he could get schoolwork from his desk. The officer hovered over me, but deliberately let the inmate wander to the other side of the room out of sight. Then the inmate yelled across the room to him, "Okay if I take out my notebook, boss?" The officer nodded, relaxed as the inmate tore out the door. The inmate grinned at me as he rushed passed, whispered, "I told you so," and went straight to his dorm without being patted down as was the procedure.

Years later, I asked some men why the officer might have done the inmate the favor of retrieving some illegal materials. I was told perhaps the inmate was a "snitch" and the officer was paying him for his help. Maybe there was a sexual connection between the two. Maybe the inmate was getting his gambling records and cutting the officer in on his earnings. I got rid of the clerk soon after, but never talked to others about what happened. I had to work there and knew I was in dangerous waters. And such reasoning, of course, is why illegal things continue to happen.

In prison, many of the illegal activities that will get inmates into serious trouble are not illegal on the outside. Having contraband (cell phones, money, cigarettes, items not on the inmate's property list), making and drinking hooch, getting a tattoo, charging extra for doing a job, having sexual relationships and, now more recently, smoking or chewing tobacco are all considered serious infractions and can bring heavy penalties.

Other activities winked at on the outside are strongly verboten within the institutions. Gambling and loan-sharking are two big ones.

And then there are drugs.

Drugs and Contraband

Drugs and contraband provide the biggest challenges to the administration. They seem to be fighting a losing battle, but watching from the outside, it sometimes looks like a game of wits for both sides. The inmates, many of whom are extremely bright, resourceful, and creative, can get just about anything done that they set their minds to. They can make big money in the institutions and can make things happen out in the free community as well. Some make impressive businessmen.

The officers and administrators, when interested, go to extraordinary lengths to locate contraband. At times, I heard a hint of admiration in their voices as they talked about unique places where they found things hidden—or couldn't find something they knew was there. But it really is more than a game. The drugs and the weapons are not funny.

Weapons are hidden everywhere. One prison had a framed display of all the shanks—scary-looking lethal knives—that had been found during shakedowns. Any item—even a toothbrush—could be sharpened into a weapon. One of the men told me he had named his blade, and when young guys gave him trouble, he asked them if they wanted to see "Johnny Walker." Most of the men feel they need some form of protection at hand, even in the more peaceful institutions. A lock in a sock makes a lethal weapon should trouble come their way.

A gun was even found recently in the visiting room. It was brought into the institution hidden within a visiting woman's vagina, removed, and placed under the vending machines. An inmate cleaning the room found it, left it untouched, and notified the officers. The action was caught on surveillance tape and the woman charged. The ultimate plan was unclear. Perhaps someone was going to force himself out of the visiting room with the gun, or perhaps it was being hidden to eventually find its way onto the yard. A frightening possibility either way.

Drugs and other illegal items often find their way into the institution through the visiting room. However, it's a delicate balance for administration to search visitors without excessive and inappropriate intrusion into their privacy. Most visitors are there purely out of love and concern, but others are willing to help their incarcerated loved ones continue their lives of crime. Probably the most common form of smuggling is when women carry a bag of drugs within their bodies. If a woman is suspected of that, she can be made to squat naked upon a mirror. If she refuses, she is not allowed a visit. At some institutions around the country, such indignities are required of all female visitors.

Bags are removed in the restroom, and then deposited casually in an open sack of chips that the couple shares at the table. The man nonchalantly pops the bag of drugs in his mouth and swallows it. Once back in his room, a swig of shampoo will help him vomit it up. And the transfer is complete.

There really are no depths to which the smugglers won't go. Drugs have been found stashed on visiting children and even hidden in an infant's diaper.

One warden had the handles to the main prison door replaced with handcuffs that served as the door handle. I never liked the frightening symbolism for visiting children, but he said they gave a message to people as to what will happen if they break the law within the facility.

The visiting room is only one way drugs are brought in. They might come over the fence at night inside a baseball thrown onto the rec field. One man recounted them being shot in with a bow and arrow. Drugs have been found in the chapel, tucked away among the hymnals, brought in by a member of an approved visiting church group. Every time something is found, additional procedures go into place to rectify the problem. In the case of the chapel, hymnals were removed and a projector replaced the traditional songbooks. It really is a losing war, but the battle of wits is interesting to watch.

Visitors are not the only source of drugs. A far more common smuggling method is to tuck a small bag of some drug under a sandwich in an employee's lunch box. There are big bucks to be made by underpaid and overworked employees.

The men claim there is no drug that can't be found or obtained within the prison walls. More than buying or selling it, I find it harder to understand how people in such a compact living situation can use drugs without being noticed. I'm told that officers involved look the other way. And even with the best of motivations, the system is hindered by serious understaffing, which is a problem nationwide. The men smoke dope near air ducts, carrying the odor outside. Inmates are stationed as lookouts while joints are passed around. And the routine schedule of required duties informs the inmates as to the usual location of the officers.

The officers themselves told me that much drug exchange and use goes on around the weight piles, but those areas can't be monitored as they should be because of lack of staffing. They also mention that they know who the main dealers on the yard are, but those men are clever and hard to catch with the goods. The experienced dealers know how to spread their goods around among the less noticed men in order to hide them. The young and seemingly innocent "fish" are used to pass the drugs after a sale. The young guys get in the debt of those involved in illegal activities and have no choice but to help in the exchanges.

The young men are not always victims within the prison setting. Sometimes they begin their incarceration angry, knowledgeable, and with little to lose. If they are intelligent and strong, with natural leadership ability, they quickly find a place and build a reputation. Doug arrived in prison at age twenty-one. He had escaped the death penalty in his shooting of an undercover policeman, but he was facing sixty-five years of imprisonment. He remembered his first years of incarceration:

> My first day in the joint a guy came up to me and asked, "You're Mather, right? You're the guy who had the shoot-out with that rat cop? Do you still have drug connections? Do you want a hit of acid?"
> I took that hit of acid and for the next several years, I would continue to take. I was involved in almost every nefarious activity known to prison life. I even invented some they didn't know about, which is hard to do because in the joint with enough time on your hands, they have thought of damn near everything.

I would love to say I learned my lesson and when I came to prison, I was determined to live right. I'd love to say that, but prison has its own little sub-culture and its own little rules and way of life. I fit right in—hell, I was practically prison royalty. I tied up a big share of the gambling. I ran a lucrative loan-sharking business, and I was responsible for the yard being flooded with dope on a pretty regular basis.

If you are naïve to prison life, let me explain this to you. If you want to bet on anything you can name—football, baseball, basketball, horse racing—there was, and still is, a guy that will take your action. Drugs, as much as you want, are smuggled in either through the visiting room or other ingenious ways, or brought in by correctional officers or other staff.

We even have our own currency—cigarettes at the time (now it's stamps and food items). Back then, you would sell drugs for cigs, then exchange sixteen cartons for a hundred dollars in real green money that was also smuggled in. It was nothing for me to keep two hundred boxes of cigs at all times. I would just have guys hold seven boxes apiece for me in their lockers and I would look out for them from time to time. What does a twenty-one-year-old kid do with two hundred boxes of cigarettes? Anything he damn well wants to.

One day I was walking down the loop, and out of the blue, I started thinking about my life. I started to think about all the people I had hurt. I believe God just started working on me. I had been lucky so far in prison not to get busted, but I knew eventually that would change. If caught doing the stuff I was doing then, it would hurt my mother. She would have had to visit me behind the glass. She would have to drive farther to see me. She would have to…. It was that simple. I had to stop being an idiot and become the man my mother could be proud of. That minute right there, by myself, I made a choice to stop it all. It's all about decisions and choices. I had made incredibly ignorant and stupid ones in my life, but right now, right then, I made one that would forever change my life for the better. I looked around and nobody was there. I smiled and was proud of myself. My new life began that moment. I found I was crying like a baby.

Getting out of the game would not be so easy. I was running a little economy in prison so to speak. A lot of guys were making money off of the stuff I was getting and doing, and they did not feel me at all when I just decided to quit. To them, we are all convicts and it was my duty as a convict to keep on keeping on. They never viewed me as a sell-out, but they just didn't understand I had gotten sick and tired of being sick and tired.

When I walked away, I did it alone. A lot of my "friends" couldn't understand. They were mad at me for quite a while because they made their hustle off my business. They didn't have to stay mad because someone else eventually stepped in to fill the void. In prison, just like the streets, there is always someone willing to take your place. That's why the war on drugs has been such a colossal failure. There is simply too much money involved.

Prison Currency

A few years ago, many prisons were declared smoke-free and it is the unintended consequences of that policy that interest me. When the movement to eliminate smoking began, I thought there would be big trouble. Both the staff and the inmates were furious. I could just imagine the tension and violence that would occur from individuals in withdrawal. But the transition was done well, with cessation classes and medication offered to help with withdrawal. But while successful, the new rule changed the whole prison currency and added a more menacing level to the law-breaking.

Cigarettes previously had been used as the currency of exchange. Any item or service could be purchased with cigarettes. Occasionally, a non-smoker could get in trouble for having unexplained cigarettes in his cell, but for the most part, the underground economy was left unscathed.

Suddenly with the smoking ban, the price of cigarettes rocketed. While prices may differ between institutions, the going rate today in Kentucky is a hundred dollars for a pack, a thousand for a carton. Moneymaking moves on down the line where a single cigarette sells for a large jar of peanut butter. The single cigarette is broken down into smaller units and sold for more profit. Officers and outside workers can easily carry a pack of cigarettes into the institution in their pockets. Helping the inmates with cigarette dealings doesn't have the same personal compunction as drug dealing, and the easy, relatively harmless activity is extraordinarily lucrative and easy to justify. If discovered with cigarettes in their pockets, employees just plead that they are smokers and forgot to leave them in the car. I asked the men an open-ended question about the effects of the smoking ban. The response: "The officers are driving nicer cars now."

Cell phones are the most recent headache for administration. Most are smuggled in by staff and contracted workers. The phones offer the inmates privacy they don't have on the recorded institutional phones. Some want them because it is a cheaper, more comfortable way to talk with their families. But one has to assume that the popularity of the cell phones has more to do with illegal activities than convenience. Before cell phones, when they were reliant on the institutional phones, the men learned to talk in a form of code when making illegal plans with those on the outside. To a monitor, the calls sounded innocent enough, but words, phrases, and topics came to mean something else to those talking on the phone. One man with Native American relatives was able to arrange drug transfers by talking in Navajo with his brother until the phone tape was monitored and he was ordered to stop using the language.

Prisons house a bored population with a large proportion of very intelligent inmates who want things that they are told they cannot have. A never-ending intriguing game of cat and mouse keeps everyone on their toes. There is no stopping the illegal activity, but it could be lessened. Several officers and administrators in the prison told me that some of the wardens don't care. They seldom step a foot on the yard and have no idea what is going on—and don't want to know. Others stay on top of things and devise programs and activities that discourage involvement in the illegal activities.

"The hole"

"The hole" is not a hole in the ground—it is a term for a separate building that houses the prison within a prison, but the vivid name sticks wherever it is. Also referred to as "seg" or "segregation," this area differs in appearance between institutions, but it is not a pleasant place no matter where it is located. Nor is it designed to be. In seg, men are isolated, allowed little or no time out of their individual cells. They are allowed two showers a week and the severity of their punishments often depends on their behaviors. Policies may differ by institutions and states.

Men can be sent to the hole for a number of reasons: breaking rules, a fight on the yard, isolation until an ongoing investigation is complete, and anticipation of trouble just after a man is denied parole. Some inmates even request protective custody there if they are threatened by others on the yard. Men can be banished to seg for a few days or a few months. There are some who have spent years within the area, and that is not a pretty picture.

There is too much to say here about segregation and the policies surrounding it. But no one—inmates or administrators—likes the concept very much. It's just an unavoidable reality of dealing with a criminal, often very disturbed, population. Segregation presents a troubling situation. Men are kept isolated with little communication. What happens behind those doors is supposed to be regulated and the men allowed certain civil rights. But it is a place of secrecy and often trouble. It brings out the worst in everyone.

I was given a tour of one seg unit in a prison in the state. It was state-of-the-art. Solid steel cell doors had slots for meals to be passed through and a small closeable window in the door through which to view the inmates. The men could not see me, but there were random, continuously echoing screams and yells all around us. The officer with me checked in one cell first to make sure the inmate was clothed before I could peep into his cell. I was told a chilling story about the troubled man. The individual was in a barren cell with no sheets or coverings, supposedly for his own protection. He had a "dry toilet," no water. He had lived there for years and was completely out of control. They were trying to find a way to rationalize releasing him and were offering him three days off his seg "sentence" for every day he served without incidents. But he couldn't do it. Whenever given the opportunity, he acted out and got more time. "Truth is, we've driven him crazy," the officer confessed quietly to me, out of the hearing of his superiors.

At that time, the institutional doctor, unlike his counterparts at other institutions, refused to prescribe any psychotropic medications, and they had a number of very troubled individuals living in seg. "I wouldn't take my cat to that doctor," another officer there told me.

Seg units are different between institutions. I've been inside three different ones. At one facility, the unit was a nightmare, with old barred cells, broken windows, and loud echoing screams. On the outside of the building, whenever I walked by, the inmates yelled sexual comments at me through the gaping holes. Inside, the noise was deafening and troubling. Those were not the sounds of sanity. Now renovated, the new unit sports different windows, with things more sterile and isolated. The internal noise and cries remain unchanged.

There is much more to be said about the challenges of segregation and supermax prisons, but this book is not the place. Punishment within a prison could be a story unto itself. Misbehaving, and often unbalanced, inmates offer enormous challenges. They have to be dealt with. But isolation leads to more insanity. When the inmate has nothing left to lose, the challenge is how to control that individual. Each administrator I talked with is troubled by the segregation practice. It is here to stay, but it offers big challenges to those in charge.

Money

It is important to understand that the issue of prison misbehavior is a complex matter. It does not occur simply because this is a population of lawbreakers. That is a factor, of course, and a good many of the inmates—not all—do not have the moral compunctions that keep a lot of us on the straight and narrow. It is more complex than that, however.

Inmates are motivated to have money by the same forces that affect us all—greed, jealousy, peer pressure, power, and a desire for comfort. Even without those forces, there are very limited ways to make legal money while incarcerated. Inmates are expected to furnish a lot out of their meager eighteen-dollar monthly paychecks. (In Kentucky prisons, janitors make eighty cents a day. A more skilled job like maintenance can pay a maximum of two dollars a day). The men buy their own stamps, writing supplies, basic medication, and have to purchase anything other than their standard prison uniform. Sweatpants and sweatshirts, comfortable tennis shoes, knit winter hats, radios, TVs (which have to have transparent backs), all come out of the inmate's pocket. They even have a co-pay to see the doctor. Basic hygiene supplies are provided, but are of low quality; quality supplies are offered for sale in the canteen. The indigent inmates are furnished with basic supplies and a small number of envelopes and stamps each month. In some states, they quickly build up debts to the state with the doctor co-pays, postage, and other legally required items and services. So if a friend or family member sends them twenty-five dollars for Christmas, the state takes it to apply toward the debt. There is a huge incentive, almost a necessity, to find other ways to earn money.

Some states, such as Georgia, don't pay anything for inmate work. One of the men in our study is now incarcerated there and is indigent and basically out of luck. His lack of money is a constant source of tension and trouble for him. He feels that he has little choice but to break rules and cut corners. Even then, he is depressed by his pervasive deprivations. When he is finally released, he will have to pay back Corrections hundreds of dollars for the years of debt he has piled up.

Most states have something equivalent to Prison Industries, which does contract work with governmental or outside agencies. Jobs there are highly sought after because of the wages and the skills learned. Inmates in one Kentucky Prison Industries make twenty-five to eighty-five cents an hour. To keep a job in industry, an inmate needs to have perfect conduct. Trouble on the yard will cause a man to lose his prized job.

If he can't get a job, there is no legal way for a man to come up with money on his own other than to take it from his family, who may already be strapped financially. Living with some comfort becomes important in this stark life. One of the men in the study found an illegal way to live well while incarcerated. With his ill-found money, he decided he wouldn't be more miserable than necessary and his body ballooned into an unhealthy mess—well over three hundred pounds—by eating all the sweets and comfort junk food his money could buy. When he was released, he realized what he had done and found that he wasn't able to physically handle the needed activities of a free life.

Tensions on the Yard

All of this feeds into a system that perpetuates a dysfunctional and tense atmosphere.

It must be emphasized that many, even most, of the inmates work hard at their jobs or school and aren't involved in the nefarious activities. But even when their activities are totally aboveboard, the men are always under stress because of the forbidden incidents that surround them. The problems generally won't come looking for them, but the men need to be like the three monkeys—see nothing, hear nothing, say nothing. That generally works well for everyone, and is the reason all the inmates so despise a "rat." Someone reporting on someone else's activities just upsets the applecart and the smooth functioning of the institution.

These days, things are tenser because of the young guys who have no respect for anyone, including themselves. They do not respect the informal systems that are set up by the older inmates. They increasingly gather together and pressure those who are minding their own business. At times, it is necessary for even the best-behaved person to stand up for himself, which can lead to an altercation and time in the hole. Some men, like children on a playground, are prone to being bullied, while others carry a persona that keeps people away.

There are constant troublemakers who most men despise. For whatever reason, those men keep things off-kilter by stopping up the plumbing on purpose, starting fires in the ventilation system, and breaking the community TV. One man told me with disgust of finding human feces in the shower room for the fourth time that week. The difficulty for the majority of the inmates who just want to do their time as easily as possibly, is that they live in close quarters with the troublemakers. The trick for them is to find the delicate balance between staying to themselves, ignoring the illegal and disruptive things going on, and making sure they aren't seen as pushovers.

One young man who did his time well entered the prison system as a scared teenager. He emerged twelve years later having served his sentence, never having been in trouble or given trouble. He did his job, went to school, and read in his cell at nights. His best friend and cellie was known as the "king of porn," whose underground money was made through the selling of pornography of all types. The young man had learned well to mind his own business.

"It was John's way of making money," he explained. "It didn't involve me."

No one pretends to have all the answers to the dysfunctions that occur within prisons. But both the men in my study and the most successful administrators agree on some interesting points.

The increasingly long sentences being passed down by the courts contribute to the illegal activity. A nineteen-year-old facing a life sentence with the possibility (not probability) of parole after twenty-five years, doesn't have much to lose. Then, as the men grow older and have done their twenty years, the parole board frequently extends a man's sentence another ten years or more. A good number of the men in our study have no hope of ever being released, although none of them had a sentence of life without parole. A former warden muttered, "How do they expect us to control a prison when they don't leave the men any hope?"

The men and administrators also agree that increased educational opportunities are crucial to a settled and improving population. Incentive programs that encourage correct behavior are useful. Men value better housing opportunities and meaningful work that give them an ability to earn money and reestablish a feeling of accomplishment. Inmates need a legal way to earn enough money to furnish necessities. Without that avenue, many who otherwise wouldn't fool with the danger of illegal activities will become involved. There will always be underground activities within the prison setting, but there are ways to reduce it and to settle down an institution.

Issues to Think About

1. What should the author have done when the inmates presented her with the clock?
2. Considering that contraband often comes in during visits hidden in female bodies, under clothing, and even upon children, what policies and procedures would you implement if you were the warden? What might be the unintended consequences of your suggested policies?
3. What would you suggest to reduce the illegal involvement of the officers in the underground economy?
4. Does illegal activity in prisons have any impact on free, law-abiding citizens?

Six

Power, Respect
and the Convict Code
Surviving Behind Bars

Basically, you don't see nothing, hear nothing, or say nothing. You mind your own business. You don't run to the guards and tell them anything. If you have a problem with someone, you deal with it yourself or you lose respect.

—*Wayne*

I believe there are two things at the heart of the prison experience: the need for power and the demand for respect.

Power

The bureaucratic structure of Corrections is similar to that of the military. Positions of sergeant, lieutenant, and captain are rungs on the career ladder. Current emphasis is on professionalizing the ranks. New officers graduate with formal ceremonies from their initial schooling and all employees regularly attend "training," which includes a variety of classes, martial arts, and practice on the shooting range. The officers wear dark uniforms laden with accoutrements of handcuffs, radios, utility belts, micro-shields (for doing CPR), flashlights, and pepper spray. Many in the ranks are former military, and they fit comfortably into the strict structure of command.

Once established in their positions, most officers are caring, sensible individuals who know how to manage a troubled population with consistency and common sense. Those are the officers on their way up the career ladder. Those with a mean streak or wrong mind-set often remain in the lower ranks, dealing daily with the inmates, and that is where the problems germinate.

Unfortunately, certain authoritarian personalities gravitate to Corrections and they cause problems and are often hard to work with. For the most part, I found the top administrators above the level of officers to be well educated, caring, and concerned. They had an interest in rehabilitation while emphasizing safety and security. They were respectful to me and often surprised me, making themselves freely available whenever I jumped ranks to ask for their help. That access did not sit well with other people in the rigid chain of command, but it worked for my program as long as I kept the wardens well informed about everything.

At all levels, I found if I acknowledged the staff's power and showed deference to it, things were more likely to get done. I enjoyed the employees I worked with in the prisons, but there was much more game playing required than I liked.

The officers are still referred to as "guards" when the older inmates talk about them, especially when they are angry. The officers on the yard have complete authority over the inmates, collectively and personally, and some make overt and subtle use of that power. The inmate who recognizes the authority and accepts his place as physically powerless will serve easier time. The inmate who constantly rails against his status and things he sees as unfair will spend his years figuratively knocking his head against the wall and doing harder time.

In writing this, I realize how my own emotions have been influenced by my time behind bars. Of course, I had good experiences with officers who were kind, helpful, and sensible. They followed DOC's "firm, fair, consistent" philosophy, and showed respect for the men under their care. They deserve to be highlighted, but they tend to be invisible as things around them are quiet and uneventful.

In prison, I learned a lot about myself, and I find that I would not make a good inmate. When I witnessed or experienced actions by an officer that were unprofessional and personal, I could not let it roll off my back. I felt red hot anger whenever one flexed his/her muscles with me, deliberately letting me know where I stood in relationship to their unquestionable power.

Like the inmates, I was often treated disrespectfully, forced to wait much longer than needed, refused help that would have made things much easier, ignored when I was waiting to speak to an officer. I let the incidents sink into my psyche where, to my surprise, they still burn with the same anger that simmers within the men. As I write my memories of the years spent on the various prison yards, and particularly when I think of the power-hungry officers, it is the piercing anger that comes to the forefront. I never reported any of them. I never talked back to any of the rude ones. I just simmered with things I saw and experienced. Had I done otherwise, it would have brought trouble to my own house as Jack wrote earlier. I understood the feelings generated by the struggle for power and respect. And I started to understand the convict code.

In spite of the move to professionalize the ranks, there are problems throughout the country. As prison populations burgeon, money becomes an issue and prison salaries have not kept pace as demands for more officers eat into the budget. Long-term officers say that there is no longer an incentive to make Corrections a career for those who start at the bottom as officers. Pensions have been taken away; salaries are low. Turnover is extraordinarily high. Both long-term officers and inmates say the quality of the officers is falling.

"If they are breathing, they will get hired," one career officer noted.

Because of the high turnover, staffing is at dangerously low levels in many places and regular mandatory overtime is required. Money is at the heart of the problem.

This is not a book about officers, but as I interviewed officers, staff, and administrators, I found I had opened a can of worms. In today's prisons, there is as much distrust, rule-breaking, and anger among the officers, administration, and staff as there is in the inmate population. I learned very troubling things. An incredible amount of ugliness goes on behind the scenes. Cliques form and influence what information is passed upward to administration. Administrators support their friends, ignoring their shortcomings. A former administrator explained, "If the warden or officers feel they are invincible because they are friends with those above them, then ultimately the men suffer because there is no accountability." All the resulting tensions, anger, and mistrust is carried downward, often lying upon the shoulders of the powerless inmates.

Men and women, unhappy in their work setting, uncommitted to the importance of their jobs, quickly learn to build up their own egos by flexing their muscles in a system designed to let them do so.

When it comes to power, the inmate is going to lose. A prisoner with an attitude will be subjected to close scrutiny (some call it harassment)—frequent shakedowns, strip searches, and even body cavity examinations. The physical abuse has lessened greatly over the years, but it still occurs. The men have little protection against personal vendettas if they make enemies of the officers. The officers have to follow rules, but there are many ways to get at someone. Bill was not a man to handle officers with tact, and he paid the price:

> During the counts when everyone is locked in their cells, the officer uses a flashlight in order to see inside the darkened cells. Most use a small flashlight that has a very dim light. This not only allows the officer to see, but also doesn't cause the disruption of sleep of the inmate. We have a few officers who wish to use nothing but the biggest possible flashlight and they purposely adjust the light so that it is at its

widest and brightest setting in order to do just that; wake an individual up from a sound sleep. The "rules" state that they "must see flesh and movement." While most understand how to interpret this, a few use it to harass. They will shine the light directly into your eyes and shake the flashlight back and forth until you finally wake up. When I was experiencing this, they were counting every hour. He would repeat this scenario at every count, thus you would not be afforded a good night's sleep. The following day, things that would not normally upset you were suddenly irritating. They created a hostile environment through deliberate harassment.

He continued:

With the cell doors isolated at night from midnight to 5:45 a.m., one must press a button to get the tower guard's attention in order to have their cell doors opened to use the restroom. I have had the officer up there ignore my buzzer for as long as twenty minutes. There has been more than one occasion over the years in which I ended up going to the bathroom in a food container and just going back to bed.

Leslie, who was in the same institution as Bill, handled his incarceration differently, and thus managed to stay out of trouble with the officers. They basically left him alone.

I don't get into trouble with the guards. I don't cause them any problems, and usually they don't give me any problems. It's a matter of common sense. I know what's right from wrong, so if I do something wrong, I have no one to blame but myself— right? A lot of guys come in here and give the guards a hard way to go; then they get mad when the guards write them up. That's stupid. I believe you "get" what you "give."

Yes, I've experienced the so-called harassment of having a light shined in my eyes, not getting let out immediately to use the bathroom. Personally, I don't let little stuff like that bother me. I've got enough to worry about. Those things are minor to me.

One of the most difficult things for me over the years was to have to stand by and watch, and thus subtly be part of, the cruel mistreatment. We had an officer at one school who took delight in making the men miserable. He would make all the encounters as difficult as possible. On the days of advising, for example, he locked the door of the school, making the students wait outside in long lines in a freezing sleet storm or pouring rain. Another more humane officer firmly set guidelines for behavior in the crowded setting, but made arrangements for the men to come into the warm building to sit and wait.

When vocational students leave their classrooms, they have to be checked and patted down for possibly stolen tools. One day, my least favorite officer, with another officer in tow, picked out one young, less savvy man to taunt. As the students were leaving for lunch, the officer stopped the line and went after this guy. He had him take off his belt, put it back on, empty his pockets, fill them back up while he was barking out more things for him to do: "Turn around; stick out your tongue; take off your belt again." The young man was fumbling, trembling like a leaf before they let him go. As soon as the inmate exited the door, the two beefy officers doubled over in laughter. One of them said, "I love doing that."

There is no question that the inmate is at the mercy of the officers and staff, and he must learn to swallow his pride at times to get along. In the early days of our program, for example, the college students frequently were taunted by some officers who felt they should not receive a "free" education, and the student had to act submissive during their ridicule. Generally, however, the two groups get along well, and informal friendships evolve between the officers and inmates.

> I feel there are things in here that do get on your nerves a lot and that is the uneducated guard hiding behind a badge, and also the inmates themselves making unnecessary problems not only for them but everyone in general.—Al

> There are good and bad correctional officers. The bad ones are like drill sergeants, not police officers. Most, however, are friendly and have some understanding of how the inmate might feel. Some of the young ones are over-zealous and hide behind their badge.—Don

However, if a conflict does arise between an inmate and officer, the inmate can file a grievance. It is similar when an officer writes up an inmate for a rule infraction. In both cases, the defendants appear before a court-like committee.

It is more difficult for the accused prisoner. As one inmate who used to be a correctional officer himself told me, "If you testify against a corrupt officer, there is no one to side with you. You don't testify against a brother, and they think they are like brothers."

One of the grievance counselors says inmates seldom ever win officially in staff conflicts, but sometimes they will win without knowing it. The "innocent" officer might be assigned to hated tower duty for several months, for example. Officers insist that inmates sometimes win against the write-ups if there is not enough proof to support the officer's charge.

Respect

The concept of respect comes up over and over again, but it is initially difficult to understand within the context of the prison environment.

There is, of course, the constant struggle for the individual to find something within himself to respect. Other chapters examine that in more depth, as the internal conflict is ongoing and ever pervasive. The man who has failed so miserably in life does, most of the time, know, or at least hope, there is something salvageable within himself.

Some of the men have found the inner confidence and peace that allow them to not judge their worth by their powerlessness within the correctional system. They are the ones who don't sweat the small stuff, as the expression goes. If they are talked to rudely, they see it as the other person being a jerk, rather than feeling belittled. They accept their lower role without it affecting their psyche. Those men, to me, have found a sense of self-respect. But that is my interpretation from watching and listening over the years. They do not talk in those words or concepts. And those reactions, so helpful in free society, do not translate into respect from the other men.

To men in prison, especially the ones who have served many years, respect is something else. It is the difference between an inmate and a convict.

Some of the basic rules of respect as defined by us on the outside are understood within the prison setting, but are heightened in intensity. More than once, I've had to jump in and defuse a situation before one of the men got in trouble, thinking an officer had disrespected me. The men might accept a curt or sarcastic answer or an order without explanation, but they were protective of me and got their hackles up when I was spoken to that way. They didn't seem to understand when I explained that I could take care of myself or that words didn't matter as long as I got what I needed. It was the act of disrespect that bothered them so much.

Tensions from the visiting room often reached my ears. Depending on the captain, the warden, or who was on duty, families were frequently subjected to a variety of searches. When the fathers saw male officers laying their hands on their pre-teen and teenaged daughters to frisk them for contraband, sparks flew, tempers rose, and grievances were filed. (Today in these institutions, mostly female officers pat down other females.) The same happened if family members were treated curtly or rudely. One man refused to allow his family to visit because he couldn't stand to let them see him being treated disrespectfully. He was afraid it would make him less of a man in their sights.

It is an ongoing tension, and issues of respect fly around all aspects of visitation. There is another side to that, of course, when the inmates take advantage of the situation.

The men seemed particularly sensitive to how visitors were treated; all of our college teachers mentioned with surprise the protectiveness and respectfulness they experienced. It was always a puzzling contradiction to me, considering the many acts of the men that resulted in imprisonment. But the contrast between students on our main campus and the students within the prison was startling. Each semester, I struggled with boxes of books, lugging heavy loads into the institution on campus. But at the prison, once I left the sally port and entered the yard, men always approached, without exception, to take the boxes from me and help me along to the back of the institution—even men who were not part of the program. It was like stepping back into the 1950s; doors were opened, men moved back to let women go first, and all needs were immediately cared for. I often noticed men quietly shifting chairs around so I had the one padded, comfortable chair while they sat on the plastic or metal chairs. They did not usually have a sexual motivation. Their actions emerged from a politeness and appreciative respect for those who came to help them and who treated them respectfully in return.

But there was another facet to prison respect that took a long time to understand. It was respect among the men and it didn't depend on administration, visitors, or officers. It went back to the days when the convict code ruled.

The Convict Code

I met David many years ago. He had already been in prison more than half his life and he hasn't been a free man since. Short and scrappy, a prison tattoo on his forearm, David hated to be called an inmate.

"We're convicts," he would say with some pride.

He was assigned to work with me and he took his job seriously. Always convinced that women weren't safe in the prison, he watched me like a hawk, sitting outside the door when I needed a private conversation with a man. His fears were exaggerated, but were grounded in years of experience in some of the country's toughest prisons.

David started his prison career at the infamous Angola facility in Louisiana. He later served time in the notorious maximum-security prison in Michigan City, Indiana, before he came to Kentucky. He told startling tales of murders, gang rapes, violence, and sadness. At Michigan City, he was stabbed above his eye as he stepped out of his cell—a misidentification in a hire-to-kill situation. The attacker was trying to run an icepick through his eye but missed.

"For a carton of four-dollar cigarettes, you could get a man killed," he said.

In the 1990s, when I first knew David, things were peaceful in the Kentucky institutions. The prison system was under a strong consent decree—a federal court-ordered cleanup of the state's prison system. Programs were in place, old guards were replaced with more professional officers, and the facilities were clean.

Yet David kept insisting he'd rather do time in Louisiana or Indiana. In Kentucky, he felt physically safer, but he claimed, "They play games with your mind."

I came to realize he was distressed about the gradual change from the days of convicts to the new atmosphere for inmates. He was not alone. To my surprise, even the officers I interviewed wanted to make sure I understood the difference between the old convicts and the younger inmates who inhabit the prison today. And, they agreed, the difference had to do with respect—however twisted that respect was.

Convicts had a code of conduct that centered on respect for one another—the old "honor among thieves" that we hear about. If a man broke his word, it was a sign of disrespect and he was "taken care of." If he owed money and didn't pay it back, if he stole from another, if he ignored the unwritten rules of prison life, the other inmates dealt with him. They didn't go to the officers for help; they handled it themselves. To rat on someone was a weakness. If a convict refused to rat, he might end up in the hole, he might catch another charge, but when he re-emerged on the yard, he was more respected and not to be messed with. The unwritten rules were strengthened.

Weaker men broke under that system and there was certainly more violence. However, those who survived and followed the convict rules were proud and strong—and respected. And there was a predictable order to things both for the men and the officers.

In preferring that old system, David was railing against the new population where officers use men against one another, finding "rats" to tell on their fellow inmates in return for special privileges.

Today, with the convict code dwindling, you can trust no one—even those closest to you. And there was an unspoken order to prison life that is now missing. In David's words, "There are really no convicts these days. Convict is an old-school name for a man or woman who has morals and ethics in a prison setting."

I had to smile as David struggled to explain the issue of respect that is such a different thing within prisons than it is outside. But what he says is worth repeating as long as you read it carefully. I asked, how is respect in prison different than the concept outside?

Outside, right is right and wrong is wrong. If a man steals your car, you can call the police. You have to. In prison, if a man steals my radio, I don't call the cops/guards because, unlike on the streets, it's wrong to call the cops. Respect kind of works the same way. You get respect in prison by handling your own problems. If you use that concept/scenario on the streets, you go to jail—no one out there respects you for breaking the law (to handle your own problems). In here, they do respect you for it.

I'm not explaining this well. Try again. On the streets, if you do the right thing, people respect you.

In prison, "the right thing" is often the wrong thing. You get no respect for doing the wrong thing in any setting.

So it comes down to the fact that between the streets and prisons, what's right and what's wrong is completely different. Therefore, so is the concept of respect.

Let me know if that makes any sense to you, because I don't really understand what the hell I just wrote, but I'm pretty sure it's close to right!

In another letter about the convict code, David told me the story of Dick, who committed the only murder at that particular institution in the twenty years I worked there—at least the only one that I knew of. David's conclusions are extreme—almost bizarre—to those of us on the outside, but they are helpful in understanding the convict code.

Dick was my cellmate at the time he killed a guy in the print shop. That story might help to explain the difference in inmates and convicts. A more respectful and respected man I've never known anywhere in any prison system. At Christmas that year, Dick stole three Christmas cards from the print shop. An inmate saw him and told on him. Another inmate heard him tell and informed Dick. Keep this in mind. In the old days (like my years in Michigan City and Angola), a snitch was killed for snitching. Also killed were child molesters.

So, we were searched and our cell tossed until they found those cards. Afterwards Dick told me he knew what the deal was and he'd have to handle it. I had no clue what was going on. Picture the yard in your mind—the grievance office was in education and the print shop two doors down. Dick and I walked to work together as usual. To make a long story short, Dick walked into the print shop, checked out a ballpeen hammer, and beat the snitch to death. After doing so, he reached down, snatched the wristwatch from the guy's wrist and held it up to the cop, who wisely watched it happen and did nothing, and said, "Now get it right this time. 'Robbery-murder.'"

I know what he meant. Robbery-murder brings the death penalty in Kentucky. He told me before he wished they had sentenced him to death the first time. He said something I have said many times, that he didn't have the guts to commit suicide.

At that time, if you'll remember, I was a grievance aide and my job was to go to segregation and handle grievances for the seg inmates. Dick was in the observation cell, which had a big Plexiglas window. He didn't have any of his property, just a jumpsuit. He asked me to get him something to read. I asked the unit manager of seg if I could bring him a couple of books. He said no. I tried to talk him into it and he finally said, "He killed a man. I'm not giving him anything."

To make a long story short, I told him that Dick was a convict and what he did, he honestly believed (right or wrong) was what he had to do, what he was supposed to do. Regardless of what you think, in Dick's world, he did what was needed and expected of him. In your world, he's a monster.

I told him that unless Dick is disrespected again or snitched on, assaulted, etc. you'll probably never have another problem out of him. He'll accept whatever punishment you and the system dishes out and won't hold a grudge about it because he, unlike you, understands that what's right in *his* world is wrong in your world. Not allowing him a book or a magazine isn't accomplishing anything.

I went back to seg the next day and Dick was reading a book.

I'm not saying that Dick was right to kill that boy. I'm just saying that he thought it was right. I remember the day clearly. He wasn't angry or vindictive. It was like, for example, a sniper shoots a kidnapper. It may be murder, but it's his job as a sniper. Dick felt it was his job as a convict. I personally wouldn't have done it, but to be honest I guess, though I have portrayed myself as such, I have never been a real convict. I draw the line short of killing and/or bucking the system to the point of rioting.

In short, an *inmate* just merely exists in a convict's world and, if he's smart, stays out of everybody's way. He's loyal to no one, staff or inmate, but tries to straddle the fence and make both factions happy, and that never works.

A *convict* lives by a code and won't be disrespected by any inmate. He also won't accept disrespect from staff when they go over and above their job description. He understands and accepts that staff members have the responsibility to make sure you serve your sentence as ordered by the court. He understands enforcement of most rules and regs.

That being said, that's the way it used to be. It's no longer that way. These days the word "convict" simply means you don't tell on each other. You do your thing and keep your mouth closed about other people's business and, truthfully, these days most so-called convicts will tell whatever they have to, to get or keep what they want. Pretty much these days, inmates are inmates. Back in the old days, if you had a problem you knew it and knew where it was coming from. These days you have no idea.

The bottom line is that for the convict, rules for successful living on the outside are turned upside down within the prison. That makes the transition back to the community difficult. Years ago, David's supervisor was complimenting his work ethic to me. He's smart; he is conscientious; he is capable. He knows prison life and operates very well within the prison environment, she said. Way better than he probably will when he's finally released, she added.

When I first met Al, he had already been in prison almost twenty years. He's now at the forty-four-year mark. The parole board served him out on his life sentence, meaning he can never be considered for parole again; he is in prison until he dies.

He was one of the men I had hoped most would answer my letters. In 1994, he was straight-talking, tough, and proudly declared himself a convict. I was anxious to see if he had changed and wanted to get his unique take on prison life. I wanted to see what had happened about some of the things he had talked about twenty years before. Someone told me he'd never participate—he considered himself too tough to do something like that. "He's an old convict and thinks he's better than anyone else," I was told.

It took several letters, but I finally got an answer. It was a short note written in a shaky, disconnected print. It was obviously difficult for him to write. Al's letter read:

> Ms. Holman, I have received all of your letters. I am sorry for being so negative and unresponsive toward you and your project. Yes, I will help you, but only if we have a one-on-one conversation. My writing over the years has kind of hurt my hands. Too much fighting in here over the years.
>
> This will be short. So do let me know and I will answer every question you ask

me. But, I will only answer them honestly and to the best of my ability. Again, I hope you forgive me for being so selfish. Hope to hear from you soon and see you.

He got his way. I got permission to meet with him privately and we talked for three hours. I know now that the old con "conned" me. Most of the later letters have been written in a smooth cursive hand, no sign of debilitating arthritis, although I noticed his knuckles were indeed swollen when I saw him. But I didn't care if he had conned me. Like conversations with him years before, it was time well spent and a fascinating look into the mind and life of a man who has spent most of his sixty-five years behind bars. He doesn't have visitors except for a rare visit from a brother. He enjoyed the conversation as well. Like years before, he was straightforward with his thoughts on a number of subjects.

I asked about the difference between a convict and an inmate. He said: "I'd a hundred percent rather be a convict. There aren't many old-timers left. These new guys have no morals, no respect for selves. They don't care who they hurt. Sixty to seventy percent of people here are sex offenders. They don't have any morals. I hate sex offenders."

That negative feeling about sex offenders is indicative of the convict and was pervasive years ago in prison—that was the one crime (especially if it was child sex abuse) that inmates kept very quiet. They did it for their own safety. It still isn't openly admitted. Al went on to emphasize that he treats women right. Indeed, he showed a lot of respect for me, watching his language, carefully choosing words as he explained how things work that had a sexual context (like the smuggling in of drugs by females).

Like some of the other older guys, he had a disdain for programs. "The guys ain't learnin' nothin'. Either you are or aren't going to change. You can't teach that." He and David use almost the exact same words.

He continues about the life of a convict today.

> I have no close friends. A close friend is going to cut your throat. With enemies, you know where you stand. Friends cut your throat—it's a matter of time. They will get jealous. They will turn you in or steal from you. It's a different breed today. In the old days, I could leave ten dollars on this table and come back in a week and it would still be there. Not today.

I asked him what advice he would give to someone coming into prison and facing a long sentence like his. It took him a long time to answer. He was unusually silent. "I'd tell them to be prepared to handle things differently here than on the street. It's a mad house. It's crazy here—off the handle. You have to be tough. I'd tell them to buckle up and do things best they can."

Interestingly to me, the old-time officers also liked the days when the convict code ruled. It dictated the informal rules of the prison and there was violence among inmates as a result of it. But the old convict was (and maybe still is) the best ally of the staff, one long-term officer told me. They used the convict code to help run the prison and keep things in line.

"At any one time, we might have sixty-eight staff supervising fifteen hundred men. They can take the prison whenever they want," he admitted. The situation is dangerous with the understaffing that occurs with budget cuts. One of the old cons told him in a friendly conversation, "We let you run the place." And he knows it's true.

This man and others—officers and inmates alike—want to see things run smoothly. They respect the situation when rules and officers are fair. This particular officer, who later became an administrator, enjoyed working in the living units, whereas others hated it and talked about the danger.

"If you treat them right, follow procedures correctly, there will be peace and order," he said. "The old convicts will help you out if you're doing a job correctly. They will back you up. It's like 'treat a dog mean and he'll bite you.'" If you treat the men mean, you'll have trouble. They'll help you if they know you are fair, firm, and consistent."

He went on to tell about a time there was trouble brewing and there was about to be an uprising in the dorm. He was ready to call for backup when one of the old cons stepped in front of the men and, facing them, started cussing and yelling at them about their behavior, telling them to settle down. The convict emphasized that anyone who caused trouble would answer to him. All went silent and peace reigned.

I heard similar tales from a former female officer who told of incidents where men stepped in when their fellow inmates were getting out of line.

I was surprised by the number of staff who said that especially in the old convict days, they were sure that the convicts would have protected them in case of a riot. That aligns with what I was told during my years inside the prison. Both the men and older staff said that if trouble came up, the men would not let harm come to me. But they emphasized that wouldn't hold true for some of the staff.

All older staff that I talked with verbalized the same respect for the old, traditional convicts. They broke rules, ran stores, dealt drugs, caused headaches for the administration, but when caught, they never complained. They respected the fact that the rules were in place and calmly accepted their prescribed punishment.

The old convict code is fading away. I'm told by inmate and staff alike that the new group of young people bring more discontent into the prison. They say the young inmates won't take responsibility for anything. They blame everyone else for their crimes and their present condition. They keep things stirred up. They ignore the informally prescribed codes of conduct and cannot be trusted. It is all a matter of respect and they have none.

The new emerging order of things troubles the older long-term inmates.

But still, there are portions of the old code left in place, and danger still lurks for those who don't understand or ignore them.

Issues to Think About

1. How is "respect" different in prison than in the free community?
2. Do you understand the difference between a convict and an inmate?
3. What are the advantages and disadvantages of the disappearing convict system?
4. In some countries, prison inmates are deliberately treated with extreme respect. Their living conditions are pleasant. Harassment or sarcasm by officers is strictly forbidden. The recidivism rates in these countries are low. What is your reaction to that approach?

SEVEN

The Past That Clings
to Them

Scars of Child Abuse and Neglect

My father has beaten me with his fists, mop handles, rosebushes, belt buckles, and on one occasion, I was beaten with a speedometer cable until my shoes were filled with blood. Yet I would often cry myself to sleep wondering what I had done to make my "daddy" not love me.
—Charles

Whenever we got to the discussion on child abuse in our Modern Social Problems textbook, the atmosphere in the prison classroom invariably changed. Usually responsive students became quiet. Eyes dropped to the desk or the floor. The students' body language screamed of anguish and hurt, as many twisted backwards in their seats, sometimes even covering their faces. It was clear from the very first that abuse played a significant role in too many of the prisoners' lives.

Dry statistics support the premise that both physical and sexual childhood abuse has occurred significantly more often among the incarcerated population than in the general population.[1] But the statisticians agree there are problems with the figures. Abuse statistics are based on self-reporting, and people often don't share such painful personal experiences with strangers. Men, especially, have difficulties admitting to childhood abuse. It was immediately clear to me in the classroom that mistreatment, especially by parents, was not something the men were readily willing to admit. Their private responses verified that.

"It's just embarrassing," one man mumbled as he explained why the men had trouble discussing the topic.

And then there is the definition of abuse. The men understand the nature of sexual abuse, but in describing severe beatings and other forms of physical discipline, they do not all define that as abuse—it is just the way children are appropriately disciplined, they say. I found in my study that as they aged and were more distant from the actions, the prisoners came to define actions as unacceptable that they previously thought of as appropriate but painful discipline.

Delving into the men's problems in childhood was a big part of my first study. I did not place the same emphasis on it in asking questions twenty years later. But to my surprise, the subject came up more times than expected. It became clear that this was something that some of the men had been processing as they grew older. I learned of some incidents I hadn't heard about the first time around.

It bothered me twenty years ago, and it still does today, to realize the level of violence that regularly occurs in families. There may be less tolerance of domestic violence today, and more help for women wanting to escape impossible situations, but it is still there, erupting daily, injuring and killing children both in body and spirit. We hear that children are resilient, but perhaps not as much as we hope. I heard numerous accounts from the men of uninvolved and verbally cruel parents, even in situations when the parents weren't physically abusive. The prisons are full of angry, violent men who were once scared children crying themselves to sleep at night.

In this chapter, I am using much of the material gathered during the initial 1994 study. Many of the men quoted here have since been released, but I will indicate when they are the men still imprisoned and will explain how their attitudes towards their parents have changed over the years.

Charles

This chapter started with Charles's words as he described the almost daily torture he received at the hands of his father. He recalled his confusion about his father's actions and his need for his father's love.

At the time I knew Charles, he had grown into a large, solidly built middle-aged man. One could tell at a glance that he was not a man to mess with. Quiet and isolated from others, he was also smart. Sometimes pain showed through his uncertain eyes and shy smile, but you never knew what he was thinking. He shared little in person. He would not communicate about his childhood experiences except by writing. Face-to-face conversations were too difficult for him.

He wrote:

> As a child, my alcoholic father (also the son of an alcoholic who abused him) physically abused me almost daily.
> Throughout these incidents, I blamed myself for what he was doing to me. As I grew older, I felt abuse was the nature of things and every child must be going through the same treatment.

Although I accepted what he was doing to me as natural, what he was doing to my mother was something altogether different. I can't count the times my father would come home from a night on the town with his drunken friends, beat my mother within an inch of unconsciousness, and then raped her in front of us kids.

The abuses continued until I was fourteen years old. By that time, I had worked out and had grown exceptionally strong for a boy of that age. One night my father came home drunk and once again started to rape my mother. As her screams echoed through the house, something snapped within me. I jumped out of bed, ran into the living room, jerked my father off my mother, and beat the living hell out of him. Needless to say, what love I held for my father was lost that night. However, one good thing did come after that incident—the beatings stopped.

Regarding the role abuse played in my life, it's still there buried deep within me. You see, I associate love with pain and I still express my feelings in the wrong way. Although there are times I feel a rage building inside, I have never pulled the stunts my father did…. Yes indeed, abuse has and continues to play a big role in my life.

Cal

Cal is one of the men in the current study. He has been in prison for the past twenty-five years. He did not write after his first letter in which he told me that his mother had died in the years since I had been in touch with him. However, in that letter, he helpfully answered a number of questions. He did not know what she died of, which makes me think there was minimal family contact in the last years. He added that he lost his father, aunt, and first cousin during the past year, "so my thinking isn't up to par as it used to be."

In spite of what he wrote twenty years before about his mother's problems, he loved his mother and understood and forgave her weaknesses. He felt her loss deeply. As I remember, she had stayed in touch with him during his early years in prison and regretted her part in his return there. His father was another matter. Neither parent gave Cal what he needed.

My mom and dad got a divorce when I was about eleven or twelve years old. I can remember them always fighting and arguing all the time…. My mom always used to call me stupid and after a while, I believed that I was really stupid. If I would ever try to tell her how I felt about how she treated me, she would smack me or grab me by my hair because she thought I was being a "smart ass."

Drinking played a part in my family because both my mom and dad drank as well as both of my brothers and sisters. Mom would always tell me not to drink, but she did, and I could never understand that. If I would come home drunk, she would smack me around and talk really awful to me. But on the other hand, she would always drink, and she wondered why I got drunk all the time.

I don't want you to think my mom was all bad, because she wasn't. I think she raised me the best way she knew how, and I never went without anything, thanks to her. I think she raised me the only way she knew how and that's the way she was raised.

Cal spoke gently of his loving but naïve mother who turned him in to the police, thinking he would be treated fairly and helped. But he turned angrily to the subject of his father, a career military man.

My father, on the other hand, never really has shown any love towards us—except in his own way.... He has never, to my memory, told any of his children that he loved them with the exception of my sister by his first marriage. He has cheated on our mother and generally treated us like dirt.

Many times, Mother started to leave him, but like so many other wives and mothers, she couldn't earn enough to feed herself and her four children, not to mention losing all the governmental insurance her continued marriage provided.

As the firstborn son, I was expected to be rough and tough and follow his footsteps by joining the army. One day, on my return from basic training, he got his wish—I was not only rough and tough, but I was also mean.

We were arguing. I came off with a smart remark and he tried to kick me, but my instincts and reflexes were faster than he knew. I caught his foot, executed a maneuver, and put him on the ground. Before I could apologize, he grabbed my aluminum softball bat and tried to kill me. I deflected a shot to my head and I blinked out. What happened next, I don't remember exactly, but my mother's screams brought me out of it and I saw my father laying on the ground, out cold, and I was on my way down with the bat in my hands. I caught myself, threw down the bat, and left the house.

What is strange about all of this is that I still love my father in spite of what he has put our family through. I believe very firmly that my father was the controlling factor in my incarceration and my fear of underachievement. As children, all of us were subjected to negative communication and slanderous remarks every single day until we convinced ourselves he was right.

Early exposure to a related mixture of violence and sex is a dangerous prescription for later mental health. Psychologists say it can lead to twisted understanding of love and sex and leads the victim to sexual aggression in later years.[2]

Sexual acts upon children leave their own ugly brand, a scar hard to erase in adulthood. Far more boys are sexually abused than we know; the embarrassment of reporting makes it difficult to get a handle on the exact figures. In a self-reporting study, twice as many men in prison, as opposed to the general public, admit to being sexually abused as children.[3]

I asked my male prison class once about having a treatment group for sexually abused victims. The idea did not go over. "Who would ever admit it?" one man mumbled.

Max

There are treatment programs for those men who have sexually abused others, and in that setting, some have come to grips with how they came to be abusers themselves. They are willing to talk more openly about their child-hood situations than others not in therapy, but their language is usually couched in stilted treatment lingo. They use their childhood abuse to under-stand, but not excuse, their own crimes. Max is one of those men.

> My father was an alcoholic and my mother was co-dependent, both with fairly aggressive attitudes. Their talks normally ended up in full-blown arguments with me caught in the middle trying to play peacemaker.
>
> My father started working out of town and my mother started to see other men, leaving me with a babysitter. The babysitter had a sixteen- or seventeen-year-old son who got his kicks by slapping me or twisting my arm or choking me until I passed out, while the sitter's fourteen-year-old daughter got her kicks by sexually abusing me. This happened without my parents' or the babysitter's knowledge. People believed that family life when I was growing up in the sixties was like the Cleavers on *Leave It to Beaver*. It was not, and right now, I can see no living happily ever after.

Max was six when his father started messing with him.

> I was so young when it first happened, I guess being shown some love by a father who was not around much was better than being shown none at all. Also, it was a way to show him (my father) that I loved him.
>
> As I got older (ten to twelve), I knew things that he was doing was wrong, and I know that I had some of the signs of being abused. I became belligerent, and I became a loner. I used alcohol and drugs. I even went as far as trying to commit sui-cide at the age of twelve.

Max remembers getting drunk when he was just ten years old, and was into a regular pattern of drug and alcohol use by the time he was twelve. When he was sixteen, he and his father had a fight.

> I ran to Tennessee and got married to get out of the house. Being sixteen and with so much anger and hate in my soul, I would have killed him if I hadn't left—no ifs ands and buts about it.
>
> While my father was not the only one to sexually abuse me (besides the babysit-ter's daughter, there was also a teenage aunt), his actions probably had more effect on me than the others. The only thing I can say about Father is that he was a victim too, and the closest he ever came to telling me he was sorry was when he told me what happened to him when he was ten years old.
>
> Why I have not told anybody about this is two-fold. First, I believe my pride would not let me. I was a man. I could handle my own problems and all the other male macho crap we men like to tell ourselves.
>
> Second, my father is dead now and for the last twelve years of his life, fully dependent on me to help Mom take care of him…. So for the unresolved issues between me and him, there was no way I could resolve them with him for he was sick and limited in his functions.
>
> I could point and blame him for my situation, but what good would that do? I could say he caused me problems that were not addressed until now. But the facts are that I have to live with the situation and be responsible for my actions.

As a result of abuse, the emotions I lived on were hate and anger. (As I learn more about myself, I find that fear was really my main motivation.) This meant that most of my relationships have been very one-sided with others giving while I could not give of myself. When I felt that a situation was becoming one where I had to give of myself, then I would in turn become abusive—fear of being hurt again turned me into a monster.

I do not offer my abuse as an excuse for my crimes. I am not insane, and for whatever reasons the choices I made, I have to pay for them. But being aware of my history, it is easy to see that abuse led to some ill-rational choices.

My files are filled with heart-wrenching tales of frightened, sad, and lonesome children. Each story, so personal and difficult in the telling, is tied with a face I know. Today, the men's earlier anguish has crusted over, encapsulating the pain deep within. They have grown into adults—adults who are locked away for their own illegal and twisted actions.

Tony

Some of the stories, like Tony's, leave us scratching our heads, wondering how the situation might have been handled better. He feels that in trying to help him, people made his life worse.

As a child, I lived through a brief, unfortunate experience of being in an orphans' home and a foster home. To the best of my recollection, I was five years old when I first entered the orphans' home. The feeling was that of confusion and rejection, for no one attempted to explain why I was taken from my home and family. It left me feeling as though I had failed as a child in the eyes of my parents. The orphans' home was run by very strict guidelines. Corporal punishment was enforced for any infraction of their rules and policies.

Tony said he was slapped, pushed, and spanked with a half-inch wooden paddle at age five. I suspect he was older than this and the facility not quite as closed as he remembers—but these are his experiences, and how he interpreted them as a child is what matters.

The only thing I felt in common with was the other children who shared the same fate as I. The institution in many ways was like a prison camp for children, for I knew my freedom was blocked. Just like prison, there was a high fence up around the institution. All movement was controlled and all visits were monitored.

I think I remained at the orphans' home for about six months, then I was transferred to a foster home. Foster home wasn't home either. I always detested when the foster parents would push the issue that I could refer to them as Mom and Dad. They both would drink heavily on weekends. I was very rebellious because all I wanted was to go home to my real parents.

I finally got reunited with my parents, but growing up, I always felt like an outsider instead of part of the family, but at least it was home.

Tony admits that his family didn't do much to meet his needs, but interestingly, like so many of the other men, he doesn't blame his parents. He does blame the social welfare system.

> My parents neglected me unintentionally with their silence. I never heard many words of encouragement or acceptance. They always enforced what I couldn't do—like if I had an ambition, they would say things like I'm too small, not smart enough. They were unaware of the effect on me of their lack to nurture me as a child. I don't hold any resentment against my parents. I know they raised me the best they knew how.
>
> I do believe that through the combined efforts of the social workers and their system to protect children, my childhood was scarred.

Jones

Jones, mentioned earlier as the hard-scrabble knowledgeable convict who handles everything through humor, entered his first institution when he was only four years old. He was the youngest child ever accepted in the institution, he said. He lived there until he was eight. He and his four siblings were placed in the children's home when his father ran out on them and his mother couldn't support the family.

> It was an abusive orphanage. Back then I didn't think so, but I do now. They'd crack your hands and knuckles with pointer sticks.
>
> I used to wet the bed and they couldn't figure out why. They thought I was lazy and didn't want to get up to go to the bathroom. So they'd pull me out of bed and make me eat those dried red peppers for punishment. They made me puke, and I remember standing against the wall pukin' and crying.
>
> I was in the little boys' hall and when we acted out, they'd put us in the older dorm and line up the bigger boys and let them punch us in the arm.

"But not all of them were mean," Jones said, his face visibly softening. "I remember Sister Marian Frances. She was so nice.... She cared about us. She was a real nice lady—Sister Marian Frances."

I have to confess that since that conversation I could never think of this man who once started a prison riot by clubbing a man over the head, without first seeing him in my mind's eye as a frightened little kid crying in wet underpants with vomit dripping down his face and stomach.

Jones and his brothers and sisters returned home five years later when his mother had remarried, but it was not to a good situation.

> My stepfather was abusive too, but I respected him. Why? Because he accepted the responsibility my father wouldn't take. He took in my mother and her five kids. He was abusive with me and my brothers and sisters, but I could leave the house when I needed to.

I was nine when I was running in the streets. He was an alcoholic and drank on the weekends.

Whenever his stepfather was drunk, Jones would leave home. On a few occasions, he spent the night in a neighbor's doghouse. They had a big Saint Bernard, and the boy and dog would curl up together and keep warm, he explained. Once, the woman who owned the dog saw him and brought him in and gave him breakfast. He recounts that memory with a happy grin. He was in about the third grade.

Jones continued to run the streets and his behavior became more out of control. "I've been in every youth institution in Ohio," he says. "The abuse was bad, but back then you didn't call it that. Even the courts hit you. I remember the judge spanking me."

Jones was moved from institution to institution as a teenager.

I wasn't into crime when I was a kid. It was mostly for truancy. I didn't go to school. They sent me away because I wouldn't go to school, and then the places they sent me didn't make you go to school. That never made sense to me. I mostly did things like truancy—I was out of control of my parents. I fought a lot, too.

When I was seventeen, I did crime and they put me in an adult institution 'cause none of the youth institutions would take me back. I did bank robberies.

Emotional abuse can be worse than physical abuse because it eats into a child's soul. When children are continually run down and discouraged, and have troubling upheaval in their families, they develop low self-esteem and a sense of hopelessness that they carry with them to adulthood. The childhood homes of many of these men were chaotic, filled with physical and mental violence. As an educator in prison, I frequently heard men marveling at their unexpected successes. "They always said I was dumb," and "I never dreamed I could do this," I heard repeatedly.

The conversation that sticks the most in my mind came when I stood talking to a grizzled man in his late fifties from the mountains of Eastern Kentucky. He talked in a slow mountain drawl. I had just told him that he had the highest grade point average in the graduating class, and therefore would be the one chosen to give the graduation speech. His eyes brimmed over, tears dripped down his creased cheeks and fell onto the floor. He was so overwhelmed, he made no attempt to stop the flow. "I always thought I was stupid," he choked out.

John

It's not always words or physical violence that do damage to sensitive children. Being ignored and isolated can do as much psychic damage as the raining of fists. John wrote:

My mother was a very dominant factor in my life. She handled most of the punishments. I never received hugs and kisses as a child. I was very shy and timid. I thought there was something wrong with me. No one in my family was very close.

I have three older sisters who used to beat the hell out of me.... All the neighborhood boys beat me up too, so I isolated myself from almost everyone. I came to live in a fantasy world where I never got beat up. My mom never noticed my low self-esteem or isolation. She and Dad both drank too much. I knew they drank too much, so I stayed away from them and played with my Hot Wheels or my GI Joes with the Kung Fu grip. My fantasy world was strong.

Now, Dad. I never saw Dad. He worked long hours and when I did see him, he would be drinking, so I stayed away. I felt rejected from my family.... I was also sexually abused by a cousin at age six or seven. I was threatened with death if I told, so I kept quiet. I wanted to tell Mom, but I was afraid. I began to repress all feelings after that. I did that in adult life as well.

I idolized my dad, but I never saw him. He has never taken me fishing, hunting, or anything. We moved to a farm when I was ten. He still didn't do things with me, but he found plenty of work for me to do. I resented him for that.

My parents' attitude towards school was mixed. They wanted us to do well, but they never took an active role. Mom would make me do my homework, but seldom helped me. I was pretty much on my own. They never went to school functions or sporting events. I wanted to play sports, but I had no way of transportation, plus everyone told me I probably wasn't good enough to play anyway. So you see, my low self-esteem was instilled at a young age. I don't think it was intentional; I just don't think Mom and Dad knew what they were doing. In my opinion, they were teaching me the way they were taught.

Already lonely and living largely through fantasy, John as a young teen turned to the rural liquor store and the men who hung around it. He caught the school bus there and as he waited, he got to know the regular clientele. He worked there after school.

Being young and impressionable, and wanting desperately to fit in and having no male role model, I was susceptible to anything. I spent a lot of time at that store and even got a job there. I fit in and was accepted! I was taught many wrong things. This is where I learned about sex, hearing all these old men talk. I absorbed it like a sponge. It truly shaped my future. My parents never noticed what was going on. They continued to drink. Dad continued to work.

I even saw less of him because he had two extra hours of drive time now. It's like everyone in my family went their own separate ways and I was alone. My childhood definitely shaped my adult life. I don't blame my parents for me coming to prison, but it did contribute. So many things and factors added together like a puzzle until I finally broke and committed my crime. It's very sad to think about.

Of necessity, John spent most of his life escaping through his imagination. As a child, he used fantasy to escape the reality of his loneliness and sexual abuse. As a young teenager, he entered the fantasy world of porn magazines and exaggerated stories of debased sex told by the alcoholics who taught him a depraved view of women.

A few years later, he set up a sexual encounter based on a fantasy scenario. He explained he awoke with terror from the act, realizing the reality of the rape he had just committed. Apologizing repeatedly to his victim, telling her repeatedly that it wasn't her fault, he dashed out of the building into his truck. Tears streaming down his cheeks as he drove, he pulled over to the side of the road and put his gun in his mouth. Years later in prison, he said it was a vision of his family members finding him with his head blown open that caused him not to pull the trigger.

Shak

In 1994, Shak was a young, handsome African American inmate, smart, verbal, simmering with anger but wanting a better life. He was trying to find his way. His story, I suspect, is one found over and over in the inner cities of our nation. Bitterness imbued his words.

> I had the opportunity to be raised up in a single-parent home. My unwed mother happened to be unfortunate enough to raise three misguided young boys. At the time of my father's departure, I was eleven years young, the eldest of two brothers, ages seven and one. No great experience other than the fact that my only male role model was gone away, leaving my mother with the responsibility of supporting four with less than half the income.
>
> Instantly I moved through the ranks from the little boy who couldn't be allowed to walk to the corner store after dark, to the man of the house who knew little about being a man. I knew even less about raising two younger brothers who shared the same loss of parental guidance—a father.
>
> My mother was laid off from her job. Already a fourth-rate citizen, my once strong independent African American mother of three became a downtrodden, subjugated, uneducated, unemployed Negro woman with three Negro bastard children all perpetually dependent on welfare.
>
> Many days didn't pass that my mother's anger toward my father was redirected to me because I favored him so much. I couldn't see it then, but it distressed my mother greatly when my younger brothers imitated the things I taught them of the father they never knew. My mother was strong because my father wasn't man enough.
>
> There were many nights that I sat and watched my mother cry from all the overwhelming anxieties that she faced daily. It's hard for a son to see his mother cry. I vowed that I'd never again watch my mother continually suffer, working on a job all week that simply didn't make the ends meet. In my spare time away from home, I learned a new trade. I learned the drug trade. It was one thing that would change my life forever. It wasn't the greatest life, but we now had steak with the red beans and rice.
>
> Now I'm locked away in prison trying to figure a way out. My two younger brothers have two poor role models to follow: a runaway father and a convict brother. The cycle continues unless either I or my father can step up and stop the madness.

I have a difficult time not pontificating about how our society treats children or allows them to be treated. It is impossible that neighbors, teachers, social workers, ministers didn't suspect some of these problems or know something was wrong. In some cases they did, and did nothing. Sometimes they contributed to the difficulties. The stories stack up, waiting to be told.

Bruce

Bruce was also from the first study; he was a large man, in the six-foot range, heavyset, pudgy rather than solid. He was not a pushover, but I could tell he was sometimes unsure of himself. He was friendly and helpful, but became upset when people were irritated or critical of him. His feelings were hurt easily. He said an experience he had in the seventh grade had lasting effects on him. His crime was of a sexual nature. While he told of an appalling situation, if his parents and school officials had worked together to help him through the crisis, the outcome might have been different. Most thirteen-year-olds are insecure and easily embarrassed. The situation he found himself in was overwhelming.

> I didn't know an English word during class and Mr. P____, who had, I realize now, been molesting me and nine other classmates, made me stand in front of the class, take my pants and underwear down, and made me turn around and paddled me until my bottom had welts on it. He was later fired and the abuse covered up by the town council, but I carried the mental scars the rest of my life. To my knowledge, the subject was never brought up or discussed by family or anyone. I guess people thought the memories would just fade away.

Although the vast majority of the men in my study report unpleasant and painful experiences in school, the all-too-few good experiences stand out clearly. I asked the men to tell me about their best teachers. Alarmingly, very few could remember any.

Gene

Gene was an exception even though his life story did not turn out well. To hear this angry, often hostile older man talk softly about someone kind in his long harsh life, brought home the importance of kindness to troubled children. His African American teacher actively worked to become the second line of defense for a child with problems at home. He remembered her many, many years later.

The best teacher I had in school was Miss Weaver, my fourth grade teacher. She had to be the sweetest woman in the world. Even when I was beaten by her, I soon got over it, because she was so nice. My mother and father died at an early age and Miss Weaver knew this. At different times while in class, she would call me off to the side and comfort me. I lived with my aunt and uncle, which wasn't completely pleasant. Miss Weaver also understood this. On Saturday, many times she would let me come to her house and cut her grass so I could have extra money. I would also eat lunch with her. She was tall, neat, and very attractive. She never petted me. She was one of the most lovable women I have ever known.

It is appalling to listen to story after story of lonely children, of scared children, who in only a few years grew into lonely, scared, and angry men. No one took time with them as children to teach them, talk to them, laugh with them, or show them how to live with any semblance of dignity.

People cannot live in families filled with violence, neglect, and hate and suddenly. as teenagers and adults, know how to act responsibly, think rationally, and love appropriately. These things have to be learned. The question of where it is to be learned remains. In a dysfunctional family mired in pain, where does appropriate behavior and responses to tension begin?

Most of the men in prison know right from wrong, but they do not know how to control their inner turmoil in order to function appropriately in stressful situations. They do not know how to delay gratification, how to plan, or how to work through difficult, discouraging tasks. These are things we learn gradually as children from people who carefully teach us. Most people from deprived backgrounds who have been successful in spite of it, can point to individuals in their childhoods who gave them hope, love, and guidance. Many of these men in these pages cannot point to anyone they knew like that.

I have talked to scores of prisoners over the years, and one man, Ken, always remains among the most vivid in my mind. He talked openly about his feelings, experiences, crimes, and his hopes for the future. But it was when he talked about his childhood and what is happening to children today that his passion emerged and the listener had to remember what he said. Raised by an elderly, overwhelmed, and resentful grandmother, abandoned by his mother and father, running with gangs in a large city, and finally homeless at age eleven, he begs us to think of the children.

Man, kids are important. If we would start with the kids and show them somebody cares. They shuffle through foster homes, reform schools, group homes. Kids are smart. They know nobody gives a shit.

I wonder how society could look at that little boy I was in the eyes. A bleak child who needed something. They had to see it.... And a few years later they say, "Damn, why did he do that?"

Issues to Think About

1. Did your attitudes toward the inmates change as you read of the abuse and neglect some of them suffered as children?
2. Do you think that a man's past should have any influence in his sentencing or parole?
3. Do you feel society holds any responsibility in the crimes that are committed?
4. What policies or practices would you propose to help alleviate the problems of abuse and neglect?

EIGHT

Desperate Connections
Family Ties

*Prison is punishment for you and your family. It is punishment for every-
body. The kids go through hell every weekend. They will for eleven years.*
                                                                    —Andy

*My family doesn't care for me. They don't visit me or send me money.
But when you come from the sort of life I did, what do you have but
family?*
                                                                   —Jamal

The Families

The power of it puzzles me still, but the connections and expectations
of family are central to a man's concept of self and his experiences in prison.
Most men, it seems, are clinging to family, hoping for family, or embittered
about family. It is the subject most likely to bring men to tears.

For men so isolated from the outside world, emotions in the prison are
surprisingly dependent upon what is happening outside of the correctional
facility. Families and friends "do time" just like the inmates. But after a while,
the time grows longer and harder, and those on the outside start to drift away.
Within the walls, there is a continuing saga of anguish over deteriorating
families, impending divorces, and illnesses and deaths of loved ones. Prisoners grow increasingly angry in the earlier years of incarceration as they
have no control over these events, and they see the results of their illegal
actions causing even more destruction and sadness until they are left with
absolutely no one at all.

In looking at changes in people incarcerated over a twenty-year period,
the most apparent changes are in their physical and mental health and in
their attitudes toward their families. During the early years, I heard much
about wives, girlfriends, and children. I was shown numerous pictures, learned

about their children's activities, and heard concerns about their marriages and wives. Twenty years later, most of the first letters that arrived in my box had news about their parents—their illnesses, their deaths, their faithfulness. There was very little mention of wives. And surprisingly little about children who were now grown.

Marriage and Children

The pain first starts when the men enter prison and are separated from their families. Much is said about female prisoners and the heartbreaking situations they face being separated from their children. But few statistics are available about the number of men in prison who are fathers. And little is written about their parenthood. The father/child relationships take a back seat to the mother/child relationships in our society today, and the parental status of men is not a consideration in the sentencing or parole of the men as it sometimes is with women. That special consideration for women has lessened in the past twenty years, but at times is still a factor in lessening women's sentences, depending on the state and laws.

Unlike in the women's facilities, there are few parenting programs for fathers that facilitate visitation of children. The incarcerated fathers seem to suffer by the separation as much as the women, but they don't show their emotions in the same way. Most of them care for their children deeply, regardless of their past actions. Free society is not well designed to keep men involved in their children's lives after marital separation. Imprisonment finalizes the break.

Soon after incarceration, most of the men are acutely aware that their masculine role of caretaker has abruptly changed. Now their wives and girlfriends, who are extremely vulnerable and who may be struggling with serious emotional and physical hardships themselves, must care for the men. The problem of family separation is so multifaceted that it is difficult to pinpoint the part that is the most problematic for the men. The men worry about their family's safety, how they will survive, the effects of their imprisonment on the children, and whether their wives will be faithful. Cal wrote in 1994:

> We worry about our loved ones all the time as we think of them, and we ask ourselves questions like: Are our children getting enough to eat? Do they have adequate clothing to wear? Is my spouse committing adultery? Are they safely tucked away in the house at night with the doors and windows locked? Most of us have had many family members die while serving our sentences and many of us wonder how many family and friends will be left alive when we are finally released.

Twenty years later, Cal made no mention of his children or his wife. He talked about death—the deaths of both his parents, an uncle, a first cousin. His aloneness and bitterness bled through his handwritten pages.

The early concern about family is widespread among the men and crosses racial and socioeconomic lines. The men carry a quiet anguish with them that is especially acute when they think of their children. Jeff wrote:

> For me the worst thing about being in prison is that I can't be the father that I want to be to my two children. Yes, having to come to prison stops a person from being a good role model for their kids. You know, prison takes away the love that one needs to show to the children and the guidance that a child needs from the parent.

Ken shared similar thoughts about his children:

> As for my children, they are the ones that suffer the most in my opinion. They have to live for the next thirteen and a half years without a father being there whenever they need me.... I am sure that they have asked the question if they were the cause of the criminal activity even though I have assured them they were not. It has affected them that their father will not be there to see them celebrate many special occasions, including graduations, birthdays, and major achievements in their young lives.

Almost without exception, the men agree with Ken. The children seem to pay the highest price for the men's mistakes, and the knowledge of that fact remains with the fathers. Once imprisoned, they play and replay scenarios of good times with their children. They yearn to redo their lives to make up for past parental mistakes. They want to make their family whole again.

Another man, Andy, wrote:

> My incarceration has had a quite dramatic effect on my family as I see it. Before I was locked up, I was able to be involved in raising my children, but incarceration is a strong deterrent for this. I miss the small things like just being around to teach them how to ride a bike or tie their shoes. My mother has helped a great deal with my children (girls four, five, seven).... As a matter of fact, if it wasn't for her I don't know what would be happening with them.

When I saw the gentle attitudes many of these men now show towards children, and witnessed the pride with which they share their children's achievements, I knew they were probably caring fathers in some respects. Obviously, if they were the kind of fathers they should have been, they wouldn't be in prison, but in their own ways, they tried to be good parents.

In 1994, Ken was in his thirties, a handsome, dark-haired man with expressive eyes. He was thoughtful, sincere, and a favorite of the teachers. Twenty years later, I ran across a former college instructor and we were reminiscing. She first asked what ever happened to Ken. He was an engaging, introspective man, afraid of little, but with a compelling, gentle side.

He had grown up on the streets; both of his parents were in prison. A resentful grandmother threw him out of the house as he entered his teenage years and he hinted at the unthinkable ways he had used to find shelter and money to survive. But somehow, he held onto his humanity.

You ask if my early experiences have affected my parenting skills. What parenting skills? How can a person who had no parents have parenting skills? I can tell you that when I was out, I really tried very hard to be a good parent. I told myself what I was missing, or thought I was missing, as a child, and tried to give my children things I didn't have. Things that I thought were important—stuff like open house at school, Mommy and Daddy career day. I would drive my big service truck up to the school and let the kids walk through it while answering all their questions, or most of them anyway. I let them blow the big air horn, one time each, of course....

I tried to teach them responsibility, like when my oldest son got tired of his old bike and wanted a new one. I helped him fix his old one up and took him around to different bike shops until he sold it. That was really cute. Then we used that money, and of course, a lot of my money, to buy the bike he wanted.

I show them love and respect. I want to get my children to thrive in society. I want them to be part of society even though I don't want to be part of it myself.

At one point in our acquaintance, Ken was distressed as his ten-year-old son was looking up to him too much, wanting to be just like his dad. He talked about going to prison someday. His behavior was becoming a problem. In one of our college classes, Ken learned about parent resource centers in the public schools. He got the needed information from his teacher and persuaded his wife to call the school and seek help from them. He son started to improve.

Ken remained very involved with his parenting although his involvement was not always legal. In prison, he ran a parlay business and arranged to have the earnings sent to his wife and children each month, which helped supplement the wife's welfare payments.

I asked him what effect that would have on his son who already was glorifying his father and his actions.

They only know Dad works in prison—not that he runs a parlay business. They knew I was in the hole. [Ken occasionally got caught with his business dealings.] I tell them I did something wrong, and you have to be punished when you do something wrong. About being in prison, I tell them I took something from someone else. That was wrong because it wasn't my money to take. I made a mistake and you have to pay for your mistakes.

For a while, by being able to contribute, Ken was able to hold his family together and keep a balance with them, but he admitted that might be more of a problem the longer he was locked up and away from them.

I do not know what happened to Ken after he was extradited to another state to serve another sentence for bank robbery. I saw a man on Facebook with the same name who looks much like Ken used to. I wonder if it is Ken's son now grown. I wonder but don't ask. Family relationships over the years are touchy and I hesitate to stir the waters.

Like Ken, many of the other men worry greatly over their children. They understand that their wives are left holding the bag, forced to support the family alone financially and psychologically. They must also deal with the stigma that imprisonment brings. In 1994, Bill, a man whose wife had stayed with him for the almost-ten years he had been incarcerated, said:

> Outside of myself, my wife is the one who has suffered the most. She testified at my trial on my behalf, so from the beginning she has been called a "liar" and "co-conspirator."
>
> This will be our tenth wedding anniversary and we have yet to spend one together. We went from a family of four to a single working mother with two daughters and a husband who became dependent on her for nearly everything. Our roles in life changed drastically.
>
> She could no longer depend on me to do the maintenance around the house.... They quickly had to learn how to get by on less. The children felt the monetary effects immediately. I honestly don't know what effects, if any, the children endured in school. The fact that these children are not biologically mine probably helped ease their pain. It still devastated their mother, thus it had an emotional effect on them because she had to divide her time up in so many places.

A lot of women, like Bill's wife, stick with their husbands for a long time, picking up roots and moving whenever their husbands are transferred between institutions. They are the exception rather than the rule, however. The men get involved in their own problems and start to ask too much of the women who are getting little emotional support. In an attempt to stay in control and hold their place in the family, the men too often tell the women what to do, trying to manage the home from prison, and criticize the decisions their wives or girlfriends make. They argue angrily during phone calls. The men don't remember the demands of everyday life and can't understand why the women don't have time to do a myriad of tasks for them, or why they aren't waiting at home every time they call. Nor do they understand the heavy financial burdens the institutional phone calls place on an already strained budget. During the time I first talked with the men in the '90s, there was much anger and hurt expressed towards their family members whose lives were moving on.

Since those days, courts are now giving longer sentences, and parole boards are giving longer deferments (the amount of time the men must wait until another parole hearing). The wives may be willing to wait another two years, but ten or twenty more years seems a lifetime. When a man receives a large deferment or setback, he knows it involves more than his freedom. It is usually the death knell of his marriage, as well.

Sometimes the men understand their wives' pain and continue to care for them even though the marriage ends. Greg, a second-time offender, was one of those young men.

> When I left, my wife and I had a four-year-old, a five-month-old child, and she was pregnant with our third. She came to see me often, but I still didn't take the time to

understand what being incarcerated again did to her, my Mom, and myself. I quickly learned how hard it was and still is for them, especially my wife. She needed me out there, and eventually I lost her.... She's a beautiful person. I just hope that she realizes that she is somebody and don't need me or anyone else to tell her that.

Many of the men become angry and bitter toward the women they feel have abandoned them. They seem to adjust better to the inevitable breakups if visits with their children can continue, but more often than not, that doesn't happen. Gary talks of the emotional pain involved in losing his family and friends.

> The most painful time was after I was here. One day my wife and children, ages ten and five years, came to visit me. They left and said, "We love you and always will." I did not have contact with them again for eight years. My wife of fourteen years did not even say goodbye. It is most difficult to feel helpless to defend your family, but it even feels worse not to say goodbye.
>
> Eight years after I lost my family, I got a twelve-year deferment. When the deferment came, every other person I had met left me.... I feel dead.... There is no light at the end of a long tunnel.

Tom also has been in the system long enough to watch contacts with his family and friends disintegrate.

> Prison separates you from those close to you not only physically, but spiritually, piece by piece over time from their lives, feelings, thoughts, and emotions. When you are first locked up, visits are frequent, letters plentiful, and phone calls many. As time passes, the visits become few and far between, letters never arrive, and there is no one to call. You are no longer an active part of their lives, their activities, their joys, and their sorrows—the very things that hold a relationship together and allow it to grow.
>
> For friendship, as well as for intimate relationships, there seems to be a magic cutoff point at about two and one-half years. Interactions slowly, almost systematically, decrease until this magic point, then abruptly stop as if some inevitable button has been pressed.

Norman had been in prison about three years when we talked about this. He had not yet hit that "magic cut-off point," possibly because his conviction was so controversial. But it was getting closer and he knew what would happen.

> I have many friends who support me and believe in me. I have my family's love and support, and I probably get more mail than most people here from former students, friends, and acquaintances—many people. But I know that as time goes by and life goes on for everybody except us in here, correspondence will slow to a gradual stop, contact with friends will cease, old friends and relatives will die, and I will suffer the loss of loved ones without the chance to ever see them again. This is a lonely and forlorn thought, and my heart hurts to think about it, but the fact remains, this will happen. This has happened.

I have not noticed any significant differences that the type of crime plays in whether the wife stays or leaves. Wives of rapists and child abusers seem to hang around about as long as those of robbers or drug dealers—at least among the men involved in this project. This is an area that would be ripe for research and might be better conducted by psychologists than sociologists.

Prison Marriages

Incarceration does not stop attractions between the sexes; in fact, it may increase it. Prison marriages are common. It is easy to envision how incarcerated men are drawn into new relationships, as they are desperate for warmth, affection, and affirmation while in prison. It is harder to explain the women's positions since they have more to lose.[1]

In a way, the attractions are understandable. Most of the men involved in prison marriages are at their prime. They are clean and well-groomed according to prescribed institutional standards, and are usually in good physical shape. Women are attracted by their appearance, cocky confidence, and emotional vulnerability. I do not agree with those who say that the men only establish relationships for what they can trick the women out of. I think, like everyone, they are looking for someone to care for them, to reinforce that they are worth loving. No doubt they also realize the advantages that come from having someone committed to them on the outside, but in most cases that is not the main motivating force.

The relationships that start while men are behind bars can last longer than their marriages did that began before incarceration. During their weekly visits, each party is at his or her best. There are no painful memories to get in the way of the developing relationship. Unexplored sexual tension and innuendos keep the connection electrified. Their relationships are based on their hopes for the future, not the failures of the past.

All types and all socioeconomic levels of women get involved with incarcerated men. There are various ways couples can meet. One of the men in this project ran a national pen pal matching service while incarcerated that brought many couples together. Staff, volunteers, and officers can get romantically involved with inmates during regular prison activities. Many men meet outside partners through friends of other inmates whom they get to know in the visiting room. In some cases, the men knew the women before they were incarcerated and the notion of rekindled love added to the romance. In several cases, the women's mothers even served as matchmakers.

Our faculty used to watch with amazed interest each time we had an occasion where the men were allowed to invite a friend or family member.

One particular man showed up each time with a different gorgeous woman, each of them classy and personable. He was charming himself, with average good looks, but we couldn't understand where he met and wooed these beauties.

Another man, Stuart, talked about getting a letter from someone he knew long ago. They later married in a prison ceremony.

> It was very exciting for me to know she remembered me. Her letter was really powerful. She said she knew it was a difficult time in my life and she said things like she wanted to help me and wanted to be a friend. We don't get many "fuzzies" around here. It was wonderful to be told by an outside normal person that she wanted to be my friend.

I have talked with some of the men who have been married while incarcerated, and although the men and their crimes are very different, there are some surprising things they have in common.

In each case, the men felt they were in charge of the relationship, unlike those who struggled to hold together a previous marriage. In the new relationship, the men have a feeling of control and of being needed. Unfortunately, these relationships are not developed amidst the realities of everyday life, and when the man is released, it is a rare couple that remains together more than a few years.

Policies allowing marriage ceremonies within prison differ between states, institutions, and chaplains. Most do allow it and help with formal marriage ceremonies. The number of institutions allowing conjugal visits is decreasing.

Unlike the men in prison who were married before their incarcerations, the men married while incarcerated declare they have no doubts about their wives' fidelity. In most of the men I talked with, they tie that trust to the wife's religion. Al wrote: "She's a Pentecostal girl brought up in the Pentecostal church. I lucked out when I got her. It's the best decision I ever made. If I get out of line, she gets up my behind and points a finger at me. I don't let anybody do that but her—at least up to some point and I say 'that's enough.' I'm a very fortunate man."

That trust does not always lead to the long-term success of the marriage, however.

I had expected to find that the men were using the women to supply some of their economic needs in prison, but that does not necessarily seem to be the case. The men who married while in prison report their wives are struggling financially and can't help them out. I expected these relationships to be very short-lived, but the men I have talked with have been married or at least seriously involved for three to twenty years. One relationship that had lasted nine years had never been consummated. There are longer relationships that have survived, but the couple managed to get together sexually surreptitiously within the institution. However, no matter how long the couples hold together, the end result is often hurt and disillusionment.

The men in this study all disclosed their criminal charges to the women early into the relationship, or else the women knew before they became involved. The men I interviewed included a serial rapist, a man who kidnapped a former girlfriend, and two murderers. The couples argue about the usual things other married couples do—monetary decisions the women are making, the men trying to be too controlling, and in one case, sex. The serial rapist shared with his wife when he had sexual fantasies that aroused him.

"As a wife, she feels jealous. Instead of being threatened, I wish she could see it as more therapeutic," he wrote.

Still, as the years roll on and the parole deferments pile up, many of the men regret having involved the women and realize it is selfish to hang on. Al said: "I haven't told her this, but if I don't make parole this time, I'm going to let her go. Why should I deprive her of her own life? I would set her free and she could find someone else. I have no alternative but to do that. We've never discussed that. All I'd ask is that she would raise my son."

Although he is a man totally different from Al, Jonathan echoed his words almost exactly. He hoped to get paroled in a few months; it was his second time up for parole.

> If I don't make it, I wouldn't want her to wait. It was hard enough waitin' three years. I don't think our marriage would work. I'd give her her freedom. It's the best thing I can do for her. Every woman has her needs. I can't give her her needs. Giving her freedom is the best I can do. All I can ask is for her to take care of my little girl.

Jonathan was not released for another nineteen years. Al remains incarcerated.

Parents

As spouses and friends gradually depart, the inmates' mothers seem to offer the most continuing security and strength to the men. They often stay in touch long after others have abandoned their sons. It is a contradiction in one sense. The same men who have recounted troubled childhood memories of mothers who drank too much, didn't hug enough, and whose tongues had a painful cutting edge, now tell of loving families who give them strength. The sharpness of unpleasant memories dulls with time, and they cling to what love they believe is there. Each side tries harder to make the short visits pleasant ones.

Twenty years ago, when the men talked more with me about parenting and childhood issues, many said they didn't blame their parents for the mistakes they made. Most of the parents, no matter how horribly they treated them, apparently loved their children—they just didn't know how to be good parents or to communicate positive feelings to them. But once their sons were incarcerated, they had less personal contact. The sources of daily hurt and stress were minimized, and they were better able to express love in their brief, controlled contacts with one another. Perhaps the parents tried harder as they came to grips with their own guilt in the difficulties their sons had encountered.

"My mother raised me the best she knew how.... I think she raised me the only way she knew how, and that's the way she was raised," recounted Davis. He had told me of a mother who drank too much, who knocked him around, and who often insulted him. But once he was in prison, she became a main source of support for him. In 1994, when we were conversing about this, Davis was only twenty-two years old, but he had already served four years in prison. He got a two-year deferment from the parole board when many of us expected him to be released. He was very upset but said, "It's the hardest on my family—they are taking it the worst." I've heard that a lot over the years.

The things parents can do for their adult children in prison are clearly spelled out in regulations and many do the most they are allowed to, often at great personal sacrifice. Maybe if good parenting skills could have been reduced to a procedural manual, they would have been more successful.

It is easy to be too judgmental, however. Just out of college, I worked in an institution for emotionally disturbed children. While railing one day about the parents who had mistreated the children so badly, I was stopped short with a gentle reminder from my supervisor that changed my outlook for the rest of my life.

"Just remember," she said, "those parents are these disturbed children grown up."

The men's internal conflicts toward their families flickered through their early conversations and many of them felt that it was the duty of their families to help them once they were incarcerated. Cal, a man with a ninety-nine-year sentence and a very difficult childhood knew twenty-years ago that he would eventually be eligible for parole, but had no idea when, or even if, he would ever be released. He worked hard in school to achieve, and always said it was his primary motivation to get a degree for his mother's sake. Yet, at another time, he callously said his family would pay for something he needed although their money was tight. "They owe me," he said.

Cal eventually saw the parole board, which deferred him for another twenty years. Today he is an embittered man. His mother and all his family members are dead. It is the first thing he mentioned when we reconnected.

He serves his time alone and mourning the family that never treated him well, but whom he loved.

While poor parenting is a common thread that runs through most of the men's childhoods, that is not true in all cases. Some parents agonized as they watched their teenagers get involved with drugs and rough crowds. They tried hard to help but were unable to save them.

Billy is such a case. He says his parents were great as he grew up. His trouble began when they moved to a large city where the young African Americans living around him were tougher than his former small-town friends. As a teenager, he had no juvenile record, did well in school, and held several jobs. But he drank too much, took on the ways of the street, and didn't learn how to walk away from a fight.

One night, armed with a gun, he retaliated against an acquaintance who earlier had attacked and robbed him. The man was injured but not killed. Refusing a good plea-bargained deal, Billy insisted on a court trial and got a surprisingly heavy sentence. Then, while being initially assessed in the prison system, he got into a fight with another new inmate and was classified to the maximum-security facility, which is where the most hardened, hard-to-control men are sent.

At age twenty-one, a kid who had never been in trouble before "went straight into the hard core of it all. I will never forget the sight of that building once it came into view and stepping inside of it. I was scared to death."

Billy learned about prison life quickly. In those days, Kentucky State Penitentiary was a rough institution (it still is) and this somewhat innocent youngster was surrounded by stabbings and killings.

> Constantly, waking up every day was a living nightmare, but I learned to adjust. I had to if I was going to live.... The faith and determination that my father and mother bestowed on me got me through it. I felt like a child. I called them every day. It was long distance, of course, and the bills mounted up, but they always took the calls. Hearing the sound of their voices made me closer to them. My father said to be strong. He said, "Remember you are as good as they are. You put your pants on the same as they do—one leg at a time." My mother is real religious. She would tell me to take care of myself. I have always been surrounded by the love of my family.

Billy was later transferred to the medium-security facility where his parents, girlfriend, and son visited him every weekend without fail. But as the years rolled by, his mother died and other contacts dwindled.

Cam is another man whose parents stuck by him. Although he says they should have made him go to a counselor when he was a teenager, they tried everything else.

> My father used to tell me, "Cam, if you keep this up, you'll end up either on the streets, or in jail, or dead!" Evidently he was right about one of those, but you couldn't tell me anything. I thought I knew everything....

My family had no idea what was really going on. I was living a double life. My parents would always be there for me, and always supported and provided for me. I took it for granted and took advantage of it. I was too blind to see what I was headed for—exactly what my father had said.

In 1994, four years after his incarceration began, Cam recognized what his family had done for him. "Without them, I could do the time, but it would be extra hard. They support me financially, give me the clothes I wear [back then, men were allowed to wear personal clothing], and give me love. They visit every weekend. I call them every Wednesday. Mother sends at least one card a week."

He leaned more on his family as his young friends scattered and faded away. He wrote that his life was like a big X, with one stroke being his time in prison, the other his number of friends. "It's like a big X. My time goes up; my friends go down."

Now twenty years later, his parents are still by his side. Without fail, he says, they still visit him every weekend.

I recently got a letter from Cam. He was awakened in the middle of the night and moved to an institution far away in the state. He claimed he has no idea what the move was about and he recognized the difficulties this move would bring to his parents. He said, "I'm mad still."

As parents age, the distances matter even more.

Women support their sons or grandsons for as long as they can. It's poignant to watch the older stooped women going through the degrading personal searches and slowly shuffling into the visiting room. After a while, they lose their ability to travel or walk the needed distances, but they try to stay in touch through phone calls and letters. Bill was a middle-aged man in 1994 when he had already been incarcerated for more than ten years. His mother was one of those elderly women.

> Mother goes out of her way to ensure that my life is as comfortable as possible. In a way, she blames herself for not doing more to prevent my incarceration. While we all can easily see the things that we should have done to prevent the tragedy in our lives, I wish my mother wasn't so hard on herself for what happened to me.
>
> She is a very emotional woman, and it was many years before I would talk to her on the phone and say "goodbye" without hearing her cry. I cannot begin to tell you how much this hurt me. I wanted to do something to ease her pain, but could not. The devastation of this incarceration could not begin to be measured.

As the men get older, their parents age, and illness strikes. When their parents are sick and hospitalized, the incarcerated men become quite upset. I have seen them temporarily self-destruct at those times, dropping or failing out of school. They know there is nothing they can do to help their families during the difficulties. It is the sense of helplessness that drives them to the edge emotionally. Jack wrote: "My mother went into the hospital for open-heart surgery. I was left without knowing for two days, and that has been the hardest time I have had adjusting to being incarcerated."

When David learned that his mother had unexpectedly died, he said he "hit the fence"—climbing up the chain-link, blindly trying to get out. "I hoped they would kill me," he said. But instead, the officers pulled him down. "They gave me a break because they knew she had died. It was the only kindness they ever showed, but they did then."

When parents are dying, the men are officially allowed one visit with them, provided they are living within the state and they can afford to pay for the escorted trip. The men must choose between a bedside visit before death or attendance at the funeral.

Winston visited his mother in the hospital as she lay near death. Afterwards, he told me about the experience. It pained her to see him in his orange jumpsuit, he said, but after a while, the officer guarding him removed his handcuffs, and he was able to hold her hand and forget about prison for a short time, although his legs remained shackled. He said they were able to talk over some past issues and say goodbye. Winston died in prison within a year after his mother's death.

Cam had two grandparents die by the time we talked in 1994. He was able to attend the funeral visitation, but he had to go in shackles and handcuffs. One time, the officer guarding him removed the cuffs so he could interact more normally, but at his grandfather's funeral, the guard refused to release them. The decision is at the officer's personal discretion. "I felt ashamed and embarrassed. I was more embarrassed for my parents. They still loved me, but the relatives looked at me strange."

I talked with Leslie a few weeks after he had attended his thirty-one-year-old sister's funeral. She had died unexpectedly from a brain aneurysm. His anger from the experience was still evident, disrupting his usually quiet, gentle demeanor. The staff at the prison gave him much support and help, he said. Their unexpected hugs and reassurances touched and comforted him. But recounting his trip to his sister's funeral made fire flash in his eyes and his face redden.

"I was chained like a dog. My travel rules said full restraints, though I don't understand that," recounted the man with a perfect prison record. Full restraints meant that his legs were shackled with chains so that his walk was reduced to a shuffle. Heavy chains were placed around his waist, and his hands were cuffed in place with the "black box," which unlike regular handcuffs, holds the hands completely immobile and attached against his body with the waist chain.[2]

As he talked, it was easy to feel his humiliation.

> We pulled up at the funeral home. The men were standing outside smoking, and immediately everyone knew it was me. The marked car, the big lights on top, the policemen in full dress blue with their guns, of course.

I begged him to take the cuffs off. I said leave the shackles on, I can deal with that, but please don't make me go in like this. The son of a bitch said, "If you give me any shit or your family gives me any trouble, I'll take you right back." Can you believe that! Oh God, it was humiliating.

As soon as my family saw me, they knew I was fuming and knew how I felt. I have another sister who loves me, but she has trouble with where I am. She has visited me only once in five years. She came to me first and hugged me and whispered, "It doesn't matter." I got lots of hugs. I couldn't hug them back, but it worked out okay.

I'll never forget that bastard's name. Someday I'll see him on the outside, and I'll look at him and tell him I remember him. I won't do anything, but I want him to know I remember. If he has no more compassion than that, he shouldn't be doing funeral trips.

And on top of it all, the sons-of-a-gun charged me forty dollars to take me! It's not the money, it's the nerve.

Some men refuse to go to the funerals of relatives because of the humiliation to themselves and their families. Or they don't have money, or they are out of state. Norman was unable to attend the funeral of his mother as she lived in a neighboring state.

To be as close to her as I was and not be allowed to attend her funeral is a crime in itself. I will probably never get over it. It is not natural to be deprived of natural ways of grieving, but in here, any grieving you do best be in the deep and dark of the night ... away from the view of the other inmates. One must not show weakness in this place. Isn't that a crock???? To be comforted by your loved ones, to be held and touched and feel the warmth of human compassion is part of life, and to be deprived of it is a prison to itself.

Men usually take deaths extra hard. Perhaps it is because they are unable to grieve in the usual manner, or maybe it is because the death ends the dreams they had of close, normal family relationships.

When the parents die, very often that is the end of all visits. Parents are often responsible for pushing siblings and other relatives and friends to visit and write. They are the one who bring their grandchildren to see their fathers. Without their influence, already fragile relationships break or just fade away. Most of the men in my study who remain in prison have no visitors at all. They are totally on their own in a lonely place.

Issues to Think About

1. Why do you think family is so important to the prison inmates even when an inmate's family is dysfunctional?
2. What do you think would be the biggest strain on a marriage when one of the spouses is locked up?

3. What do you think prison visiting policy should be concerning the children of inmates? What are some of the issues that need to be considered? Should prison marriages be allowed?
4. What was your reaction to the men's accounts of visiting or not being allowed to visit a parent's deathbed or attend a funeral?

NINE

Two Sides of a Coin

The Man and His Crime

Sometimes I see a vivid picture of him lying there with his hand over his mouth, as if he had been in total awe. Many times I pray and tell God how sorry I am, even though I know I've been forgiven. Probably the most haunting thing about that night was just as I stabbed him, he screamed, "Oh God!"

—Leslie

Men in prison are extraordinarily diverse, as are their crimes, but the one thing they have in common is that they are convicted felons. They have all been found guilty by the justice system of our country, and they will forever carry the label with them.

Behind every man and crime, there is a story. It may be a story of red-hot anger, of fuzzy drugged memories, or of revengeful hurt. The crime may have been well planned and executed over a period of months, or it might have been a singular reactive incident, thoughtlessly destroying lives in a matter of seconds.

Some of the men in our group have long rap sheets illuminating criminal behavior stretching over decades. They do extra time now because of past crimes. They are considered persistent felony offenders (PFOs); the designation requires enhanced sentences in most cases. Others had no records at all until the moment they reacted wrongly. One, still imprisoned, declares his innocence. Others admit to some of their actions, but deny other charges that were piled onto their convictions, adding to the number of years they must spend behind bars.

To discuss their crimes is to open Pandora's box. For me, clearly the most difficult part of coming to grips with the prison experience was reconciling the men I came to like with the horrific reality of what they had done. The contrasts tore at me.

For some people—and I include the general public as well as the victimized—it is easiest to label men convicted of horrendous crimes as evil. They deny that men who rape women, kill others, and steal at the point of a gun, can do those acts and also have feelings of gentleness or caring. These people can see no good in those convicted of such crimes.

We see this attitude during well-publicized trials. If the defendant cries or makes a statement of apology, he is accused of acting and being insincere. If the arrested sits stoically in the courtroom with his emotions carefully hidden, he is accused of callousness. One seldom hears a nuanced middle-ground opinion. The all-too-common feeling is that no one who commits such a horrific crime can ever be rehabilitated.

On the other hand, there are thousands of people seeking to help or connect personally to these inmates. They come into the prisons to bring a variety of programs or to save souls. Some seek intimate pen pal relationships. Many of those outsiders are also blinded to the nuances of criminal behavior. They rationalize, speaking of the men's indescribable childhoods that explain, and even excuse, their behaviors. They consider the inmates victims of an unfair and unequal justice system or their crimes as anomalies. They see the prisoners as personable men who surely will do better when given another chance.

Neither perspective is entirely appropriate. The most difficult challenge to understanding the causes of crime and the criminal himself is the necessity of seeing the inmate as a whole person. It's easy to dismiss the perpetrators of crime as "evil people," animals to be locked into cages. Or it is easy once you get to know them, to feel sorry for them and trust them completely. But as most who work within the prisons can tell you, it's not that simple.

Most of the men in our prisons in many ways are very much like our friends in the outside community. Once they trust someone, they are fun and interesting to talk with. They have warm and caring feelings for selected people, and they yearn for a better life for themselves and their families. As law-abiding citizens, we have much in common with them.

But we cannot and must not forget the illegal, and, in some cases unthinkable, acts they have committed. At the same time, we must neither forget their humanity nor ignore the sparks of goodness that flourish within each of them. Within the prison walls, I saw "bad" people display extraordinary kindnesses, and I have seen "good" people be unspeakably cruel. If we are going to find workable answers to crime and subsequent rehabilitation, we have to understand the full complexities of the individuals involved. Few people are truly evil with no redeeming qualities, just as few people are truly righteous with no personal weaknesses.

The public fails to understand the diverse nature of the men in our prisons and this lack of understanding keeps us from finding effective solutions to our problems. This topic is further complicated because of the widely differing motivations behind various categories of crime. Child molesters have entirely different motivations from drug dealers, for example. They require different treatment programs and present different security issues. Yet in our criminal justice system, these people are housed together, treated the same, and share the same labels of "felons," "criminals," and "inmates."

The situation becomes increasingly complex as we find that the men themselves are also confused by their actions and their own seemingly two-sided natures. Many of them struggle to honestly accept responsibility for what they have done while fighting against internalizing the damaging labels society has placed on them.

For various reasons, the men are often reluctant to talk about their crimes. Some, like Wayne, are private people and deal with their crimes and incarceration by withdrawing even more emotionally. The emotional with-drawal does not necessarily mean that the men don't think about their crimes, but a number of the men have always been uncomfortable with sharing any types of thoughts or emotions. That tendency may have contributed to the crime in the first place. Wayne wrote:

> I've heard men talk about the crimes they committed like it's something to be proud of. But that's not who I am. I'm a very private person.... After I committed my crime, and the realization of what had happened sunk in, I realized a part of me died on that day as well. I've never talked about what happened on that day, not even to my parents, and I never will talk about it. I figure it's my own personal demon. It happened, and it's not going to help by talking about it. The way I figure it, they can keep me locked up as long as they want to, but having to live with my crime is the ultimate punishment.

Taking Life

The label of murderer is perhaps the most feared by the community at large. The sentences are understandably long, and the murderers often begin their incarcerations in the harshest of prisons. Yet statistically, we know that those who kill are the least likely to reoffend.[1] The sober, cold-blooded killer of strangers is more an anomaly than a pattern.

Most of the men in my study who have killed are average representations of those in that category. They had been drinking or were on drugs. They had some personal connection with the victim. The murder was the acci-dental result of an argument, fight, or romantic triangle.

Leslie's experiences are typical. Increasing drug use and mounting inter-nal anger are ingredients for violence.

> I remember when there were years that went by when I really wasn't conscious of time or things around me that should have been relevant. But because of the drugs

and the constant quest for a good time, I neglected those important things in life, even my family.... A very large proportion of the drugs I consumed on a daily basis, and to what extent I stayed high, they (family and employer) never knew as I built up immunity. Looking back on how dangerous I was, it scares me.... There came a point in time just before my crime took place that I couldn't stand myself.

Leslie had a long-term drug problem and seethed with anger. He and his wife went to visit a friend who had his own problems. The friend, recently released from psychiatric care, was a collector of weapons and had been drinking throughout the day.

When my wife and I arrived, he welcomed us in and locked the door behind us. We sat and talked for a while until Bill's personality began to change. At the time we had left to go to Bill's, I wasn't high, but I had done several Valiums earlier that day, which probably still had some effect on me. I had been noticing for a year or so prior that the Valium I was taking daily was beginning to make me very short tempered....

The conversation that Bill and I was having turned into an argument. Bill left the room and [in] a few minutes entered with an entirely different look and attitude— one of a crazed person. Bill began to shout at Kathy and cornered her. I grabbed him and he pulled a knife and stabbed me. I ran over to the counter where I had previously seen another knife laying and grabbed it.... I attacked him and stabbed him. He turned and we engaged in a stabbing, slicing match. He backed me over a chair and was trying to stab me when Kathy picked up a baseball bat that was lying in the corner. She hit him in the arm and he dropped the knife and turned to her. He grabbed the bat and swung it at her. I attacked him again, stabbing him many times. He turned to me and shoved me, and I dropped my knife. It was dark in this place because the only light was a small black-and-white TV. I was able to get one of the doors open and as I pulled it back, it hit Bill and slammed closed.

Kathy at this point was totally in shock, screaming and hiding in the corner. I made an attempt to drive Bill into a door casing. As I drove him towards it, he moved over fast enough to hit the window; we both went through and were cut up severely.

I got Kathy out of there and we left Bill on the ground in a puddle of blood. I really didn't know whether or not Bill was dead, nor did I care at that particular time.... Instead of calling the police or ambulance, we left, and I went to the hospital.... Later we returned home to find detectives waiting for us.

Leslie and his wife each got thirty-five-year sentences. Leslie served out his sentence without parole in twenty-two and a half years due to good-time credit. His wife served out a few months later, having served twenty-three years.

I knew both of them well over the years. They were ideal inmates in their respective institutions. Attractive, intelligent, and personable, both worked to find their way out of a rocky life with help of some counseling and programs. They got their associate degrees, and helped other inmates along the way. By 1994, Leslie was tutoring in a literacy program for disturbed inmates housed in a closed dorm, and later he became involved in a hospice program for dying inmates. Although they divorced, Leslie only said good things about his ex-wife and continued to emphasize that she was a bystander and not part of this crime. His testimony did not help lessen her sentence or her time served, however.

Leslie was released in 2012. He obtained a degree in pastoral counseling and has started a ministry for ex-offenders who are struggling with reentry difficulties. He has been allowed to go into the local jail as a chaplain. He married a supportive woman who shares his religious and social passions. He spent twenty-two years in prison off drugs and changed by a religious conversion.

Al is at the other end of the spectrum. He is such a colorful character that he warrants discussion in several chapters. Where Leslie is now gentle and soft-spoken, Al is aggressive and direct. Al has been around the block, as they say. When I talked with him in 1994, he had already served twenty years on his murder charge with a life sentence with possibility of parole after twenty years. He did not make parole and his attitude about his crime changed little over the next twenty years. He says now, as he did then, that he feels badly about what happened. He wishes he could take it back and change things. But he does not agonize over it, because he cannot take back something that has already happened. In 1994, he had hopes that he would soon be released and could enter society with his debt paid and an opportunity to start a new life.

Here is his account of his crime from 1994. As is typical with Al, no holds are barred.

What led up to this murder charge was a fight at the beginning. Our friend knew this guy, so we went to his house to burglarize his house, but he was home, so he invited us in. I didn't want to go in, but the guy who was killed insisted. We all were drinking very heavy, even the guy who invited us in offered us a drink. We all started talking, then one thing led to another. Him and I started fighting, but my brother and our friend never helped me. So to keep this guy from hurting me, I told my brother to go to the car and get the pistol. So he did and he handed it to me. I shot him while holding him in the head with the first shot. Then, as he turned loose, I shot him several more times until he fell outside the garage door. I had emptied the pistol in him and I reloaded the pistol and shot him several more times.

Then in a rage of panic, we went through his house, taking what we wanted. We took a TV and his pickup truck. We sold the TV and we took the truck out on a country road and set the thing on fire.

Even right today, if the guy was to walk up to me, I wouldn't even know him. I didn't know him before I shot him, and I wouldn't know him now. This would have never happened if I hadn't been drinking. I had been drinking heavy for about two months before this occurred. I regret that this happened, but I can't change what has happened. I will never have no more alcohol in my system ever. This I know!

> I have paid for my crime and I am starting a new life. I cannot let anyone put a label on me when I know I am above any label.... I feel I have learned that whatever crime a man or woman commits, they can always become more and better than what they were. But it has to be within them to change.

Al will never get a chance to start that new life or prove to the world that he can be a better man. He has now been imprisoned more than forty years and the parole board declared that he should never be released. His life sentence is to be served out.

There are other types of killings that are revenge—pure and simple. Well-planned and deliberate. But seeing the murderer sitting in prison for the rest of his life leaves some observers uncomfortable still.

Picture a nine-year-old boy standing on a street corner holding his mother's hand. The child watches as his mother falls dead, still clutching his hand, shot by drug acquaintances for cheating them in a deal. As a teenager, the boy sought revenge, traveling state to state to find those three who had killed his mother. He shot the first, ran over the second with an automobile, and beat the third, a woman, to death with a hammer. He was imprisoned as a juvenile with a third-grade reading level. He has been in prison ever since, nervous, on medication, and still searching for a mother figure to look up to.

Even the clear-cut, unquestionably guilty cases are often hard to judge.

Drugs

Entire books are devoted to our nation's struggle with drugs. Since President Nixon declared the War on Drugs in 1971, our prison populations have burgeoned through vain attempts to stop this scourge in our midst. Lengthy mandatory sentencing, wide sweeps of both users and dealers, and constantly changing laws have done little to affect the influx of drugs into our society. The prisons are filled with men who have committed their crimes while under the influence of alcohol or drugs.[2] Charges of murder, manslaughter, burglary, and assault are more often than not associated with substance abuse. Many people are locked up—especially in the African American population—for drug-dealing offenses.

The answer to eliminating drug dealing is not found solely in enforcement. There simply is too much money to be made, and too much power and prestige to be gained in a community with few other avenues to respect and success. And there is the psychological rush for the dealers—the thrill of the tension, the building of an empire. Make no mistake. Many of these dealers are highly intelligent businessmen running a lucrative and complicated business. It is just that their goods are illegal and their business dealings are shadowy.

The dealers enter the trade when they are young. Some are users themselves, but those are not the successful ones. Sam explained: "Selling drugs is a rough business. Being under the influence of your product is no way to conduct your illegal trade. There is a saying in the business that 'Don't be your own best customer' and 'Don't get high on your supply.'"

Most of the drug dealers and users I talk with think drugs are dangerous and they don't want to get hooked on them, but they seem to have little remorse about selling them. Like many on the outside, they argue that drug use is a victimless crime and should be decriminalized. The dealer wants to sell; the user wants to buy. They see that as a personal, not governmental decision. "If you don't sell to kids, then no one is being hurt," they say. Even those who have spent most of their lives in prison, returning continually through the revolving doors to serve more time, and those who are imprisoned for life because of violence from deals gone bad, argue that more problems arise from the illegal nature of the sales than from the drugs themselves. They regret getting hooked on the drugs, but many do not regret selling them, other than getting caught. Their responses are problematic, but interesting to contemplate.

Most of the men responding here were involved with cocaine. At the time of their involvement and arrests, it was the drug of choice. Today heroin and other drugs are the scourge and involve both the black and white communities. But younger men currently involved in the drug trade have told me that the issues are much the same; the adrenaline high in selling has not changed.

Wayne sold drugs when he was just a kid. He was a user as well as a seller and is in prison for murder, not drugs. He began using drugs when he was very young, and was first busted on a drug charge when he was only in middle school. He is remorseful about the life he took, but he doesn't blame it on the drug dealers.

> At the time, I didn't see anything wrong with selling drugs, but I didn't really think about it. I was only selling to certain people, usually my friends, and I would just sell it to people we knew that used. I would never sell to people I didn't know and to people I knew didn't use drugs.
>
> I can't really blame the sellers, because even without the sellers, the people who wanted drugs would find some way to get them, even if they had to steal them. Selling drugs in America is a multi-billion-dollar business. The sellers are no more to blame than any other man, woman, or child in America. Drugs are always going to be around, just like the people who sell them and people who use them. I believe parents have to take part of the blame instead of laying it all off on the people who sell it.

Another young man, Shak, got hooked first and then began to deal.

> I was seduced into using cocaine. My first encounter with it was in the dark. I didn't know what it was. I was handed a joint.... The joint was laced with cocaine.

The smell was different, the taste was different, and definitely, the high was different.

Once I learned what it was, I was already hooked. After all, it was the "cool thing to do" anyway. The whole time I was using, I was being reeled in by a so-called friend of mine. He eventually had me doing runs for him to pay for my usage. For almost a year, I was dealing drugs to make just enough money for a pair of shoes maybe and the rest, well, "went up in smoke..."

At the time, I felt no remorse. I felt that the drugs sold me so it was time for me to sell them. At the time, I was only eleven years young and most of my customers were adults who could well have been my parents. I felt that they were able to make the decision on whether or not to buy my drugs. I was only a child. After some time, I began using again and the end result is prison. I now realize just how great a control the drugs have on people.

Collectively, the men's accounts show the difficulty of solving the problem. It is a multi-level issue of wayward youth, lucrative business opportunities, limited paths to success, the thrill of the challenge, and a cultural divide on attitudes about drug use. Here are comments from some of the other men.

I got started by draining the leftover liquor bottles that I had seen grown-ups use. Then I went on to experiment with marijuana, speed, LSD, pills, cough syrup, and as time passed on, I went on to cocaine. I was once a drug dealer. I also used them too. I got involved for the money. Though I don't choose to be involved with this anymore, I cannot honestly say that I had any real personal concerns for the buyers because they were all of legal age. I never sold drugs to any minors.—Jeff

When I finally got out of the army in January 1974, I had a wreck that netted me a large sum of money. I started selling marijuana for a living, eventually growing pot and selling it. I moved on to selling harder drugs.

Money is the root of all evil. I had the money to start with. I just wanted to keep the game going as long as possible. I did go flat broke four different times, but I always made it back again by working, investing, and using my head.

I never did feel any personal concern for my customers, because none of them was involved in any mishap from smoking pot or using drugs. Nobody got killed in any kind of a wreck and my little business went strong off and on for four years, till I finally did get busted for drug trafficking in late 1977 and did one year for it. So begins my criminal career.—Allen

You make money so quick and fast. That is my way to success. Since I was fifteen, I never had a job. I chose the drug culture to make money. I have a daughter and son to take care of in two different households and have my own household. A minimum wage job—even a high-paying job—is not going to get it. You want to be a decent father. You want to get the kids set up so they won't have to struggle like you did. You can start with nothing. Start dealing cocaine, and within four to six months, you can have forty to fifty thousand dollars. It's like an executive who is making money. You get used to the lifestyle and you don't want to give it up. You can make $1,000 a day.—Jeff

Yes, I sold drugs. I sold drugs for about fourteen years before my incarceration. I was as addicted to selling as a user was to using.

Selling has the same effect as using. I would feel down in the dumps when I ran out of dope to sell. I would feel as if the world had stopped. Customers would come to you looking to buy and there would be nothing to sell. You start to add up the money you have missed and this would cause me to become very sick.

There is a lot of work involved in trying to keep a supply of drugs to sell. I would go places I never been before. Not knowing anyone there made the job of buying large quantities of drugs very dangerous. This was necessary to cure the sickness of not having drugs to sell. Yes, the sickness led to many dangerous trips to states I had never been to. Each trip was an adventure filled with fear. The unexpected was always your first concern.

In the life of selling the poison, you can see the effect of the poison in your customer. Each time you see them coming, you find yourself being on the defense against what might happen.

They might want to rob you, try to con you, promise you the world on a silver platter. All for the drugs. No, using drugs was something I never really cared to do. I don't drink any alcohol at all.

What got me involved in selling was the glamour of it. The power that came with selling. Also the fast, large sums of money.

You could get a drug user to do things for you that they wouldn't do for God. I mean anything for the dope! The female user would constantly offer her body or any sexual favor for the dope. I have seen them lick the whitewall of a tire for a shot of dope. The male user was strong on con games, whatever they thought you wanted to hear, they would say. The thieves would bring you the goods they have stole. I have purchased a six-hundred-dollar suit for fifty dollars or less depending on how sick they were. My personal feeling for the customer was one that I would keep locked so very deep inside. Any feeling that I may have had was for yours truly— me.

Like I said before, selling drugs is a dangerous business. And I respected it as such. I took an approach to selling drugs seriously. For if I didn't, I would not be here today. There is always the fear of being robbed, arrested, played on, and even killed. The customer wanted the drugs and I wanted the money. With this in mind, I would do whatever to ensure that things went the way I wanted them to go. In the drug game, the customer never, ever, is right!—Sam

In our Modern Social Problems class, I showed a film about street prostitutes strung out on drugs. With a pained expression, Sam asked to be allowed to sit in the hall until it was over.

"I seen too many women like that and took advantage of them. I can't stand to see it anymore," he said.

One of the African American men who interested me most once said within my hearing, "I'm a criminal. I do criminal acts, and I will do criminal things again." His clear-cut honesty rang true, but it took almost a year before he would sit down and talk with me about his statement. Then he agreed to help only after I promised total anonymity.

Yes, I look at crime as a problem, but sometimes people got to convert to crime to make it; it's rough in the world and it's called survival.

African Americans come from poverty. Their families have to struggle. You see an opportunity. It is practically overnight success and it is happening quick. I know we are killing our own people, but you are thinking about bringing your own family out of poverty, so you don't think about it—the big picture. You can drive a big car, buy a hundred-thousand-dollar house [in 1994 dollars].

A guy knows he's taking a chance of losing his freedom. When you have five or six people to take care of, and you don't know where the next meal is coming from, you see this opportunity out there. The average guy is going to take it.

When you get out of here, you have strikes against you. They say they will consider you equally for a job, but they will hold prison against you in their mind. It leads you back to it. You have to want to rehabilitate yourself. Nothing here is mandatory. Some men will be here four to five years and do nothing but go to the gym. I tried to do more. School gives you a changed attitude. I'm going to try to do right and see if there is a job to take care of my family, but if I can't....

If you be careful with your money, you'll be okay if you get caught. If you get the right lawyer and pay him twenty- or thirty-thousand dollars [1994 dollars], you'll get four to five years. But if you're messin' your money up, you'll have to take a public defender and then you'll do a lot of time. If you have money to pay the lawyer, you'll just get your hand slapped. He shuffles the money on to the prosecutor and some on to the judge. They are all just racketeers.

"Do you really believe that?" I asked him. "I *know* that," he replied, furnishing me with names that had come up in similar conversations with others.

This speaker was younger than Sam who regretted the pain his drug sales may have caused. This man agreed his dealing caused pain, but he tried not to think about it. And like so many others, he truly believed that in our world, each person must take care of himself, and that we owe each other nothing, except to the children perhaps.

Everybody is suffering behind my behavior. But I didn't hold a gun to their head to make them buy from me. I would help their children if I could. I hate to see the children suffer behind my behavior. But they know they have kids they should take care of. You must take care of yourself. They's grown. That leaves you where you have to keep your feelings out of it.

That feeling of personal isolation, the attitude that no one cares or has the responsibility to care for anyone outside of their family, is an attitude that appears constantly in the prison population, especially among the young African Americans. It extends beyond the individual isolation of prison life. The emotional isolation has been part of the prisoners' upbringing, built into their immediate community. Many of us avoid the temptation of crime because of our connections to others. We feel a responsibility to do right because of a broad social awareness and a connection to our family, friends, and community. Many of these men have none of those loyalties that would deter them from crime.

The comments above were gathered in 1994. The men in my 2014 study, as well as the officers who guarded them, consistently said that the situation was getting worse. They claimed the young African Americans were entering prison with little sense of self-respect or feelings of responsibility to others. As drugs and poverty splintered their communities and lives, they expected to be in prison—just as their father and brothers had been.

I recently had a heartbreaking conversation with an African American man, well-respected by his prison peers. Jamal was released in 2014, just before I reconnected with those still incarcerated. He is a man who found a new life in prison—he sought out education, and joined in healthy, forward-moving activities during his long years of incarceration. His parole was a long time coming, but when he finally reentered society with renewed hope, it was harder than he thought.

We reminisced about his young son—about eight years old when I first met him. The little boy was at his father's college graduation ceremony, and we have a precious picture of the young boy, his daddy's mortarboard on his head, wrapped from behind in his proud father's arms. We talked to the little boy, making sure he understood the importance of the day, telling him some-day he would be wearing his own mortarboard. But his father was not there to help him as he grew up, and when his father finally was released, the little boy, now in his early twenties, was doing a stint in the local jail.

As soon as he was released, Jamal was surrounded by pressing needs—family members asking for financial help, a wife he married while in prison demanding his time, a stepdaughter attempting suicide, an addicted mother unable to function, and a son whose downfall he blamed on himself. I tried to talk to him about not getting drawn into all the family difficulties that led him down his long prison path.

"But, Ms. Holman," he desperately replied, "when you come from the life I did, you've got nothing but family. I have to care for them."

It's hard enough to get your feet on the ground after nineteen years of incarceration. I wondered how was he going to maneuver the dangerous waters ahead.

Theft

When I first met David some twenty-five years ago, he had already been in prison over half his life. I was told by the administrator in charge that he would be my new clerk. I didn't want him for the job. He wasn't in the college program, wasn't interested in college. He was rough around the edges and didn't seem right for the job. But the administrator insisted.

"He'll do you a good job," she declared. And she was right.

I found David to be very bright, competent, and innovative. Anything we needed done, he could figure out how to make it happen. He chafed continually at the oppression of the prison structure and proudly saw himself as a convict, not as an inmate. His thoughts about that are featured in the chapter on the convict code. His word was his bond, and he watched out for me, constantly warning me about all the other men.

By the time he was in his late fifties, David had never filed an income tax return. His few years of freedom were spent running around the country, drinking, picking up jobs on a ranch out west, stealing or robbing when he needed money. He never could explain his behavior.

"I was just too damned lazy," he said. Guilt didn't seem to be part of his thinking. The on-the-edge lifestyle appealed to him. A normal life was boring.

"'Rebel without a clue,' explains me pretty well," he said. "There's never been a good reason for bucking as hard as I have for the past twenty years." He continued:

What got me going this direction? It was a lifetime ago. Fifty miles south of New Orleans, Louisiana, is Venice, the end of the world. The road, 23, I think, dead-ends into the Gulf of Mexico, and that's where we were, myself and my younger brother, walking along the docks about half drunk.

We walked past a car. I'll never forget it—a '65 Ford Galaxy 500. Just being silly and belligerent, my brother snatched a CB microphone, which was hanging from the rearview mirror. We was walking with me swinging the thing round and round by the cord, and when we got to my truck, my brother threw the thing in the bed of the truck. We didn't know it at the time, but a night watchman saw everything and called the law.

We got in the truck and headed back toward New Orleans. A mile or so later, two police cars fell in behind us but didn't pull us over. Another mile or so later, three other police cars fell in behind us and still didn't pull us over. I rounded a bend and two more police cars were across the road. That was enough. I wasn't pulling over because I didn't know what they had in mind. I downshifted and accelerated, trying to go around in the ditch. I caught the rear end of the police car and spun it around into the other one and ran like hell. They chased me for twenty miles, shooting every time they got close enough. I was driving a four-wheel-drive Dodge that set pretty high off the ground, and they couldn't hit anything but the tailgate, though one stray knocked out the rear window. Finally, a bullet ricocheted off the road and cut the fuel line. A hell of a lucky shot, but it stopped me cold.

I ran the truck off in a yard—I wanted witnesses. The cops still beat the hell out of us, and off to jail we went—Pointe a la Hatch, Plaquemines Parish prison. To make a long story short, I made a deal for four years with the agreement that they would release my brother. He was only eighteen and not as tough as he thought he was. I didn't want him to go to Angola.

They let him go. I escaped, got shot and caught, and sent to Angola with twenty years—sixteen added for escape and kidnapping—I'll explain that later. That's how it started and it got more and more complicated every day. I escaped again and got caught and served three years in Indiana. Then I was extradited back to Angola. If I'd just served that four years, I would have been all right.

The worse part of that whole deal is that after I took the rap for that CB microphone, which was simple burglary, my brother was killed within a year by a jealous husband. I've always wondered what would have happened if I hadn't got him out of jail and let him serve four years with me. He might be alive today. And then again, he couldn't have handled Angola. I don't know if I could have protected him. It was all I could do to protect myself. I always felt responsible for my brother's death in some way.

After being released from the infamous Angola and maximum-security Michigan City prisons, David was scarred by the violence and constant danger he lived in. He learned to trust no one. He ran around the country, and was arrested for forgery and theft in Kentucky. He had an extradition order on a charge of murder to take him to Georgia after his release; he said he was innocent. Always trying to stay a step ahead before things happened, he refused parole in Kentucky, hoping Georgia would forget him. He tried to forge papers to change the extradition orders, and in every way fought being sent to Georgia. He failed and was held for transport to Georgia on the day he served out his Kentucky time.

If he had taken the earlier parole, the DA at the time had decided not to pursue the murder case because of lack of evidence. But there was a new prosecutor by the time David was released, who wanted to try the case. David, who has continually declared his innocence, felt there was no good choice but to agree to a plea bargain with the understanding that he would get credit for time served in Kentucky. However, that agreement did not make it into the final decree and he has been in Georgia prisons for the last sixteen years, still proclaiming his innocence.

Once a person gets involved in the criminal justice system, like David, they may find it a bottomless rabbit hole that swallows them up if they don't start making better decisions even while incarcerated.

The puzzling thing about David is that he has an impeccable work ethic, always seeking out meaningful jobs, even in Georgia where they don't pay inmates for their work. Yet he wasn't interested in holding down a job when he was younger and still had a free life ahead of him.

Sexual Offenses

A very large number of the men I know are incarcerated for sexual offenses. These men are personable, friendly, and clean-cut. They have no special appearance, nor do they have any personal characteristics that would distinguish them from the other men or identify them within the institutions.

But once their crime is known, the rest of the prison population looks down upon these men. They do not talk openly with the other men about their crimes, and if their crimes involved children, they are particularly reticent.

On the other hand, in private if they feel they are not in a judgmental situation, they will talk openly about their crimes and what led up to them. Many are involved in intensive programs where self-disclosure is an important part of their treatment. As a result of that pervasive treatment atmosphere, they have a difficult time talking in a natural way—their language is continually infused with psychological jargon, and they are encouraged to see their behavior as a pattern of responses. It is hard to get them to go beyond that.

As a sociologist, I easily can find certain patterns among this group. Many of them experienced abusive, unhealthy childhoods. Their parents were either cold and distant emotionally or they crossed the line from being caregivers to their children to being care receivers. The men reported that, as children, they felt responsible for their parents' happiness—even sexual involvement with their parents was seen as helping their caretakers.

Although there is still little conversation about it, there is an increasing awareness that women are more involved as perpetrators in child sexual abuse than was previously known.[3] Certainly, the men here would agree. Many of them describe abuse from their mothers, female babysitters, and cousins. In most cases, there were multiple people involved in their abuse.

Steve is in his twenty-ninth year of incarceration. He has a 201-year sentence for serial rape. He is highly intelligent, very verbal, well educated, of middle-class or above social status. He is an armed forces veteran with an honorable discharge, and before his incarceration, was employed by a well-known international company. He fully owns up to his behavior, and even after all this time, tears still well up in his eyes as he speaks of the trauma to his victims. The stories of his childhood could curl your hair.

> The first peculiar thing I remember was when I was three or four years old and mother wanted me to be a girl. She dressed me up (I still have the dress and someday I will get to cut it up). She took me to a veteran's organization. She put bows on me, patent leather shoes, and ponytails curled into blond ringlets. She laughed about it. I was real embarrassed. Everyone was laughing.
>
> She was pathetic, too. Her mother was killed when she was five and she had a real cruel stepmother. She was sexually abused by her father and uncle. I learned about that after I was incarcerated.
>
> When I was a kid, my parents would get in fights and I'd hear him hurting her. When they would get in fights, I would get distraught. When I was young, I would break down in fear and run to them crying. My mother would get me back into bed when I got up crying. I can remember my father screaming, "Shut that goddamned kid up." She would fondle me to make me quiet. Physically, it felt comforting. It didn't feel too out of the way at first. By the time I was seven, I started resisting. One

night, Dad caught her. A new fight erupted and I felt I was the cause of her being beat.

At this point, several tears rolled out of Steve's eyes and he struggled to go on. "Dad had bizarre views on women. He said he would try to teach me to control my impulses about women. To do that, he started fondling me, telling me I had to learn not to react to it. That scared me more than anything."

It has been well over twenty years since Steve first told me about his mother, sharing a picture from his young adult years. In the photo, his mother was draped sensually over him, presenting the impression she was his wife. Today, his conversation still continually returns to his childhood, his troubled parents, and the pain of his crime. All these years later, his eyes fill with tears as he remembers the horrors of his early years. He recounts his father holding a hot lamp to his genitals and coating them with burning athletic ointment to help teach him not to react to women. He tells of his mother as an old lady, still arriving at the door in a state of undress, trying to seduce him.

His stories remain the same. So does the pain.

Steve married and had three children. The marriage had problems and Steve felt rejected and hurt by his wife. They were married eight years before he committed his first crime. For his victims, Steve always chose women he did not know. If they managed to personalize themselves, he ran away, leaving them unharmed—he needed his victims to be faceless, for as he raped the women, he fantasized they were his mother or wife.

I was playing out my anger. I wanted them to feel the betrayal and humiliation. I needed to humiliate them more than to have sex. The sexual gratification was used as an indicator that I was okay. It was the same as a high on heroin. It was proof that I was being loved, while it also humiliated them.

When I would get away, I'd have to pull over. I was nauseated, trembling, and would have the dry heaves. I couldn't look in a mirror. I had a lot of internal anger.

I didn't know how much I scared them. One in particular I remember. She cried and said, "Oh my God, I don't want to die." It broke my train of thought. As soon as I heard that, it made me sick at my stomach. I didn't want to be seen as that threatening. That troubled me real bad. I thought I had talked to her in a way that it was obvious I wouldn't kill her. I didn't want to scare anyone that bad. I ran off and didn't proceed. Another one, bless her innocent heart, asked me if she could get pregnant.

At this point, tears welled up in his eyes again.

Steve was arrested after five years of offenses during a time he was fantasizing about suicide. He pled guilty to avoid a trial. He said twenty years ago that he would never appeal his sentence and he has stuck with that even though he might have grounds to do so as his lawyer has since been disbarred.

I was psychologically devastated. I couldn't see making my family endure that. I had three young sons. It would have been an enormous trial with much publicity. The women might have been questioned like they were responsible for the assault. I didn't want to put them through the degradation. I didn't want to put my family through it. Foremost, I knew I was guilty. Part of me was so glad to be stopped. I tried to stop so many times, but once I started....

I have never appealed my case and won't. In my heart, I do not like the term "I beat the charge." Beat has the connotation that you look for loopholes. If you are truly sorry and have remorse and are truly supportive of the quality of therapy you have had, how can you look for a loophole?

I have to accept my fate and hope through my work and the work offered me— I've been told by some that I have something salvageable—that I will be able to sometime contribute to my children, myself, and society as a whole.

Against his wishes years ago, someone in the extended religious community at the prison tried to call Steve's oldest son, hoping to reestablish a family relationship. The son responded by saying, "That's not me; my father is dead."

When I returned to the prison for a personal interview with Steve, I was his first visitor in fifteen years.

Steve has two personal challenges. One is recovering from his horrendous childhood. As he continues to return to his old memories, albeit with new understanding, I think that will continue to be a constant, maybe impossible, struggle. The other challenge is trying to find a sense of personal worth while still incarcerated. He once compared his treatment program to treatment for a physical illness:

Let's compare an inmate with a long sentence to someone facing a diagnosis of a serious illness. The patient, encouraged by a physician, is told there are important things he can do to improve his chances. He is encouraged to follow a healthy diet, adhere to recommended treatment: medically, psychologically, and spiritually.

I can only sum it up this way. Yes, I realize I may never get out. So does that justify my turning bitter and continuing to act out with violence and take the coward's way out? Speaking for myself, it doesn't.

If a man is truly sorry and remorseful, he shouldn't just claim so. He should *live* it by his day-to-day behavior and words. He must display his remorsefulness even in how he conducts himself in prison.

Steve is doing that. Everyone who knows him believes he would not offend again. But while he remains in prison, the message he is hearing is that he is a piranha to society, and he finds it hard not to personally buy into that definition. He has internalized the remorsefulness, and he carefully recounts the positive ways he has helped others while in prison as if to remind himself he is more than his hurtful deeds. But until he is free, he does not seem to be able to move beyond his crime and the blame that he carries as a constant heavy mantle about his shoulders. He did not take a life, but society has a harder time forgiving him than they do someone who kills. Nor can he forgive himself.

Child Sexual Abuse

Compassion is stretched even more when children are abused. I do not attempt to explain the problems of child sexual abusers here—they are best addressed by psychologists in a separate book. But I do believe that it is important to see that many of these men have had unspeakable childhoods and are most often passing on behavior that has been prevalent in their families for generations. Chances are their children will also become abusers in a few years if they don't receive treatment.

I find that child abusers have a strong defense mechanism that makes them resist facing the seriousness of their actions. But once they have broken through that, they are agonized and frightened by what they have done.

Jack, who helped a great deal with the original research, even then apologetically declined to talk about his crime. Knowing Jack and his offenses, I am under the impression that his refusal is not so much a denial of responsibility as an effort to work on his low self-esteem. "I have a difficult time dealing with my own emotions and feelings concerning my crime. I do not believe that discussing it would help in my constant battle with the knowledge that I can overcome, and that I have committed a horrendous act against another."

Other conversations with him seem to indicate a fear that I and others will reject and judge him if we know the details of his charges. As a sexual offender against children, he had trouble accepting the two-sided nature of his actions; he is sure others will, too. He was released some years ago, but returned on a reoffense a few years later.

When I reestablished contact in 2014, Jack answered with a friendly, good-natured letter and a stated intent to help with the project. But in later letters, when the subject turned to his feelings about his reoffense and return to prison, his letters stopped and he has not written since.

Other than in their treatment groups, there is little to help these men with damaged self-images. The treatment groups are not as safe an environment as therapists would like to think. Details of Jack's offenses reached the yard, probably contributing to his reluctance to talk further.

Child abuse, sexual or physical, is the one crime that is unforgiveable within the prison community. In the past—and perhaps still in some states and prisons—child abusers are in physical danger from fellow inmates. In others they are looked down on, gossiped about, and taunted, but are relatively safe. Yet make no mistake, they are noted. A high-profile offender came into one of the institutions. He had beaten and killed his child and stuffed the body into a plastic garbage bag. When he was given his institutional items, the inmate in charge of the handouts gave him two garbage bags, saying pointedly and with some warning, "You seem to need extra bags."

Of all the child abusers I have talked with, Max speaks about his crime the most openly. He sexually abused his daughter. But with him, like with the others, there is an obvious underlying fear that I will hate him for it. There is an eagerness among these men to see themselves as more than child abusers. As one man explained: "The sicker your crime, then the more likely you are to be talked about and judged on the yard. This feeds into your mentality in that if you keep hearing that you're sick or violent, then pretty soon that image of yourself is going to start playing into your daily behavior."

They struggle to explain and to understand themselves how a basically nice and caring person could do such a thing to a child. In this case, the abuse was sexual, not otherwise physical. Max struggled to explain the best he could.

> At the time I committed the offense, I hate to say I was a totally different person. That sounds like a cop-out, but after so many years of drugs and alcohol, my ability to reason was shot to hell. You can't know what it is like to get up every day for twenty to twenty-five years and hate yourself every morning. I wanted to die.
>
> It happened on two occasions and only two. After the first time, I swore it never would happen again. You have to look at my situation at the time. I was fighting to survive. The first time it happened, I was pretty much inebriated. The next day when I sobered up and realized, that's when guilt and shame hit. I thought, "Hell, I've turned into my father!"
>
> The second time it happened, I was on Valiums. It was a five- to six-month period since the first occurrence. I had been partying for the weekend. I had one hell of a hangover and had taken two five-blue Valiums.
>
> At the time, you don't feel bad about hurting anyone. You are hurting and you want to hurt others. You are a different person. Then you start to realize the emotional and mental abuse you brought on. The guilt is overwhelming. You don't want to hurt. I stayed blitzed to keep from having nightmares. When I sobered up, it was scary.
>
> Yes, I was different when I committed my crime. I was waging a war of two persons—a war between two halves. I was two sides of the same coin. The dark side is more subtle. You think at the time you are doing good things, but you aren't. You make choices that hurt others severely. People ask why you don't use common sense and just not do it. What we perceive as common sense is also learned.
>
> Yes, I am the same person physically as when I committed the crime, but the coin is flipped heads up, and I now have the tools or as society says—the common sense—to keep it there.

Max served out his sentence nine years ago and I've heard he remains in the community, law-abiding as an aging man on a limited military retirement, but he was never able to find employment due to his past charges.

Issues to Think About

1. What is the meaning of this chapter title: "Two Sides of a Coin"?
2. The author says that "it is the failure of the public to understand the diverse nature of the men in our prisons that keeps us from finding effective solutions to our problems." What do you think she means?
3. Did any of the stories about the men surprise you, touch you, or upset you? Did your attitudes shift as you read more about the inmates and their feelings about their crimes?
4. What is meant by the statement, "the parents are only these troubled children grown up?"

TEN

Searching for Blue Skies
Religion Behind Bars

I never had any guidance as a kid. I don't know the rules of how to live right. The Bible gives me those rules. What's so bad about that?
                                                                    —*Matt*

Droplets of water trickled from our touching hands. The wetness spread web-like into the worn fibers of the faded chapel carpet. I took the man's tentative hands in mine, washed them with wetness from the aluminum bowl. Then he took my hands, anointing them in the spirit of humility and atonement.

It was Easter in the heart of a male correctional facility. I had been invited to participate in the Catholic worship service where I found myself washing the hands of an inmate I had never seen before. It was a profound moment.

Only later did I wonder at the allowed intimacy of the washing ceremony. Only later did I wonder about the hands that I had carefully washed, wondering about the faces they had smashed, of the guns they had held, of the lust they had forced. Only later did I wonder about the acts we symbolically forgave and washed away.[1]

Religion in prison can be a two-edged sword. For believers, it offers the men internal peace and hope, and at times, gives them new and positive directions for their lives. It can ground them as they deal with a challenging environment.

But within the prison setting, religion also causes a great deal of ongoing conflict. Although only about half of the inmates identify themselves with a specific religion, and only a third attend any service, issues surrounding the chapel are a constant source of conversation among believers and non-believers alike.[2] Other than educational programming, religious activities draw the most inmate participation.[3]

Disagreements between groups of different beliefs are magnified in the closed community. Those who do not attend prison services deride those who do, citing examples of their hypocritical behavior after leaving the chapel. Those who do have a faith sometimes feel superior to others and show that disdain. Even among the believers themselves, there is tension. Seemingly contradictory faiths share the same worship space. With close interaction, practices and beliefs of one faith directly impact and clash with the lives of conflicting believers.

Religion can be used by inmates to assert power, which causes institutional tensions. The prisoners' legal religious freedoms make the job of the administration more challenging.

Under the First Amendment, prisons have to allow access to religion, and any number of inmate grievances and lawsuits make that happen. Most prisons have chaplains who work with the administration to make sure the inmate's religious rights and requirements are balanced with correctional rules and policies.

Prison chaplains are kept busy if they do their jobs well. While they do not always preach, they have to schedule, coordinate, and supervise sometimes dozens of worship services each week. They spend much time individually with the inmates, being involved whenever there is a death of a family member or serious illness of a resident. There is usually a designated chapel or prison area for their use, but the facilities are small and the space has to be carefully scheduled and sometimes shared with non-religious programs. Hundreds of well meaning, but often naïve, community volunteers may circulate through the chapel each month and must be trained and supervised. Church is the one place in prison that the public is eager to be involved, and that brings a lot of problems along with the benefits of their participation.

The U.S. Bureau of Prisons publishes a comprehensive manual from which each state takes its religious guidance.[4] A list of "legitimate" religions is usually approved at a state level. Inmates who hold those beliefs must be served if the prison residents request help and are willing to do the work to make the services happen. Of course, in reality, the actual practices depend on the commitment and personal beliefs of the individual chaplains, as well as the determination of the inmates to make an issue of it.

The number of religious faiths served can be daunting if the chaplain is engaged and willing, especially if the prison is situated within a religiously diverse region. Besides many versions of Christianity, approved groups include Islam, Judaism, Buddhism, Hinduism, Native American, Wicca, Odinism/Asatru, Roman Catholic, Eastern Orthodox, Rastafarian, Temple of Moorish Science of America, Sikh Dharma, and more. There are a number of groups included under Protestantism: a variety of mainstream denominations, independent evangelical groups, Mormons, Pentecostals, and Jehovah Witnesses.

Lists of required and approved religious items and practices for each group are recounted in detail in the Bureau of Prisons' manual, along with prescribed correctional guidelines. For example, only plastic prayer beads are allowed, and dress items such as ties and kurda shirts can only be worn within the chapel area. Sax (swords) are not allowed in Odinism/Asatru services but gandr and oath rings can be substituted.

Christianity is the major religion within the prison setting. Within that faith community, groups with differing beliefs often do verbal battle. A new chaplain at one institution publically declared the value of all religions and stated that all sincere believers of every faith will find grace in the afterlife. One of the vocational teachers who led weekly Christian Bible studies during his off-times (and sometimes while on the clock) led the inmates in troubling blowback; he believed that one had to be Christian to be "saved." This evangelical opposition to the chaplain pushed the chapel program through difficult times.

The beliefs of some groups cause a tense and exclusionary atmosphere in the religious community. Many of the religious groups openly preach against homosexuality, making it difficult for homosexuals of belief to find a worship service where they are comfortable. In the closed society of prison, contentious issues are hard to ignore, as they are always in one's face. In free society, such issues are also abundant, but there are alternative worship opportunities available.

Each of the religions has special needs for worship, and their requirements often run afoul of the regular running of the institution, causing hard feelings among many. Arrangements have to be made to provide tobacco in a smoke-free institution for the Native American ceremonies and a sweat lodge is occasionally provided. New dinner hours and food preparations have to be arranged for the days of Ramadan. Neither side is ever happy with the compromises. Institutional policies have to be reexamined. Scented oil is a requirement in some religious traditions, but it can also be used to cover up the odor of contraband marijuana. When a prisoner is in transit between institutions with no access to his property, certain religious accoutrements have to be made available to him. Religious traditions that elevate lay people to a level of leadership have to be suppressed. For example, Imams are important to help guide their congregations and young members, but leadership of one inmate over another in prison is forbidden.

Protestantism

The primary services within prisons are a wide variety of mostly evangelical Christianity. Volunteers make church services happen, and the Christian evangelical community sees the salvation of inmates as a central tenant of their beliefs. Eight-five percent of all prison chaplains are Christian, and 44 percent of them identify as evangelical.[5] It goes without saying that those statistics help explain the predominance of more emotional, salvation-based programming within prisons.

> They've got some good services here. The "Residents Encounter Christ" gives you a spiritual feeling. They bring the Spirit of God with them. The others are not bad. Sometimes they fade away from the meaning of the truth, but it's not a circus like the others told you. The ones that come in, their intention is good. They're just not able to control the environment. It gets silly, and you want to leave. The men start arguing.—Dewey

> Your perception of religion depends on how you act in the service. Some flop around, and others are real quiet. We had this guy come in and wanted us to do jumping jacks for Jesus. He wanted us to get down and do push-ups for the Lord. I have a problem with that. But if it helps the men, who am I to talk them down?—Matt

The evangelical services do not suit everyone, so the men search out the venue in which they feel the most comfortable. Norman had attended a sedate upper-middle class Methodist church most of his life. He was horrified when he attended his first prison church service.

"They were yelling, and I began to wonder when they were bringing out the snakes," he said. He eventually found the solace he sought within the more traditional Catholic congregation.

Much of the public derides "jail-house conversions," but most of the active churchgoers seem serious in their beliefs and honest in their conversations. One of the men in my study, Stuart, explained:

> It's the desolation and dire need for comfort that draw people to the church in prison. Many people turn to religion in prison. You find that because they have hit bottom. There is the continual weight of this place. Everybody hates you. There is the continual reinforcement that you are a piece of dirt.... My relationship with Jesus Christ makes me different. Now, my circumstances do not dictate my happiness.

The men find comfort in the prevalent belief that God has a purpose for everything. If a man's incarceration is seen as part of God's plan, and there is an ultimate, but yet-unseen reason for the continued confinement, the burning anger and frustration of prison is lessened.

Duane wrote this while waiting for his upcoming parole hearing:

> I try not to get over excited about seeing the parole board. But it's hard not to. My fate is in the Lord's hands. I believe He is the one in control. I have done all that I can possibly do as far as schooling and programs. There's nothing else I can do except wait upon the Lord. I have learned things happen on His time, not mine.
> The last time I went in front of the board, I knew I was going home, but I got a

sixty-month flop. About six months into the sixty, I told the Lord, "Lord, I don't understand. I don't just believe in you—I serve you." That night I woke up about two am. As I lay there, the Lord brought to my remembrance how through me he stopped a man from getting killed. How through me he comforted a man that lost his mother. How through me he stopped many fights. How through me he brought many men to repentance. I said, "Lord, forgive me." And I've never questioned Him again. I have begged him though…. I pray he has work for me somewhere outside of prison.

There is a danger, however, in the message that some of them take away from that brand of Christianity. The men often are convinced without doubt that their newfound faith will make things work for them when they are released. They believe Jesus will lead them down the right road and keep them free from temptation. They may say they know it will be tough, but I could tell they didn't really believe it would be. They leave prison convinced their lives will be free of crime because God will make it so. They return to prison humbled and confused. It is then that their religion may develop more depth.

Stuart is a serial rapist. For years, he struggled with what he called "a serious ingrained problem of lust." When he became a Christian, he thought his problems had been cured. He faced release with optimism that soon turned sour, and he returned to prison where he will spend the rest of his life.

> The worst thing I went out of here with is the feeling that all that was in the past. I felt like I was okay, that it would never happen again. So I wasn't prepared when things hit me. Then I started the cycle. I berated myself for having those thoughts. I thought, "I'm a Christian now, so it won't happen." I was beating myself up and that added to the cycle: anger, helplessness, anger, sexual deviance.
>
> My ultimate health is through my relationship with God. I honestly didn't want to do that again. I really didn't! But I didn't understand the depth of it. I thought it wouldn't be a problem because I was a Christian.

Another man in my original study felt the same confidence in his new-found beliefs. In prison for drug use and sales, he insisted when I last saw him in prison that his faith would keep him straight. Some years after his release, I ran into him. He was doing well, had settled into a church where he had been allowed to work with the teenage youth. I asked him about his earlier statement saying his Christianity would keep him free. He laughed as he responded. He said it turned out to be more complicated than that.

> Phooey. There's only a certain amount of things that you can be tempted with in prison. You get a victory over some of those temptations, and you get complacent. When you hit that gate, things are going seventy miles an hour. You aren't in a Christian community every day. You can't run to the chapel every day. When I got out, this girl came to me with a big bag of good grade marijuana and offered plenty

of sex—all those temptations. If it weren't for my religion, I would be back there already; I would.

It's a whole new game out here. You become complacent here, too. All the new things blow people away who are just out of prison. You don't go to church as much; you are not on fire like before. If you are not in a good Christian community, you will not make it okay.

I'm doing good. I'm having some problems now, but I have to work them through. I'm accountable to twenty kids in the youth group. That thought sort of blows me away.

Some states now allow Christian communities to be formed within the prison setting. They set aside a dormitory for the Christian inmates selected for the program, and well-behaved residents receive extra privileges such as food treats and extra family visits.

David was extradited to a state that did not pay inmates for their work. Indigent, he constantly struggled to provide small things of comfort that the state did not provide. Basically a non-believer, he decided to apply to the religious program for the benefits.

"I can do or say anything to get a steak dinner once in a while," he wrote.

He lasted less than a month.

"They wanted me to skip down the aisle and act crazy. I'm no damned kid; I'm a fifty-five-year-old man. They can keep their food and privileges. I have to have some self-respect."

Volunteers

The use of volunteers in the chapel programs creates an ongoing tension with administration. There is a struggle to find the right balance between the free help the volunteers provide and increased security issues they bring to the closed prison setting.

Volunteers make most of the chapel activities happen. They provide the preaching and many of the items needed for the worship services. They donate expensive items like Bibles, Korans, and hymnals. They often bring in special music.

Critics say that men come to the chapel programs mostly when visitors, music, or food is there. Female visitors are a special attraction. Lou recalled:

I very seldom go. I went a lot when I first got here. The whole setting is fake. I don't like to go with a double standard. I felt as numb when I came out as when I went in. Once you're inside the chapel, it's just a lot of paying attention to each other—not to the preacher. Someone will give a testimony and the men will sit and talk to the man next to him criticizing the speaker.

When they have a black preacher, there is a mixed crowd with a few blacks, but when there is a white preacher, it will be all white. When women come in, it's a sell-out. Also they'll sell out if they bring something to eat.

Some of that is true, but there is another way to look at it.

The presence of the volunteers serves an important function and goes beyond just making the religious services happen. The outsiders draw inmates to them because they deal with the men on an equal, respected level. They show true interest and concern to individuals who are given little respect on a daily basis. They help the men remember the best that is in them. The women remind them of gentle feminine care that isn't experienced on the yard. The food, music, and fellowship add joy to an otherwise bleak life.

There is a challenge for the volunteers who enter the prisons to understand the nature of what is needed by the inmates. There is no question the intent of most volunteers is sincere and their help is needed, but too often they get caught up in the emotion and attention from the inmates. One chaplain explained that some of the volunteers are needy themselves and their needs are being fed by the residents. An ex-warden said of the volunteers, "Many have the heart of volunteering; not all have the mind."

It is a troubling and delicate balance required for this emotionally laden area. If the volunteers are effective, they must make sure their message, not their presence, is what remains the most important.

At times, the church groups unknowingly create hurt and misunderstandings. They promise the men they will help them when they are released, but learn that process is more difficult than they are prepared to handle.

Several of the men in my original study who were active in their home churches became embittered and left organized religion while incarcerated. Although they retained their faith, they felt abandoned by their former church families. I cannot remember a single man who ever mentioned maintaining a relationship with his home church. Don wrote:

My belief in God hasn't been hurt, but my trust and belief in people who claim to be Christians have. These "friends" deserted me and my family. I'll never doubt my God (even why I'm here), but I'll always have a problem with people saying they're Christians but acting the hypocrite and turning their backs when crisis comes. Sensitive subject.

Even the chaplains complain about the volunteers' sole emphasis on salvation. One chaplain says he likes the emphasis of the nationwide program Residents Encounter Christ, but is critical locally of their unwillingness to look at the larger picture. Because of their extensive program, they attract a number of dedicated inmates—but relatively few new ones—each session. The weekend-long program requires the involvement of thirty-five staff members. It disrupts the meetings of all the other religious groups. Because of the vast numbers of volunteers who come, and the fact they are often well-connected men in the community, politics and power get involved.

"If they would take all that money and energy and help with reentry, they could have a huge impact," the chaplain said.

"Amen," echoes the warden.

Nationwide, prison chaplains report they have more Christian volunteers who want to work with the inmates than they can use, but they desperately need volunteers to help with most of the other religious groups.[6]

Muslims and Other Faiths

Although prisons are isolated, the same prejudices, suspicions, and misunderstandings of outside society blow through the steel gates. There is tension between the Christians, Muslims, and the administration.

In 1994, attention was on the Nation of Islam when there was administrative fear of their anger, aggression, and violence. After the attacks of September 11, 2001, concerns shifted to possible radicalization of the nation's Muslim prison population. The FBI even got involved, according to a man who was a warden at the time. The misunderstandings and fears today reflect society's concerns and lie in the thought of Muslims as terrorists and anti–Christians. Many of the chaplains believe that the fearful attitudes have to do with racism.[7]

There were a number of Muslims in my original group of fifty men, but none remain in prison today. Therefore, I cannot trace their personal journeys to the present, but back then, their comments demonstrated that, like the Christians, they were looking for something more in their lives.

Aabid was a Muslim leader on the yard at the time he was writing to me—serving an important role within their religious structure. He tried to explain the difference that had occurred over time in his religious journey.

> I started as a disciple of the Nation of Islam. There's no excuse for what I've done. They pumped me up with hate. They taught me the white man is the devil. My foundation was the devil. I wasn't conscious enough of what I was doing.
>
> At that time, it wasn't true Islam. It was a national movement. There really is no "Black" Muslims. This was a lie what was perpetrated. I found it wasn't true Islam. The true study of Islam tears down hate. If I had been practicing the true religion of Islam, I'd never have come back to prison. You can have all the good positive ideas and act otherwise. I left my religion in R&D [Receiving and Delivery] when I was released the first time.
>
> Islam is a very demanding religion. Religion's root word is ritual. Our religion is a way of life, a repeated practice (like bathing, brushing your teeth). Some people get spooked and think you have to be saintly. That's not right. You just have to strive. It's a strenuous, demanding practice. Why some people don't take too well to Islam is

because it keeps people from gratifying themselves. It says no alcohol, you pray five times a day, and you can make no profit. You do as much as you can.

When a person is doing time, it is like a drowning person snatching at straws to stay afloat. First, you try other things like gambling, narcotics—things like you hold onto on the streets. After that plays out and you mature, you begin to reach for something more positive. Religion plays a big part as you are trying…. It has more meaning because of your past life—it did for me.

The distinct, required practices of Islam lead to much misunderstanding and conflict within the institutions. The Muslims say that the administration and men of other faiths don't understand the depth of their religious requirements. The dietary restrictions cause the most consternation. Pork alternatives are offered at each meal, but the servers will pick up the sausage and the fish using the same hand. This pollutes or soils the food, according to the Muslim inmates. When they complain, the standard reply is "What does it matter?"

"That shows no respect or understanding of our religion," explained Aabid. He continued:

You have to realize our position being incarcerated. Some compromises have to be made on both sides. We have restrictions on the raising and killing of food. It has to be a quick kill and a prayer is said over various parts of the procedure. We're not in the position to raise, kill, and prepare the food. So we have to compromise and say our own prayer when we eat it.

You don't use techs (technicalities) constantly. You use your religion and make necessary compromises.

Ali, who was younger and more hotheaded, and frankly, more representative, disagreed with compromise. During Ramadan, he and the other Muslims were allowed into the kitchen to prepare their own meals when they insisted the institution wasn't doing it correctly.

"I've never cooked a day in my life," he said. "The staff was mad because we were there and they wouldn't help us."

Next year, he says, they are going to refuse to cook and insist that the institution do it for them and do it as they are supposed to do under the law.

Such conflicts occur regularly. The Muslims are seen as hiding behind their religion just to get special privileges or to make things as difficult as possible for the administration. Aabid agreed that the refusal to cook for themselves looks as if the young men are more interested in control than in their religion.

"Some individuals are going to take advantage," he said. "Anytime you have the human element involved, there is going to be nonsense."

Today, Islam, like Protestantism, is listed as a fast-growing religion within prisons, but the chaplains report they believe that most of the growth of both religions comes from "switching"—inmates moving back and forth between faith communities. The chaplain at the prison where a number of the men in my study reside estimates that one-third of the Muslim congregation are white converts.

He reports a lot of men request to switch to Native American so they can smoke in the religious ceremonies. But they want to switch back when they find the tobacco is not regular pipe tobacco, but instead a concoction that initially is unpleasant tasting. The sincere Native Americans are very offended by these new converts, he added.

In another example, only a few institutions in the state are designated to serve a kosher menu, and men switch religions in hopes of finding better food, but disillusioned, soon request a transfer back. They are allowed to switch only every six months.

A similar example is brewing in Georgia where no one is allowed to wear a beard. David, now incarcerated there, wrote: "Rumor here is that if the state allows Muslims to wear beards, that the rest of us will write the chaplain and claim to cross over to the Muslim religion. They can't stop us. So, if the Muslims get that privilege, the state will probably just make new policy to allow everyone to grow beards."

Statistics on religion in correctional facilities are hard to come by. U.S. Bureau of Justice statistics do not reflect religious preferences nor do many states ask those questions of inmates. Research projects and questionnaires about prisoners are carefully limited by Corrections these days because of the relative powerlessness of inmates. In-depth information has to come from a few academic studies and an excellent Pew Research Center study of prison chaplains.[8] The responses from the chaplains' study must be considered carefully, however, as opinions are filtered through the eyes of predominantly evangelical Protestant chaplains. However, their conclusions match almost perfectly with the results of a prisoner survey done by the chaplain in Kentucky's largest prison.

The "Unchurched"

Although a great deal is said about religion in prison, about half of inmates don't identify with any religious group.[9] That figure holds up within the group of long-term inmates of this study. Only about a third attend chapel. That does not mean that those who don't attend chapel don't think about spiritual issues. In fact, it appears from the musings of the long-term inmates in this study that spiritual subjects do matter to them as they try to figure out the meanings and values of their lives.

A couple of non-churchgoers mentioned reading the Bible alone in their cells, but confessed they have trouble understanding it. Some mentioned private prayer. Most seemed to give thought to the possibility of an afterlife.

Al, who has no hope of parole, has decided his punishment is now. But occasionally he has a flash of hope that he is wrong.

> I've gone to church just to listen to them talk. I went to Pentecostals, Mennonites, and Christians. I wanted to hear what they said. I didn't like none of them. They're not talkin' about nothing. I don't believe in an afterlife. I believe there is hell and heaven on earth. I'm here in hell. You are in heaven. Can you prove there is an afterlife? I hope there is. I think we're just going into the hole. I didn't know things before I was born; I won't know them after I die.

David is another man who has spent most of his life in prison. He is thoughtful and deep thinking, but religion is not his thing. After railing on about the Muslims, whom he claimed received extra privileges, he continued:

> I personally never went to church except when I was a kid and sometimes (very seldom) forced to. Out of all my thirty-plus years in prisons, I've probably only been to church three or four times, and even those few times, I didn't go for religious purposes (the chapel is used for other motivations).
>
> I don't respect too much either about the Baptists, Catholics, etc. There is absolutely no proof as to what they believe, but they'll scream hell and brimstone if you don't believe what they do.
>
> That's a little of how I feel about it. I'll further say this: As for God, in any form, I have serious doubts. Every God, from every religion that I know about, demands—for lack of a better word—"Idolization." What true, loving God would want you on your knees singing his praises? Hell, the Muslims even get on their knees five times a day, put their face to the ground, their ass in the air and praise a God who has no respect for women.
>
> Even if you accept all of that, how can you praise a God who is all-powerful, yet allows children to be molested, raped, and murdered? He has the power to stop it. Why doesn't he? It would seem that all of our gods are "accessories before and after the fact" of all those charges and are thereby, by our law of the land, criminal. Of course, this is just me talking. However, in Georgia, I'd bet a prosecutor would file charges on God if he could figure out where to send the warrant.
>
> My take on religion in prison is that the biggest majority (not all, but most, inmates) are fakes. In it for the privileges. In it for the outside churches' help toward parole. In it because they're cowards and afraid to fight and the Bible tells them not to fight but to turn the other cheek. Others just want it to be true because it's all they have to hope for. I can understand this one a little because if I could find a religion to convince me that when I die, I'd be with my mother, brother, and grandparents, I'd jump in headfirst and be ready to die.
>
> Still others are the fanatics who actually 100 percent believe what they believe, and I can't figure out who the hell convinced them. But they'll tell you that you are stupid if you don't see it.
>
> Does that cover the church thing? I probably shouldn't have said some of that stuff. If there is a God, I am sooooo going to hell! But I've been shooting myself in the foot for years.

The Changed

All the men, regardless of their own beliefs, agree that some fellow inmates are sincere and their changed lives reflect their religion. Three of the long-term men in this study definitely fit that category—perhaps as many as five—but Doug is the one who stands out the most.

Doug has spent the last thirty-one years in prison. He was raised in a kind, working-class family, with both parents present and active in his life. He was a well-known high school football player at a local Catholic high school, reportedly on his way to a big-time sports career. He was sidetracked by a serious drug problem that graduated into drug dealing. He shot a cop in an undercover deal gone bad.

Twenty-six years ago, Doug glowered at me from a corner of my first prison classroom. He was angry, hostile, and intimidating with his hulking physical size. But he was silently attentive in class and made good grades. He continued in the college program for several semesters, but then I did not see him for a number of years. One day as I left the sally port and entered the yard at another facility, a huge man came bounding up to me.

"Mrs. Holman," he whooped with a bright smile. It was Doug. I had never seen such a change in an individual, nor do I expect to again.

Today, he is the favorite of many. Staff and inmates alike are drawn to his positive nature, his frequent laughter, and his open attitude. His hulking physical size and bearing give him another form of respect. Doug does not talk frequently about his faith, but the men know he is a chapel-goer. He has written a few articles for the institutional newsletter about his belief, but "God talk" does not continually enter his conversation. He also has been guided by the Shakespeare Behind Bars program, which is not religiously based, but leads men to meaningful spiritual insights. Doug is a man who seems to live his private faith and stays steady by it during his darkest moments, which—he admits—still overwhelm him at times. The first part of his story is recounted in an earlier chapter, where he shared that his first years of incarceration were filled with anger and illegal activities. He discussed the day he began to change. He said it was the day God began to work on him.

He explained how he continues day to day without knowing if he will be released before he is an old man.

> One of my earliest epiphanies was living in the moment. People in prison and in the free world put their lives on hold. "When I get out I'm going to do this, when I get out I'm going to do that"—*do it now*! Don't wait! I learned to understand that this is my life. I would not choose these circumstances for my life. I don't want to be in prison, but I chose to take advantage of every positive thing I could, not so my future would be better, but so this day would be, and so that my life in prison could have meaning to me and hopefully others as well.

Today I am forever upbeat and I suspect you know why. I believe in God and his son Jesus Christ!!! I believe faith, hope, and love sustain me in all the dark times. I thank God for his grace and mercy that he has given to me when I sure have not earned it or deserved it. I hold onto Philippians 4:13, "I can do all things through him that gives me strength," and a Psalm I lean on is 142 and if you read it, you'll understand why it's special to me.

I do at times have darker thoughts and hope you understand that I'd kind of like to keep those to myself. To be honest with you, they are scary at times, but I will let you know how I deal with them and everything really. I think of everything in terms of blue skies. ☺ In other words, my relationship with God is me and him and a crystal blue sky between us. Anything that separates me from him, I consider storm clouds. The idea is to quickly recognize that there are clouds and get them out of your mind and out of your life and out of the way. When a person has dark thoughts, his inner dialogue can be extreme. The ego will have you puffing yourself up; you can sound so tough when you plan on how you are going to say this or that, or handle this or handle that. The unwanted traffic of thoughts is tiresome and unproductive. When my mind starts to have an unproductive dialogue with itself or basically any thought that is not positive in nature, I remind myself "blue sky." I remind myself what is important. I demand that my mind stays positive, happy, and focused on God. It takes practice, but practice brings peace and it is that peace that keeps me forever upbeat and positive. At the heart of all this is my faith and knowledge that God is in control of everything.

Issues to Think About

1. The public often derides "jailhouse conversions." After reading this chapter, have your attitudes changed about the role religion plays in the prison setting?
2. How did you react to learning about the wide variety of religions that are permitted to conduct worship services within the correctional system? What are the implications—positive and negative— of the allowed religious diversity within a prison?
3. Volunteers are often thrilled when an inmate experiences a religious "conversion," but are devastated when that inmate is not successful after release. What are your thoughts about that?
4. Should an evangelical chaplain be expected to facilitate religious beliefs and practices other than his or her own?

ELEVEN

The Long Wait

The Parole Process

Have they no sense? Have they no goddamn sense?—Staff member seen kicking and hitting the wall upon hearing that several men in her treatment program had received serve-outs rather than being paroled

I could walk into the prison and know almost immediately when the parole board was meeting. The air was thick with pain, tension, and fear. The conversation of the day focused on what mood the board was in. Were they "walking" a lot of men or were they giving "setbacks"? Staff members, as well as inmates, sometimes shouted out words of encouragement as those hoping for a chance at freedom made their way to the administration building.

Two middle-aged men recently took that trip up the walkway, sat in front of a camera's eye, and talked with two parole board members in another city via video conversation. Their hands shook, their nerves were on edge. One uncharacteristically cried through much of the interview from his tension. One was serving a life sentence with possibility of parole after twenty-five years; the other had a sentence of sixty-five years. Both had thirty years of incarceration under their belts and earlier unsuccessful parole hearings. They knew what was at stake. Their futures would be determined that day in the small concrete-block room where they tensely sat behind a wooden table, dressed in their neatly pressed khaki uniforms.

The two individuals whose faces appeared on the screen held the key to the men's futures and those of their families. The day the men met with them, the parole board members would make one of three decisions:

- They could talk with the inmate and decide that he had served sufficient time, and was ready to walk free. He would be out the prison doors within sixty days after three decades of incarceration.
- They could give him a "flop" or "setback," telling the man he should serve more time before he could once again plead his case to them.

146

The time, though calculated in months, would be served out in long years; setbacks for murder charges like theirs are usually meted out in five- or ten-year increments.

- The case could be referred to the whole parole board and the inmate informed of the decision within ten days. That could mean that the two parole board members disagreed on the decision and the whole board would have to vote. It could mean they want to give him more than a 120-month setback. Or it could mean they want to give him a serve-out. In other words, he would have to serve out his entire sentence and could never see the parole board again.

The parole decisions made daily across the country are difficult. Other than the original sentencing, the parole board is the part of the justice system that consistently receives the most criticism, is hated the most, and is the least understood.

"It's a crap shoot," muttered one employee who has watched the process for years.

There are no federal guidelines, no nationwide standards. Each state has its own process, but they are relatively similar.[1] For the men waiting to hear their futures, the faces in front of them are what counts. What will they decide? What would you decide?

The two men's stories that are recounted here are chosen because they are similar but had different outcomes. Both men were in their early fifties. They each had served thirty years in prison. They committed their crimes when they were very young men living out-of-control lives, immersed in alcohol and drugs. Both were mentioned by administration and staff as being ideal inmates. Once well-known leaders of illegal activities on the yard, years ago, they made conscious decisions to live out their lives in a more positive way, shocking their fellow inmates.

Both claimed a newfound Christian faith that now played a central role in their lives, but said their personal changes began before their religious journeys were evident.

Both have had outside support that has been consistent for years—one a mother who has visited weekly for thirty years; the other a wife of over twenty years whom the inmate first met in the prison visiting room.

Each has completed every program available to him within the institution, and has taken part in optional activities. Both received several associate degrees.

Both pulled the trigger that ended at least one person's life. In both cases, the prosecution threatened or fought for the death penalty.

Here are their stories, written over time but pieced together for coherence.

Occasional holes were filled by interviews or audio recordings from their parole hearings. These are their stories, told from their points of view. One of the men insisted that it was important to remember that the inmate is never the victim.

Duane

When I was three, I was taken from my family and sent to be raised with who I later found were distant relatives in Ohio. It was an upper middle-class family where money was never a problem. They were very good to me. As I got older, I noticed I never looked like them; we had different last names, I had a sister only three months older than me, and so forth. After a while, I began to voice my concerns. It didn't take long before I found myself and my foster parents sitting around the kitchen table having things explained to me. I discovered how my birth family lived in Tennessee. And when I was little, I was sent to where I was at to be raised.

At that point, my whole outlook on life changed. I took it personally and asked myself, "Why does my family not want me? What's wrong with me?" I became rebellious and began spending most of my time running the streets.

I was maybe twelve or thirteen. I remember running with the older kids. They introduced me to acid, pills, liquor, pot, and things of that nature. We would be out riding around and they would have me get out of the car, destroy mailboxes, throw rocks through windows, etc. I noticed none of them ever got out of the car. They just laughed.

My legal guardians would try to talk to me, but I felt as though they wouldn't understand. It was me against the world.

When I was about sixteen or so, I found myself sitting around the kitchen table again. My legal guardians asked me if I would like to go spend spring break with my birth family. I was so excited. My sister and her family came to pick me up. Not much was said on the long trip to Tennessee. When we got there, everyone was waiting on us. It was at that point I discovered I had two older sisters and two younger brothers as well as a mother. The moment was filled with tears, hugs, and joy.

Over the next few days, I was introduced to other family members that lived around about—cousins, aunts, uncles, etc. I had all of these thoughts running through my head. I knew my stay was going to be brief, because I was returning to Ohio in a week or so.

I noticed my family was close to poverty. They lived off of the state. They received a check and food stamps every month. Some were career criminals.

On several occasions, my cousins came to pick me up to go riding around. I was quick to learn this wasn't any different than Ohio with the exception of the drugs being harder, and instead of knocking windows out, I was climbing through them. Everyone stayed in the car and watched though—that was the same.

My two weeks of visitation flew by. Toward the end, I listened to how I should remain in Tennessee because all my family was there and that's where I belonged. Calling my legal guardians, I informed them I would not be returning.

I tried to enroll into school, but that only lasted for a month or so before I walked in to the front door of the school and out the back.

In my mind, I knew what I needed to do. I needed to get a job and support my family. That was big talk from a sixteen-year-old. So that's what I did. I got a job, rented a place, and moved everyone in with the exception of my oldest sister and her family.

I had been in Tennessee for about five or six months when one day after work, I got picked up by the police and took to the station. An officer took me into a room and said, "I want you to listen to something." It was a tape recording of my cousin telling them how I had picked him up in a stolen truck, etc. Just so happens several days before this, my cousin came to my house in a stolen truck and asked me to go with him. I said "no."

The police officer said, "We know you did not steal the truck, but we need you to testify against him." They gave me a list of things that were going to happen, then let me go. I went straight to my older sister's house and informed her what had happened. That very night, I found myself on the way to a relative's house in Eastern Kentucky where I stayed until the case against my cousin was thrown out of court. Then my sister came and got me and took me back to Tennessee. I was eighteen by this time.

I remember when I got back to Tennessee. We were all sitting around the kitchen table. I looked around the table and said to myself, "I don't even know these people." Less than two months later, I was arrested for the charges I'm in prison for now.

My cousins and I started drinking and they told me they knew a couple who had scored some settlement money. We went to get it. They said I had to be the one going in and killing them, as I was the only one the couple didn't know.

I knocked on the door and was shocked. I knew the people who came to the door—I had met them during the time I stayed in Kentucky. They invited me in. They offered to fix me breakfast. I was scared to death, to be honest. Scared to death. I sat there a long time. It seemed forever.

Through his sobs, Duane told rest of the story.

I shot the man first. Then the woman.

You can't hate me more than I do. I wish. I wish I had the strength to not do it. I don't understand, but I didn't have the appropriate tools to know how to resist.

There was four of us involved (two cousins, one brother-in-law, and myself). I remember lying in a cold empty jail cell watching the three of them go on visit every day and wondering why I wasn't going on visits with any of them.

Each of the four people involved were charged. Threatened with the death penalty if he went to trial, Duane pleaded guilty and accepted a life sentence with the possibility of parole after twenty-five years. His brother-in-law served no prison time; the two cousins got twenty years each and served about four years. They have returned to prison several times since.

Coming to prison several months later, I started writing letters home and got no response. I tried calling home, but the number was changed.

About a year into this life sentence, it dawned on me that I was on my own. I can remember breaking down as I walked the track right here at Luckett. I cried like a baby. I was nineteen years old.

I remember saying to myself, "I see what time this is; I am on my own." I had no idea what I was going to do. I was not even from this state. I knew absolutely no one. I was scared and confused. After careful consideration, I decided what I was going to do. I put the mask on and became what the state of Kentucky said I was—a convict.

I began running around with the older cons and they taught me the way of the convict. I had my hands into everything going (stores, drugs, gambling, homebrew, loan sharking, and dope). If there was a dollar to be made, I was involved. I noticed the more I got involved, the less I thought about my family and the streets. That is until I lay down at night.

Over time, I developed an I-do-not-care attitude. At least that was the persona that I projected. The truth is, I was just a confused and scared young man who just wanted to fit in and be accepted.

With my new outlook on life, it did not take me long to find my way to Eddyville [the state's maximum-security facility]. In 1990, while at Eddyville, the officials brought a tour of children across the yard. Little did the officials know, but they were about to change my whole aspect on life. [This was part of the *Scared Straight* program which was popular at that time.]

I could not believe my eyes and ears. The officials brought a tour of children out of the visiting room area, across the yard, and down into 4-cell house. Men began hollering obscenities at the children—I mean the foulest things you can possibly imagine. I looked to my left, then to my right. You could see the excitement in the inmates' faces as they hollered; the veins in their necks bulged out as they screamed. I could not believe what I was witnessing.

Glancing back and forth between the children and the inmates, I noticed that the children were looking at me also. Even though I had not said a word, I was standing right in the middle of all the inmates. The children saw me as one of the screaming inmates.

I cannot say what happened, but I know that a feeling came over me and I asked myself, "Duane, is this what you really want?" At that time in my life, I was on the verge of giving up all hope and saying, as so many of my friends in the past have, "This is me; this is where I am going to spend my dying days." I thought hard about the question for several days and I said to myself, "No. If this is all there is, I think that I would rather be dead."

It was at that point in my life that I stepped back and took a long look at myself. I could hear the voice of my legal guardians: "Stay in school, get an education. This will bring more money, a bigger house, a better car, a better life." Being that I was uneducated and unlearned, I decided I was going to use this opportunity to educate myself, so I got into school and began taking programs, thinking that's what I needed in my life.

Over the course of the next sixteen years, I obtained two degrees, as well as [completing] many other programs pertaining to self-help and responsibility. I was doing what I thought was right.

Even though I was preparing myself for society by educating myself, I still had an uneasy feeling about me. I had no idea what it was, or how to get rid of it.

In August 2006, I found myself at Little Sandy Correctional Complex. I had only been there a week when a young man (Kevin) asked me if he could work out with me. I said, "Sure, Why not."

On a Sunday morning, about a week later, Kevin and I were sitting down cooling off and Kevin said, "Can I ask you something?" I said, "Sure, go ahead." He went on to say, "Would you like to go to church with me tonight?" I laughed and said, "Don't you know who I am? I don't do the church thing."

"I don't mean you any disrespect. I was just wondering," Kevin went on to say.

Sitting there for a moment, I felt that same feeling come over me—the same one I had felt some sixteen years earlier while on the yard at Eddyville. I look at Kevin and said, "Since you are the first person to ever ask me to go in over twenty years, I am going to go with you."

Walking into the chapel, I looked around. I wondered if the walls and ceiling were steady enough to hold my presence. Stepping into the sanctuary, I sat quietly and as close to the door as I could get. I had one butt cheek in the chair and the other in the aisle ready to move in case of an emergency.

I remember the preacher stepping into the pulpit and beginning his sermon as he glared around the congregation. I caught myself swaying with the man sitting in front of me so not to make eye contact with the preacher (even though some things are inevitable and meant to be).

The preacher looked at me and said, "If you are tired of looking and you are tired of searching, I have the answer you are looking for. His name is Jesus Christ."

I left there that night and a transformation began. For the next three months, the Lord allowed me to see what I had become. I was a murderer, a thief, a liar. I never honored my mother or father. I always wanted what everyone else had. I've lusted, never putting God first in my life. I have broken every commandment there is.

As I walked the yard at Little Sandy, never talking to anyone, over a course of three months, the Lord allowed me to see where I was headed. I was on a path of destruction. I was on my way to Hell, but the Lord showed me that I did not have to go because he gave His son to die for me, that through his death and resurrection I could have life eternal with Him.

On November 26, 2006, some three months later, I decided I was going back to church. I remember the whole day. I was sweating so much that I took shower after shower. I can never remember being so nervous.

Once again, I found myself stepping back into the chapel. This time I got a little braver—I sat on the other side of the sanctuary, all the way in the back. As I sat there, tears rolled down my face. It was the first tears I had shed since I was nineteen years old while walking the recreational field right here at Luckett.

I remember the preacher doing an alter call. But I was so caught up with what goes on in prison that I could not find the strength within myself to get up out of my seat and go turn my life over to the Lord, so the Lord sent a man to me.

I felt a man grab me by the arm and say, "Come on. I'll go pray with you." Had it not been for that man's obedience, I would still be caught up in this life. I remember walking to the altar as tears streamed down my face. Reaching the altar, I fell to my knees, cried out to God, and asked Him to forgive me—not only what I'm in prison for, but for all my sins. I accepted Jesus Christ as my Lord and Savior. It was as if someone reached down and took a thousand pounds off of me. I had never felt so much love in all my life.

I knew at that moment I would never be the same again. It wasn't something I had to wait a day, a week, a month, a year to get. When I stood up, I knew I had a life-changing experience. Some people say, "I believe in God." I don't believe. I know. I know the man that I was, and I know the man I am today and it's nothing I've done.

After giving my life to Christ, I began reading the Word, then one day I noticed that the habits I used to have I never had anymore. The first thing that changed was my mind. Anyone I wronged, I wanted to make it right. I wrote letter after letter asking people to forgive me. Then my will changed. I have a desire to serve God. I don't want people to have to wait twenty years before being invited to church. Then my heart changed. I don't want to be a part of sin anymore; not that I can't, I just don't have a desire to do it anymore.

After serving thirty years behind bars, Duane met the parole board for the second time. Two women represented the board that day. The one who led the questioning was gentle and respectful in her approach and did all the talking except for two questions. When Duane broke into tears, she quietly reassured him and told him to take his time.

He continued. "I wish I could take it back. I can't. I want so bad to honor them, but I don't know how. I can't take it back. I will not play down the severity of what I did, but I can't take it back. I only pray that one act doesn't define who I am. Otherwise I should be dead."

He was asked about where he planned to live and Duane began to tell about his wife, and his voice broke again. As he talked, he fought through his tears. He explained he met her when she was at the prison visiting another inmate.

That's another thing I shouldn't have done. I should have left her alone. I see the pain on her face whenever she comes visit. I tried to run her off, but she said that was her decision to make. I see the family going through what they have to because of what I did. I have a mother-in-law and father-in-law who are older and need help. I'd love to buy a bigger house where we could all live together. I'd love to repay her. I'd love to have a wedding—I haven't told her—a wedding, not a prison wedding, but a real one. My grandkids—her grandkids—run across the room yelling for Pawpaw. They ask why I'm here. I tell them I did something wrong and I have to be punished. They ask when I'm coming home. It's crushing, crushing to me. It's the people I'm hurting by sitting here.

The two parole officers cut off the video feed while they discussed Duane's future between them. Duane's tension and the silence resonated around the cold walls. There is no record of their deliberations, but soon they were back, telling him that they were releasing him.

Duane had killed two people in a planned murder and robbery. He served the required minimum amount of time plus another five years after one deferment. There were never any victim impact statements presented opposing his release. Although Corrections employees could not write letters of support, the general feeling among staff and inmates was that Duane was a good candidate for release. His religious conversion, while shocking to many, persisted for many years and was accepted as one of the true prison conversions. While he speaks continually with religious phrases in everyday life, he did not once mention his Christianity in the parole hearing.

Duane is now settling into everyday life. He has a good job using skills he learned while in prison. He is eagerly waiting for permission from his parole officer to be involved with a reentry program in a local evangelical congregation, helping others who emerge from prison.

Doug

When Doug wrote his life's story, he entitled it "The Thing of Darkness: The Life and Times of a Reformed Gangster."

I grew up in the suburbs of Louisville, Kentucky, in a middle-class family. I was the oldest of two kids; my sister being three years younger. I had then, and still do have a very loving family. In fact, in the category of sainthood, my mother has visited me in prison every week for over thirty years! It was through her love that I found the inspiration to carry on when I felt like giving up.

So you see my childhood was typical, and I grew up in a house filled with love and happiness, and my parents were together until the day my father passed away.

I was a big kid and so I always played sports—baseball, basketball, and football. In fact, I was full grown at age fourteen at over six feet, four. My parents were financially able to send me and my sister to private school, and being Catholic, we attended Catholic grade school and high school. So I grew up with all the opportunities a young man should have in life: a good family, education, and atmosphere to know I could do or achieve anything in life if only I applied myself.

Like a lot of young boys, I dreamed of playing in the NFL. I also was aware of what a long shot that was. I knew I would have to take school seriously so that if I didn't make it in the NFL, I would have a degree from a respected university to fall back on. I had it figured out. I had a good head on my shoulders and nobody could interfere with my goals and aspirations. Nobody except me that is....

I first got high the summer before I turned sixteen. I got into a car with two other guys in the neighborhood, both my really good friends. They fired up a joint and passed it to me, and I tried it. I remember them laughing and me laughing right along with them as I tried to inhale the smoke. A few minutes later, everything was funny. It was even funny when we went into the neighborhood store to get something for the munchies and I fell down into the frozen food bin. I was incredibly stoned, and I liked it. That day, my dreams started to fade away and my double life became reality. In SBB, we don't act—we tell the truth, but for the next five years of my life, all I did was act.[2]

I acted like everything was fine. I acted like a good student and a football star. I acted like the perfect son. I could never allow anyone to realize I was a dopehead. At least not anyone that would not be keeping the same secret.

I had separate friends and I had separate lives. I wore my mask well, but as you can imagine, it soon became impossible to keep the genie in the bottle, especially as my drug abuse worsened. I went from smoking pot (which always remained a staple of my getting high) to alcohol, hash, opium, LSD, uppers, downers, mushroom, etc. You get the idea, and I could go on listing many more.

Okay, so how does a high school kid have the money to put gas in his car, pay for dates, movies, going out to eat, beer, and all the other expenses teenagers have, not to mention paying for a pretty expensive drug habit? Certainly no one on an allowance. Hmmm. Could it may be *dealing*? I knew people that had drugs. I knew people that wanted drugs. So I could be the big shot. The guy who could get things, and I could afford to party all I wanted and I could have my dope for free and I could have two pockets full of money, and I could have girls chasing me and I could.... Did you notice how many times I just used the word "I"? Looking back, that's when I quit being me and started being all about me.

I was a nice kid. I was sweet—not a mean bone in my body. In fact, Coach would have to light a fire under my ass to get me fired up before I would destroy someone on the football field. I earned my varsity letter as a sophomore and Coach announced at the awards banquet that I was the heir-apparent to Bubba Paris, a graduate from a few years back who went to Michigan and protected Joe Montana's blind side for many years in the NFL.

Any kid using drugs has a drug problem, but to me the even more serious danger was chasing the life. I enjoyed playing football in front of thousands of people, but I enjoyed partying after the games. I enjoyed being the guy that had everything. When we needed a keg of beer for a party, I'd get one. When someone needed some dope, I had it. Looking back, I realize that I was just chasing adrenaline or a special rush or feeling of excitement. I was what we call being caught up in the game. I started paying the price in my junior year in high school.

My football coach called me aside and told me, "You need to quit hanging out with your non-jock friend." He was talking about James. James had been my friend since grade school and when we got together, we got high. Always. James just wasn't as good at hiding it as I was, and in some ways, didn't care to.

One week later, my team won the county AAAA championship and we would play in the state championship the following week. We were so excited—on top of the world—the greatest time in our lives.... Oh my God, what the fuck happened? The team buses were just a couple of blocks from getting back to school when we drove right up on a fatal accident. You somehow just know in the pit of your stomach someone died. That night that someone was James.

So there I was on top of the world one second and then completely devastated the next. How could God let this happen? I blamed God. I never came to grips with what happened while I was in the free world. My life went downhill from that time, both mentally and spiritually.

Now at about the same period of time, my father bought a bar. It was a neighborhood joint with a beer and liquor license. It came with all the trimmings—gambling was at the heart of it all. There was always something illegal going on, and you didn't have to go far to get all the action you wanted. My father eventually became a full-time bookmaker. My pop was the coolest cat in the world to me, and I always wanted to make him proud. He wanted me to play ball and go to college. Any time I would be exposed to something or see this or that, he would remind me of my education and ball. I was specifically not to discuss anything I saw with my mother. My pop knew everything and everyone in the neighborhood. Everyone treated him with a great deal of respect.

The rest of my high school days were uneventful. I even managed to be named the First Team Catholic All-American, which itself was amazing given drugs and how empty I felt inside. No football, no girls, no party, nothing was filling the black hole I felt inside.

After a game my senior year, a priest came up to my father and told him a lot of the stuff he believed me to be doing and told my father he was a bad influence on me. My father told him, "That may be true, but don't think I don't know what the fuck you and your cop buddies are doing." This priest was taking government cheese and distributing the cheese to the police to sell. Apparently, there is a lot of money in selling a semitruck load of cheese at five dollars a box. You do the math. From that point on, I was on the radar and certain police would try harder to get my father and me.

I graduated high school, but my drug use was no longer a well-guarded secret. I did not receive the football scholarship I wanted, but I was offered one by a small private college and I accepted, and off I went. The school was perfect for me. A school mostly full of squares. It was far from the "bright lights and big city" of home. It was far away from my friends, my drug connections, and the family bar. In other words, I hated it. If I had just stayed there, I would have been fine, but I didn't. The real reason I wanted to come home was to be close to the bar, the action, my friends, the life. When I got home, I was no longer in the dumps or depressed about anything. In fact, I had my swagger back. I was six feet four, 237 pounds, as big as a house, strong as an ox, and could run like a deer. I was invincible and untouchable, and I thought my shit didn't stink. I would find out soon enough that simply wasn't true.

In July of 1985, I started going with a beautiful young lady. Unfortunately, she, too, had a drug habit and she was the first person to turn me on to "crank." We had a good run, but it was doomed from the beginning. We were on again, off again, and I went to her parents' house to try to convince her to move back in with me, only this time I had a gun. I told her I couldn't live without her, and so I fired the gun to make her think I had killed myself. It seemed logical at the time. Think about that— "It seemed logical"—and you can gain insight into how messed up a young mind can get under the influence.

Her next boyfriend was a detective for the city police department. I had a phone conversation with him once and said, "You're a detective? Well, come on over to Fifth Street, and I'll give you a clue!" Looking back, it's very clear to me that I treated police with contempt, and not just police, but elected officials as well. I saw corruption and the power of the almighty dollar. You see it all in the running of an illegal poker business. Problem is, you can't pay them all, and some can't be paid.

I saw too much, learned too much at too young of an age. I saw the people in power and the people who were supposed to be the good guys really weren't. At least, not all of them, so I was guilty of judging them all. In some ways, that was the justification I used to do what I liked.

Problem was my father was a gambler, and I was into drugs, and they are worlds apart. My father always told me never do anything you can't buy your way out of. He told me if I sold narcotics that they would come out of the woodwork and get me, and there would be nothing he could do about it. I should have listened.

As Doug recounts the details of the snowy day he took the life of a police-man, bitterness enters the telling. He believes that he was set up, treated unfairly and illegally—the anger from that remains. But at the same time he is angry, he fully accepts the blame and is floored by all the pain he has caused. He was twenty-one years old.

> I saw a friend at a concert. I hadn't seen him in a while. We graduated together and played football together. He had been bringing a friend of his around to the bar on and off for about six months, but not lately. He told me his drug connection went back to Tennessee and wanted me to get him some crank. Over the next several days, he tried to get hold of me several times and when he finally did, he told me he needed two ounces. I met him at a local fast food place and we got high. He tried out the stuff, liked it, and we set up the deal. Later that afternoon, he called me back and asked if I remembered his friend. He said they wanted to go in on this together and instead of getting two ounces, they wanted four. I agreed and the deal was set.
>
> My "friend" was supposed to get all the money and meet me at the bar. The time passed for him to meet me, and so I guessed they had backed out. A couple of hours passed, and then his friend shows up and asks me if I've seen him. I say no, and then he tells me he wants to do the deal anyway. He went to get rest of the money and so off we go.
>
> I'll go ahead and tell you my "friend" was studying to be a cop—taking his intern-ship in narcotics. Basically, his friend—the one who came to me—was a part-time rookie undercover officer for a local police department, loaned out to the county police department for narcotic operations. They had me.

Doug's narrative continues in detail about their drive, looking for the supplier who had earlier spotted the sting operation going on and had left the arranged meeting place. Doug admits to taking the police on a wild goose chase to cover his tracks. He and the undercover were outside the car in a church parking lot when they got into an argument over not being able to find the supplier.

> Right before we were getting back in his car, he pulled his gun (357) and I ducked a little bit and pulled my gun (38), and from one side of his car to the other we unloaded at each other. His first shot took the hat off my head. My first shot hit him in the chest and spun him around, and one of my next couple of bullets hit him in the back and my last shot hit him in the collarbone. His last shot hit me in the right arm. He shot at me six times and I shot at him five times, and the whole thing lasted less than five seconds.
>
> They said the shot that killed him bounced off his collarbone and ruptured the artery in his neck. The surveillance team was there in about forty-five seconds. It was their job to be in visual contact with us at all times, but none of them said they saw it. He was flown to the hospital and I was trying to remain conscious.
>
> They put me on the ground, handcuffed me behind the back, and beat and stomped me unmercifully. I would have loved to have only had the beating that Rodney King took. I was so bloody that when they finally got me to the hospital, they thought I was shot in the head. And by then, I wasn't even sure myself.

They chained me to the bed and two detectives started torturing me. They were squeezing my arm (the bullet was still in there) and asking me if I knew that was a cop. They had another rookie outside the curtained area say that I said I knew he was a cop. Bullshit.

At trial, they said I knew it was a cop and I was going to rob him. Ridiculous. If I knew someone was a cop, I sure would not take him to buy dope. I sure wouldn't try to rob him, knowing if he's a cop that he's wired and his surveillance team is listening to everything.

Now let me tell you this. They said he was wired that night and they could hear it all. But they were not recording it. Do you believe that? He had a throwaway gun on him (a gun not registered to him or that he was allowed to have on his person). It was a chrome-plated Raven automatic. Isn't that convenient? The day the deal went down, my "friend" had asked me if I would be carrying a gun. He wanted me to be, under the guise that he didn't want me getting robbed of his money that night. Actually, they wanted me to have a gun so when I was arrested, I could be charged for drugs and a gun.

The trial was a circus. One officer after another taking the stand with one goal on their mind—get me the death penalty. I believe in my heart the jury knew the prosecution's case was bullshit with a brass band, but they were under a lot of pressure to convict.

And after all, even in the light of what actually took place, and with me taking full ownership of this tragedy, this has always been and always will be where the rubber meets the road: *I take full responsibility for this very senseless tragedy that resulted in an officer losing his life.* It was the poor decisions and choices I made with my life that were to blame for this. I was ignorant to how bad, how fast, my stupidity could lead to disaster.

The jury reached a compromise verdict, and I was given twenty years for robbery and forty-five years for taking a life. The judge ran them consecutive for a total of sixty-five years. That compromise made nobody happy. The police were upset I did not get the death penalty, and I sat shocked and amazed that they had convicted me of robbery when nothing was stolen.

Well, I made this bed, so now I had to lie in it. I was on my way to prison. My father had looked into the crystal ball. He told me not to do anything you can't buy your way out of. He told me that if I sold narcotics, they would come out of the woodwork and get me, that I would go to prison, and there would be nothing he could do about it.

As I think back to how this affected my family, I remember how strong and courageous that they all were under the circumstances. I know it killed my father that he was not able to "fix" this and make it go away. Sometimes things cannot be fixed and all you need is someone to empathize with you—someone to be with you in your pain or whatever you're going through. That's what my father learned, and what my mom knew from the onset of the tragedy I set in motion.

My situation could not be fixed, so they all just joined in on my pain. They bore it upon themselves, and basically became incarcerated themselves. My family did not miss a visit in thirty years. Wow! Talk about being there for you! The love and support from my family is what helped me get through each day. It's not just my family's love, but so many people that have taken time to be here with me. I am truly blessed and I carry their love with me always.

Doug has developed an unusual and outstanding positive reputation among his fellow inmates as well as with the administrators who watch him. He has been mentioned in well-known national publications because of his acting skills in Shakespeare Behind Bars. A warden, breaking precedence—and perhaps rules—voluntarily wrote to the parole board in favor of his release. Doug's name came up in a number of my interviews—the inmates, staff, and administration spoke of the rehabilitative power of prisons and mentioned him as an example of where the parole process is flawed.

Doug has seen the parole board three times. The first time he received a deferment of 144 months (twelve years). The second time, he was given a five-year deferment; the last time ten years. He applied for a commutation of sentence from the governor after his last deferment, but was turned down, in spite of a large groundswell of support.

Those with an eye on the board say privately that Doug will probably serve every day of his sentence. They recount what happens whenever he comes up for parole. Police officers pour into the victims' impact hearing, overwhelming the small facility. Those on the parole board who were former police officers place strong pressures on their fellow board members. Those speaking up for his parole are ostracized by their peers. At one of his hearings, a former police officer was one of the two making the parole decision.

There is a website, the Officer Down Memorial Page, where police officers from Kentucky, Pennsylvania, New Hampshire, New Jersey, and South Carolina have posted their comments about Doug. Statements about his rehabilitation are removed promptly from the site.

But the pain expressed by the officer's family, friends, and others involved are palpable. Even those who don't know him personally are affected. A mother whose police officer son was killed in the line of duty in California wrote on the memorial page of Doug's victim:

> This site is meant to memorialize our fallen officers. It is not meant as a site for any lectures or hopes for forgiveness for the killer or to list what some see as his prison accomplishments. I feel no compunction or desire to forgive the murderers of my son. I have always said that they don't have to answer to me, but to God, and the same rationale applies to forgiveness.

In most states, under most laws, individuals incarcerated in state institutions are eligible for parole well before the end of their sentences. There is a prescribed minimum percentage of their sentence that they must serve before being considered for release. When that date arrives, it is up to the parole board to decide if the inmate is ready to reenter society. The board can specify the terms of his release, reject the release and suggest more programs the inmate should take, or they can flatly refuse the release with little explanation. They can even specify a serve-out, insisting that the prisoner serve the full sentence. In many cases, that action is the same as declaring the man will spend the rest of his life behind bars.

While the parole process differs from state to state, the basic concept is the same. Most often, the cases to be considered are assigned randomly to those on the parole board and only a couple of members review the file or interview each inmate. Because of the overwhelming numbers of cases coming to the parole board, only the more serious offenses warrant face-to-face meetings.

The board is composed of regular citizens, ideally with some experience in the criminal justice system, although that is not always the case. In most states, it is a paid, usually full-time, position. Members are usually appointed by the governor, and in most states, the parole board is responsible to the governor rather than the Department of Corrections.

In the best of circumstances, there is an attempt to achieve balance on the board in terms of gender, political party, and race. This does not always work out. As of this writing, on the nine-person board in Kentucky, there are only two men and two African Americans, which is far from reflective of the inmates who will come before the board. Since each board member brings his or her own personal biases to the table, it is inevitable that an unbalanced board will produce unbalanced decisions.

A former police officer is going to bring one perspective on criminals, a minister another. Someone abused as a child will have a hard time making an objective decision about someone who has harmed a child in his crime. Some years ago, there was a female parole board member in Kentucky who was quoted as saying she would never vote to release a sex offender. The men's futures were often determined by the possibility that she would be assigned to hear their cases. I asked if that could be true. "I wouldn't doubt it," several people in a position to know responded. Vetting of parole board members doesn't necessarily include questions to determine if the prospective member has been a victim and has a personal agenda.

Parole boards frequently turn over as members rotate on and off after relatively short prescribed terms. Sometimes the boards seem to have a conservative bent; in other years, a liberal one. Members are most often appointed by the governor, and are sometimes chosen on the basis of their related professional experiences. Other times "they don't have a clue," a person close to the boards said.

Regardless of the state or its procedures, the parole process everywhere is fraught with problems, fears, and high emotions on all sides. Much is at stake, and the impact of the decisions made about release roll far beyond the walls of the prison. The secret nature of the mostly subjective parole process is at the heart of the problem. Neither victims, their families, nor the inmates fully understand how things work, and each group feels the system is stacked against them.

Long before the scheduled date of the parole hearing, the men and their victims start their preparations. The prisoners solicit letters of support from anyone who knows them, and carefully collect the letters and precious certificates of program completion in a well-designed and thought-out folder that they take with them to the hearing. Others pay attorneys to collect the materials and send them to the board early. To the frustration of the inmates, the people who know them best—their teachers, their bosses, the officers—are not allowed to send letters of support in most states.

At the same time, victims and their families are lining up support on their sides, sending letters opposing the release of the inmate and recounting the lasting harm he has done to them. Media is contacted and news stories may be printed or broadcast, letting the public know the high-profile offenders are being considered for release.

Before the actual parole hearing, there can be, if requested, a face-to-face meeting between the assigned parole board members and those people who have been victimized. The victims are able to tell their stories in detail, air their hurt, and plead for the continued incarceration of the perpetrator. There is no way to overestimate the influence of the victim impact statements on the inmate's future. If victims are angry and persistent enough to show up at each hearing, they have the potential power to keep an inmate incarcerated many years beyond the time they would have normally served. If the media is involved, the inmate's chances go down even more.

Only occasionally do the victims' statements help the inmate. John killed his younger brother in a drunken fight. Their mother, a feisty personable little lady, appeared at the victims' hearing to tell of her painful ordeal. The incident caused the loss of both of her sons, she said: one dead and one in prison. She begged for John's release. He was released on the first time up. Any other decision would have punished the mother even more.

There are also occasional letters from victims indicating that they have forgiven the perpetrator and do not oppose their release and the second chance they hope for. Sometimes victims and their families move on, piecing together their lives as best they can, trusting the justice system to make appropriate decisions without their input. They do not get involved in the parole process. But if a victims' impact statement is submitted, the chances of parole declines dramatically.

In some states, the victims are allowed to speak only at the first parole hearing.

On the day of the parole hearing, two or three parole board members sit down with the impersonal correctional files of the offender in front of them. They review the man's institutional record, look at his risk assessment scores, and read the official report of the crime. Again, the process is not transparent. In Kentucky, for example, the assessment tool used for parole purposes is different from the one used in DOC's more public settings and which is available to the men. Without knowing more about the parole board's assessment tool, the inmates have no ability to question the instrument that plays a large part in decisions about their release.

For fifteen minutes to half an hour, the parole board members talk to the prisoner they've never met before. They thumb through the correctional file as they talk. Some members admit they read the files for the first time as they are talking. Others say they have reviewed them beforehand. One admits to not always reading the letters of support. "They all say the same thing—'My son's a good boy,'" one member said with a laugh. In a few states, the warden sits in on the meeting and can participate. In most states, however, the employees who know the prisoner best are not allowed to weigh in on the decision for fear of corruption in the process. The men often complain that the parole members decline to look at the personal file of accomplishments they have so carefully compiled.

I have listened to the audiotapes of the men who have been up for parole during the writing of this book. I have been surprised to see how differently the interviews are conducted. In Duane's case, the lead questioner took a gentle approach, giving him time to think, compose himself, and talk about his accomplishments. The second female questioner present asked only two questions, which were just requests to make him repeat details about the crime.

In another case, both questioners were aggressive, non-sympathetic, their comments bordering on sarcasm. Other interviewers push the inmates, seeing if they can keep a steady head under pressure. Board members can request to work together, so often the pair are like-minded, thus eliminating the preferred give-and-take of different thoughts that would lead to a more balanced decision.

I found the men were correct in saying they are made each time to repeat the gruesome details of the crimes committed thirty years before. I became uncomfortable listening to some of the insistent prodding for lurid details that seem to have little relevance so many years later. All the details of the crime are already in the written record. It was up to the inmate to skillfully express great remorse while recounting the gruesome details of the crime, and managing to shift the conversation to his accomplishments and personal changes that had occurred in the ensuing years.

"It's as if I will always be judged by the worst five minutes of my life. Nothing else seems to matter," one man said.

In less than thirty minutes, this conversation between previous strangers will culminate in a decision that will affect the inmate, and those who know him, perhaps for the remainder of their lives.

For the parole board member who takes his or her job seriously, the decision-making is a heavy burden, especially when passing judgment on those who have already spent more than half of their lives incarcerated. There is also a burden on the sincere inmate to explain a crime that today seems inexplicable to him. Both inmates and parole members know there are plenty of men appealing for parole who are not sincere in their rehabilitation. Some already plan future crimes; others haven't gained the needed desire to change. It is a challenge to know the true character of the man pleading for his freedom.

When a man is refused parole and given additional years to serve, he is to be given a reason and a suggestion for how he should live the next years of his life. It is here that the non-transparency of the parole process creates the most confusion and anger. If they have a number of institutional problems, the men understand how this affects their parole. But most (not all) of the men in my study have aged out of criminal activity on the yard. They have hunkered down and done their time—some with more positive flair than others. They have completed every treatment program suggested by the parole board. They have established a work record at the institution. To the man, they say they do not know what more they can do to earn their release. Too often, when the long-termers are refused parole, they are simply told to go back and keep up the good work. They do not understand, and are angry and frustrated. They do not know all that transpires behind the scenes.

There is an attempt to professionalize the parole process nationwide, with the Association of Paroling Authorities working with up to forty states, helping them train members and develop committees to work towards nationwide standards for parole. Some states are moving towards presumptive parole, where parole board members operate less on opinion and more on a model of accomplishment by the inmate.

But the big sticking point remains at the top of the state food chain. In most cases, the governor has the ultimate authority over the parole board, which keeps the process in the political realm. When problems arise, the governors seldom publically stand behind their parole boards and their decisions. If a board releases a high-profile inmate with a lot of media attention, it is displeasing to the powers that be. Or if a released person with a serious background reoffends, there is tremendous blowback. All boards know this and know they will take the brunt of the anger, explained a person who works closely with parole boards across the United States.

When it happened in Massachusetts, all the board members were fired. In Pennsylvania, all paroles were stopped until the process could be reevaluated. In Oklahoma, the prosecutor didn't agree with a parole release and criminally indicted the parole board members. They were part-time employees and didn't have insurance, so they had to pay for their own attorneys.

Knowing that no one has their backs, parole boards are reluctant to release anyone who is high profile and in the media's eye, or anyone who has someone with power speaking against his release. Other more anonymous cases may initially be given longer sentences, but the parole boards do not seem to be as reluctant to give them parole when the time finally comes. Those men from communities where life is cheap, or where their victims' families fall away after years or who do not know how to use the system to their advantage, may be released earlier. The parole board is more likely to free someone who can go quietly than someone who will have TV cameras waiting at the door for them.

Reforms in parole are beginning to get the public's attention. Young offenders are given many chances and treatment opportunities. More justice reforms are being considered and implemented. Better risk assessment instruments, based on scientifically supported data, are being developed to help with release decisions. But the reforms still are not touching those with violent or sexual offenses—those who have served decades in the penal system. Even though murder has one of the lowest recidivism rates of all crimes, the men in this study who have killed are the ones ignored in the proposed criminal justice changes.[3] Someone involved with parole issues nationwide explained it this way: "Think of it as a bell curve. Most serious crimes fit under the larger curve, but the politicians and parole board members are most worried about the 2 percent outliers who cause the most trouble. So they develop policy that deals with *all* serious crimes as outliers. Nothing is going to be done to change the procedure in terms of them."

Mel is stuck in that impossibly difficult situation. A former minister who had never broken a law until he killed his wife in a momentary flash of anguish, he has been incarcerated for the past twenty years. During that time, he has had only one minor write-up and has piled on certificates from all possible educational and treatment options. Family members have appeared at each hearing to object to his release. Mel talked about his quiet fears as he waited for his fourth parole hearing.

One particular line from the *Shawshank Redemption* has been resonating in my mind lately: "Hope is a dangerous thing. It can drive a man insane." The longer I'm locked up, the more I understand what that means.

The last few years since my deferment have been particularly difficult, with the past six months being some of the darkest times of my incarceration. I'm trying to wrap my mind around the very real probability that I may never get out of prison. Trying to hope for the best, yet prepare for the worst, becomes more difficult by the year.

If I live well into my 80s, as have my folks and many aunts and uncles, I will die alone, unable to take care of myself in a prison nursing facility. Dying alone in prison is a very real fear for me, and as things look now, a very clear possibility.

Mel recently saw the parole board again. He was given a ten-year deferment. He will be sixty-nine the next time he can hope for a chance to start his life again. But by then, he will have no way to support himself.

I have shared his plight with people who do not know him to get their reactions.

Often, I get blank stares and the same response: "It's sad, but I don't care what happens to him. He killed someone. I just don't care."

Issues to Think About

1. What do you see as the strengths and weaknesses of a policy of parole that shortens sentences?
2. What part do you believe victim impact statements should play in parole consideration?
3. How does the public, individually and collectively, influence the parole process?
4. If you were given the power to design a state's parole policy, what would be the major (if any) changes you would make?

TWELVE

End of the Journey

Illness and Death in Prison

If a man urinates in his cell and doesn't even realize he is in prison, what good is it to punish him more? I tell them to just find a mop and get someone to clean it up.

—*Deputy warden*

Larry seemed an unlikely person to die.

He came to me in prison one spring afternoon, ostensibly to talk about a school issue, but the conversation shifted, as it often did in those private times with the inmates. I was an unusual confidant, but he needed to talk.

I already knew that Larry grew up in Cabrini-Green, the infamously grim Chicago projects that once held thousands of violent, crime-ridden households. He was a muscled, ruggedly handsome African American man who knew the streets and who made good money in his youth selling drugs. When his own drug usage outstripped his income, he turned to guns and small businesses for his cash. His life got more complex as he grew older.

As Larry unloaded his thoughts, a tear formed in the corner of his eye and began a trail down his rugged black cheek. He turned his head and pretended to look at something on the wall while he furtively dabbed at his face with his muscled hands. But soon the tears welled too fast to be hidden, and he fought to keep control as he gave way to the truth.

> I wasn't trying to quit crime. I knew right from wrong, but I did what I wanted to do. I wanted pretty cars, pretty clothes, pretty women.
>
> I've used people all my life. I used women. I used my family. I always done things the easy way. I took the easy way out. I never worked for anything till I been here. And now it's too late. I think I'm getting sick again.

Larry was serving his ninth year of a twenty-five-year sentence. It was his third incarceration and his last. Unknown to most of us, he had been diagnosed as HIV positive from his days of shooting cocaine. Soon after our

165

conversation, his health problems increased and he was hospitalized. Although his days were numbered, the parole board gave him another thirty-six-month setback. He feared it was a death sentence. It was. Larry died alone in shackles within the year.

For him, prison was a desperate place to die. It was also a desperate place to live.

Health Care

Health care in prisons is uneven. The quality of care differs between states, institutions, and even within the same institution over time. The doctor in charge may be quite skilled and caring or under the cloud of pending malpractice suits. Corrections does not pay their attending doctors the same wage a skilled physician could make in the community, so the personal reasons the doctors are working behind bars determine a lot. Some of the best are physicians just retired from demanding practices, or young foreign doctors unable yet to set up their own practices. One can't paint with too broad a brush, but generally speaking, you get what you pay for.

Many inmates are getting more health care than they would have had in their undisciplined lives on the street. They get periodic checkups, medication for high blood pressure, and referrals to excellent specialists and surgeons when their serious conditions are identified and acknowledged. Many get treatment for the hepatitis that is widespread in prisons. They may not receive the most up-to-date expensive drug for their troubling conditions, but they receive something.

Still, prison is not a place to get sick. There are abundant tales of men forced to wait until morning with serious chest pains, of ignored diabetic attacks or oncoming strokes, of pleas for help that are ignored. All too often, men are taken to medical after their complaints are ignored for too long. They never return, and a rumor of death floats back across the yard within a few days. In prison, if they can't get the sympathetic ear of a few key people, they are out of luck.

Mostly, the men suffer alone. Flu and intestinal bugs run rampant, and many over-the-counter medications are unavailable. Restroom facilities can be inadequate and overrun. In prison, illness is something to be toughed out, taking the men even further from kindnesses that define and teach how we should treat one another.

Lee is an old-time convict, now growing old in the state's maximum-security facility. He has a serve-out on his life sentence. He recently tried to explain his distant, hard, and cold demeanor of years ago. Much of it was tied to the excruciating, continual pain he experienced with his back.

That entire ordeal with my back problem in the '90s had a lot to do with my attitude back then because of the intensity of the pain I was in a lot of the time. I just couldn't believe I was being allowed to suffer like I was. There were many times I couldn't get up out of bed to do anything. I had to have other inmates help me get back and forth to the bathroom and had to depend on them for my food as well because medical wouldn't do anything.

They actually thought I was faking, trying to get drugs, for a long time. Hell, they had me so mad one time I told the head nurse, "I can get anything I want off the yard anytime I want it, so I'm not needing anything from you to get high on. I just want to be fixed." That was sometime around '93 or '94, I guess.

There was guards there and staff at the school where I worked that couldn't believe I was being done like I was. The whole thing regarding my back problem and the way they were addressing it made me feel a lot of hate and anger, and it was really hard keeping all that from controlling my attitude towards others.

There was a point where it had gotten so bad I tried to get one of my few friends to go buy me a bunch of morphine off the yard so I could OD and get it over with, and up until that time in my life, I would of never thought about doing anything like that. But that's just how intense the pain was and I needed for it to stop. Good thing I didn't, because you'd be one short for this study!

In 2000, they sent me to KSR to take the hepatitis treatment and get the long-awaited back surgery, which fixed the main back problem for then and the hepatitis, as well.

The doctor that finally did the surgery couldn't believe they had taken so long getting the surgery done because of how messed up it was. He even had to take out some pieces of my vertebrae because of the nerve damage.

My back started messing up again about three or four years ago, but nothing like before. It just comes and goes and I've been exercising my lower back almost every morning while watching *Wai Lana* on KET at five a.m., and for the last year, I haven't had any problems with it.

All of the men I have talked with praise the doctors and the medical care that they get once they are taken out of the institution to meet with specialists. They mention the embarrassment they feel going into medical centers in jumpsuits, shackles, and handcuffs with everyone staring at them. But once they get in the back rooms, out of the sight of curious eyes, they are amazed at the kindness and consideration shown them by the medical professionals.

Their hospital experiences differ from those of the public. If prisoners' conditions require surgery or hospitalization, they are taken to a community hospital, where their rooms are guarded as they lie shackled to their beds. One man talked of being too weak to turn over with the weight of the chain hindering his getting comfortable. Sometimes the chains are replaced by light leather restraints, but movement is restricted nevertheless.

Medical care, of course, produces headaches for the correctional medical personnel and administration, and the extraordinary costs devour correctional budgets. Men living a lifestyle that brings them to prison usually have not paid a lot of attention to their health. They bring serious medical problems with them that require expensive treatments and medication. The prisons are filled with men suffering from conditions of their days of drug use, alcohol consumption, and unprotected sex. Hepatitis and HIV are widespread. Men are in wheelchairs as the result of gunshots or damaging fights. One man was paralyzed jumping off a roof as he ran from police. Painful arthritis from bones broken during youthful altercations is prevalent. A few men are blind. Many are mentally ill.

Dental care is a particular problem. Men come to prison with rotting, uncared-for teeth—the result of extreme neglect or past drug use. There is not much help available, even though there is usually access to a dentist. Most prisons do not provide dentures. They do sometimes provide fillings, but recently I was told that the facility had not had filling materials for four months. Toothaches are handled by extractions.

In the years he has been incarcerated, David has lost most of his teeth. Eating is a serious problem for him, especially in the prison atmosphere where inmates are rushed through the chow hall to make seats available for others. His toothlessness has affected his appearance and will soon affect his employment prospects once he is released. His job possibilities will be limited to positions that do not put him in the public eye. He is not alone. Extractions manage pain, but don't position people for a positive future.

By law, inmates have to receive necessary medical treatment and, as with other issues, lawsuits and grievances are often filed to make it happen. Men frequently have to fight to get needed surgeries or the most current medications.

Stuart, suffering from Huntington's disease, is given medicine for his condition, but he is aware there are promising new drugs discussed on the Internet, but not available to him. Stroke victims have some rehabilitative equipment, but lack much of the help needed. Anyone requiring special diets on a daily basis is pretty much out of luck. Heart attacks are waiting to happen among the older men who subsist on the prison's steady diet of starches and processed meats.

Prescribing medication in an atmosphere where underground drug use is prevalent can be a problem. Many of the inmates have been placed on "psych meds"—medications to treat depression and anxiety. There are long lines several times each day at "pill call," each man needing his prescribed dosage, which cannot pass through his hands. A bored officer stands at the window watching as a nurse dispenses each medication. After swallowing the pill, the inmate must open his mouth and lift his tongue for the officer to verify that he has indeed swallowed the pill to ensure it will not find its way into the prison's drug market.

Physicians differ in their willingness to prescribe psychotropic medications, so at times, unmedicated inmates get combative and unbalanced, much to everyone's consternation.

USA Today indicated that a 2006 report from the Office of the Surgeon General about health within the nation's prisons had been deliberately quashed before it reached the public's attention. The suppression reportedly occurred because the Bush administration was unwilling to spend the amount of money that would be required to deal with the burgeoning problem. The report emphasized the close connections between the health of those incarcerated and the safety and health of our communities. It prophetically indicated that substance abuse and mental illness were growing concerns in 2006, as were infectious and chronic diseases, and that the failure to deal with the health problems of the incarcerated would bleed over into our communities in the future. The article indicated that mental illness is three times higher within U.S. jails and prisons than in the general population.[1]

The report itself is interesting, if troubling, reading. It emphasizes that the issues are complicated. The financial public health emphasis is not on community health, but on terrorism and pandemic situations. There is a lack of available information on prison health care. The agencies dealing with health care have different cultures and do not communicate well. As indicated by the quashing of the Surgeon General's report, needed funding is not available. And lastly, there is the lack of public support. Another 2006 report notes: "A significant proportion of people in this country would prefer to incarcerate criminals, 'throw away the key,' and are not receptive to providing effective medical treatment during incarceration or post-incarceration."[2]

Health care needs in prison go beyond substance abuse, mental illness, and disease. Other issues present special challenges. The stories behind many incarcerations are complicated.

In Kentucky, as in many states, one correctional facility is labeled the special needs institution. The range of the disabilities is wide. Those who are blind, deaf, or use wheelchairs are sent there. Physically fit inmates are given the job of accompanying the blind or pushing those in wheelchairs as the pavement is too rough for them to navigate by themselves.

The developmentally disabled who have broken the law are housed there, as well. Programming for the intellectually challenged are designed to match their mental and emotional capabilities. At one time, there was a Boy Scout troop for them and even an Easter egg hunt. The Boy Scout troop helped disabled inmates learn about cooperation and good citizenship, just like scouting programs for youngsters on the outside.

Aging

The current move to reduce prison populations is taking place at the front end of the age continuum, freeing the younger drug-addicted offenders.

It is doing nothing to help those older inmates with long sentences. The longer time they serve, the higher their health costs and the more their increasing age-related conditions become the responsibility of the government.

In our prisons, we are funding the care of thousands of inmates who cannot feed themselves or control their bodily functions. They lie in beds, sometime comatose, for years. Others languish, belted into wheelchairs, unable to communicate.

In most states, if a person is declared near death or in a dire medical situation, an application can be filed for early release. Most agree the procedure is complicated and multi-tiered and very often unsuccessful. Administration admits its frustration with the process. Even if an ill, permanently bedridden patient is approved for early release, placement presents a huge problem. Most families do not have the resources to handle the situation. Nursing homes accepting Medicaid are the only alternative if an opening can be found. Sometimes VA facilities can be located for the veterans. In the case of sex offenders, very few nursing homes will accept them, even if they are unable to move. Occasionally, a declining sex-offender inmate will be shipped to another state where a nursing home bed can be found.

Walking through the halls of the health care center of a state correctional facility is no different from walking into the sitting area of a low-cost nursing home. A visitor is greeted with blank unknowing stares. Men sit strapped in wheelchairs where they doze, drool dripping from their mouths. Others mutter unintelligibly to themselves.

Without thinking about the unintended consequences, we pay dearly for our insistence on long-term or life incarcerations.

Two of the men in our original group of fifty have died in the past twenty years. Another is permanently housed in the institution's health care facility. The rest of them are growing old.

Some of the men in our group are scared because of their increasing age, although few admit it. It is the old convicts who seem the most concerned about their declining abilities. In their youth, their power and status came from their physical abilities to take care of business. If they were messed with, they handled the situation by force. They were not afraid to use physical retaliation if someone tried to move in on their illegal businesses or to cheat them in a transaction. Awareness of these men's strength, quick minds, and alertness had others watching their steps.

These older men mention slowing down. Al chafes as he tells of the young toughs who come into the prisons and try to intimidate him. They deliberately bump against him or push too close to him on the walkway. He recognizes that there is a change in the way the young inmates see him now. Although still strong, his winning a fight is less likely.

The desire to fight or to take on difficulties is diminishing as well. The men have "aged out," which is the term for inmates who have gotten older, settled in, and are trying to do their time with as little conflict as possible.

"Give me an institution with everyone over forty and I'll have an easy life," one warden told me.

David, in his upper fifties, has recently been sent to a halfway house and will be on his own soon after spending more than half of his life in prison. He is overwhelmed and surprised by the difficulties he is facing. "All those years, I just thought if I could get free from that pen, I'd take off and would figure out how to live with no problem. But it's not that easy now that the time is here. Things have changed on the outside. I could go the outlaw route, but I'm too old to do all that. And I don't want to do that stuff anymore."

Other issues of living become important for the older inmates. They can no longer hop in and out of the top bunks. They can't read without their glasses. Their bodies ache, and they tire more easily. Sometimes institutions devise special dorms for the older men, but mostly they are part of the general population until they need nursing home care. Occasionally, there will be a dorm for older veterans. Honor dorms are usually heavily weighted with the older, more settled inmates. But often institutions count on the aging inmates to balance off the more volatile youth, and keep the population mixed in all aspects of daily life.

There is an increased influx of senior citizens into the correctional system in the last ten years, which is raising health care costs for the correctional system.[3] Courts, which were once sympathetic to age and illness, are less likely to now consider these as reasons to keep citizens out of prison.

Death

The U.S. Department of Justice produced an in-depth analysis of prison and jail deaths between 2001 and 2009. With the exception of one year, death rates in prisons steadily increased during the period of the analysis. Illness accounted for 90 percent of the deaths, with half of all prison deaths coming from heart disease and cancer, followed by liver disease. Homicides were the least common cause of death (less than 2 percent).[4]

Other statistics were interesting and relevant to this discussion. Prison inmates age fifty-five or older accounted for 41 percent of prison deaths, but comprised only 5 percent of the total prison population for the nine-year period. Also, while Caucasians represent only 37 percent of the total prison population, 50 percent of the deaths came from this group. The mortality rates for white inmates were 1.4 to 1.8 times higher than other racial or ethnic groups.[5]

I was surprised to learn how many deaths there are yearly within the institutions where I worked. Men are continually moved between facilities, and it is easy to lose track of them. Friendships generally are not lasting and are dependent on current regulations. Men often are not allowed to write to one another between institutions or even to stay in touch once they are released. So when someone is removed from the yard and later dies, it takes a while for the news to drift back. Administration prefers to keep deaths quiet if they happen at their facility, as such occurrences are fraught with questions, concerns, and false information. Of course, if there is a murder or stabbing, that's a whole other story and it becomes the topic of much troubled conversation.

Several of the men in this study were involved in the formation of an institutional hospice program at the nursing facility. Started by a forward-thinking administration, the program trained inmates to be hospice volunteers at the prison. The chosen men were assigned to appropriate patients and were allowed special privileges to visit with the dying inmates daily, and to remain all night with them as they died. They became a family surrogate, bringing comfort during a frightening and lonely time.

The procedures surrounding the death of inmates differ around the country. In Kentucky, only a physician (not a nurse) can verify a death, so deceased inmates remain shackled until a physician signs off on their demise. Bodies are released to families for private interment if the family has the funds to cover the expenses of transportation and burial. Attempts are made to locate relatives, although many of the men no longer have anyone on the outside to contact. Unclaimed bodies are buried on prison grounds. The practice differs all over the country, but sometimes there is a central state prison cemetery where most unclaimed bodies are sent for burial. In some cases, interested family members are allowed to attend the chaplain-led funeral; in other places, they must visit at the funeral home.

Of the men in my study who will talk about such things, they desperately want to be buried outside the prison grounds. Only one man seems to be content at being interred at Chicken Hill, a neatly kept prison cemetery on a green knoll overlooking acres of state land.

There is a widely circulated story about one incident involving the burial of an inmate. I heard it repeated so often that I'm not sure it's not a prison legend, but I first heard it from an administrator who claims he was there. An inmate died. The family decided to leave him at the institution but asked to attend the graveside ceremony. They stood respectfully through the Bible reading, the chaplain's comments, and prayer. At the end of the service, the wife politely asked if she could be allowed to see her husband one more time and the casket was opened for her.

She quietly took a long last look, turned and said, "Thank you. I just wanted to make sure the son of a bitch was dead!"

There are recent, more easily proven examples of the pain some of these men have caused. A few months ago, a mother and daughter visited the funeral home where the men are embalmed. They arranged the visit in order to gain closure from years of abuse, meeting the prison chaplain there for a conversation.

But every story is complex. Every life started with innocence. It is in the lonely cemetery that the troubling questions unfolded for me. I wrote the following account after attending a funeral service at Chicken Hill.

Chicken Hill

The uneven staccato of gunfire from the prison firing range echoed continually across the freshly mown fields. The sounds blew over the cattle grazing on the rolling green pastures and settled as a discordant musical backdrop to the funeral in progress at Chicken Hill.

In the far distance, we could see the soaring tower of the reformatory and the lower buildings of other correctional facilities on the vast state-owned property. The view took in miles of rolled razor wire enclosing thousands of living men within their confines.

The chaplain stood beneath a small wooden pavilion situated in the middle of the prison cemetery.

"Listen," he said. "Listen to the sounds of the world." He was quiet before speaking again. "We hear cicadas, birds, gunshots. Life is around us until death."

In the distance, the correctional officers continued honing their aim on the practice range in case a living charge tried to flee.

On that day, one man had escaped the life that confined him.

"Death is a time we look beyond the grave for help," the chaplain intoned.

The prison chaplain, wearing his liturgical collar and incongruous gold correctional badge was burying the most recently unclaimed inmate who had died in the state. He was accompanied by the funeral director who oversaw the embalming of the wizened body. Spectators were three minimum-security inmates in bright orange jumpsuits who earlier dug the grave, and who would soon lower the deceased with a backhoe into his final resting place. The parting comments were directed to the inmates who had the most to learn from this death. There were no family members allowed, nor any who wanted to be there.

The service continued.

Jerry Lakes was born January 16, 1949, in Lexington, Kentucky.[6] He was abandoned as a child and said he had no memory of any family. He said he raised himself. He declared he had never attended school for a day in his life. He spent some time in Texas where he worked with steel in a metal plating company. He was injured there.

Mr. Lakes had no criminal record of felonies until he was arrested in 2013 when his adult disabled son starved to death. With him were found three other disabled adult children between the ages of eighteen and twenty-four. One son weighed only sixty-six pounds; the other weighed ninety-two. Only the disabled daughter was not severely malnourished. The only food in the motel room where they lived was a baby bottle with curdled chocolate milk and a package of hot dogs and lunchmeat. The young men wore adult diapers and could only stand by holding onto the wall. It is said Mr. Lakes had gambled and drunk his way through the children's Social Security checks for years.

"Stop the breeding," mumbled the funeral director.

The chaplain continued. "Mr. Lakes lived with the children's mother for thirty years. They never married. She is now incarcerated."

"I struggle with this," the chaplain explained. "How can this happen in today's society? I prayed a lot for the children who are now in adult protection. I always take comfort in the verse which says vengeance is mine sayeth the Lord. But I also have hope. I hope for everyone. I hope and pray that Mr. Lake is at peace. I don't know. I hope for us all. I look for the meaning."

The short service was concluded with Christian Bible verses and a prayer. The cheap wooden casket, covered with flocked baby-blue fabric, was hefted onto the back of a pickup truck and driven several yards to the hole that would be Mr. Lakes's final resting place. While the inmates assigned to the funeral detail nailed together the requisite plywood vault that would hold the casket, the chaplain and I wandered among the small stones that marked the graves of two hundred mostly forgotten souls who died within prison walls.

Each grave was topped by a tiny one-foot-square poured concrete block—no fancy polished stones here. An attached metal plate listed the deceased's name, inmate number, and the dates of birth and death. There was no escaping the labels of their confinement, even in death.

We wandered on the freshly mown grass, wiping aside the drying green blades covering the small labels. I wondered at the stories that lay beneath each marker in the bucolic cemetery. The earliest stone was dated 1937. We found a marker—Infant J. Nichols—from the years new infants stayed with their mothers in prison. There was an A. Ratterson, born 1856, died 1942. He lived through world-changing decades. How did those years touch him? What was his life like when he died in prison at age eighty-six, forgotten and unclaimed?

The sameness of the stones, the straight lines of the graves, the lay of the land, the litany of unknown names, took my mind to our national cemetery at Arlington. The comparison gave me pause. The shots from the practice range boomed as a parting salute.

My mind turned again to Mr. Lakes and it remained there, fixated. I did a genealogy search when I returned home. His was an illegitimate birth at the time young women were shuffled off to maternity homes, their children destined for adoption or children's institutions. His mother later had a long marriage, died at an old age, and is buried with her husband beneath a fine cut-marble headstone. Family group sheets note there were no children. Did she think in quiet moments about the son she had had in secret?

I wondered, did anything good or gentle happen in the life of this man? Did he do any acts of kindness, or is his a legacy only of pain? Did the woman who lived with him thirty years and birthed four children with him care about him, or did she stay with him out of desperation? What does it mean to all of us when someone dies, and no one cares, and all the legacy that can be told at his funeral are the sins of his life?

All that I could learn of Mr. Lakes, other than his ugly deeds, was that he was intellectually slow, but he knew enough to tell a fellow inmate that he was eager to die.

Issues to Think About

1. What level of health and dental care do you think should be provided to inmates?
2. What is your reaction to the incarceration of the intellectually challenged and the mentally ill—most of whom reside within the regular state correctional institutions?
3. Do you believe that there is a dissonance between those who push for life sentences and those who resent tax money being spent on the care of inmates, especially for the older, sicker ones whose health care costs are higher? Should the potential long-term costs be considered in the sentencing of individuals?
4. Did you have any emotional or intellectual responses to the piece about the burial at Chicken Hill?

THIRTEEN

The Patterns of Change

*Results of the Study
and Suggestions for Improvement*

The seventeen men featured in this book have spent decades separated from society and locked behind prison walls. As I have conversed with them and compared them with their peers released earlier, I've contemplated the factors that have kept them imprisoned so long and thought about the changes I have seen in them over the years. Two main observations rise to the top.

First, I realize there are few basic differences in the initial stories between the fifteen inmates in the recent study and others from the original group who had similar charges, but who have been released. Many of their crime stories were alike—some of those now freed had offenses that were worse, more horrendous, than those who have remained incarcerated. Men from both groups took lives. Some who did not kill served longer times than those who did.

Much of their fate depended on the arresting officers, the attorneys, their socioeconomic levels, where they were tried, and whether they went to trial or plea-bargained. Other factors influencing the length of their incarceration were juries, judges, the persistence of their victims, the public's attention to the crime, and who heard their pleas for parole.

The inequality and subjective nature of the justice system at all levels is troubling. It is a hard system to correct. We need to examine it more closely and discuss it in public dialogue.

The second observation involves the patterns of personal changes within the still- imprisoned individuals. Identifying those patterns gives insight as to where the problems and strengths lie within the correctional processes that add to the men's ultimate failures or successes. It gives us some ideas that could improve the chances of all.

Most of the men profiled in this book began their crimes in the same way. They were angry men—often youths—troubled by personal or family

176

trials. They were fogged by drugs and alcohol. Their crimes were an extension of their personal desperation or greed. A number of them mentioned that their lifestyles would have killed them by now if they hadn't been arrested. Most had trouble settling in to prison life, fighting back at the system that had labeled, humiliated, and shackled them.

Today there are large differences in the seventeen men, most of whom are now middle-aged or older. Some of those incarcerated for decades have mellowed, reaching deep within themselves to become the men they want to be regardless of their surroundings. Others have sunk into their anger; it eats away at them, devouring them until they cannot find their way back. Each group seems aware of what has happened to them, but the men in the most damaged group seem unable to rescue themselves, and some have little desire to do so.

It is crucial to look at the cumulative effects of long-term incarceration and see what ruins some and saves others. I have identified eight factors that deserve contemplation as we discuss ways to encourage positive change among the incarcerated.

1. The Lasting Effects of Socioeconomic Levels

Observation: The lower a prisoner's initial socioeconomic level, the harder it is for him to find the needed internal and external resources for positive change.

This observation is more an indictment of our society than it is our penal system. Inmates from lower socioeconomic levels are overrepresented in prisons. Too many of the inmates were raised by poor, struggling single parents or were shuffled between foster homes and institutions. If they had a man in their childhood, in too many cases, he was someone to fear, someone who drank too much, someone who struck out at others when angry. Few men who grew up with a shortage of necessary resources remember much good in their childhoods. They don't have role models of hardworking men who met their responsibilities of family and married life in appropriate ways.

Life to these men has always been dark and painful, with pleasures fleeting and often found only when high from alcohol or drugs. For many, prison is an extension of the only type of life they have lived. They expect little from the bleakness they see as normal. In turn, they expect little from themselves. These men silently wish things were different, but they have no reason to expect more and even less of an idea how to get there.

On the other hand, men whose lives were broader bring more to the rehabilitative table. They have seen people treat one another with care and have learned by watching others around them that it is possible to achieve, improve, and overcome difficulties. They see the world differently. Even if the people in their direct lives were significantly flawed, as children they were surrounded by individuals who had better, calmer lives. They arrived in prison with serious personal problems, but they also had role models and experiences that later could serve as guideposts to change. Those are the men who report having an epiphany—often years into their incarceration— a realization that they want to be better men regardless of where they are living.

Almost all of the men struggle to find a personal set of values and self-identity. But their past, too often defined by their socioeconomic status, seems to influence the level of internal peace that they can find. This observation, of course, is not without exceptions. But all the men who have found direction in their lives can point to a person or an influence who took them outside of themselves and inspired them to find their better selves. Men have to see a better life before they know to strive for it.

Educational programs hold an important key to a man's understanding of himself and his future direction. Vocational programs, which must not be underestimated, are vital for a man's future employment should he be released. But it is the general education that opens up new avenues of thought and contemplation that will change a man. Inmates need to be taught critical thinking skills, regardless of their academic levels. School has been a place where many of them have been unsuccessful in the past, both socially and academically. A new approach to prison education needs to be tried.

Men are bored in prison and often look for variety to break the sameness of their days. If a wide range of short, intriguing continuing education classes could be offered (taught by skilled, outside instructors), men might be led toward meaningful discussions and activities that could impact their lives. Short-term classes do not always have to be life skills classes to contribute to change.

Summary solutions: Opportunities to learn and grow should be available from the moment a man enters prison. Meaningful lessons and goals in life need to be introduced to those who have missed them because of past deprivations. With creative methods, men can be enticed into useful, personally expanding activities. Not all programming has to be seen as "life skills" or steps leading to parole. Men should have chances to expand their personal talents in art, music, crafts, or sports. It is not pampering inmates to offer them some pleasurable times. It is letting them explore their strengths as individuals. In the process, inmates may develop socially acceptable attitudes that will help them in their future lives, whether in the free community or prison community.

2. Emotional and Personal Isolation from Society

Observation: The more emotionally isolated from society and acquaintances over time, the more difficult the prisoners' psychological and personal adjustments become.

I contend that the same community that isolated the men out of necessity holds the key to their salvation. The longer a man is locked up, the more he is separated from the society he needs to learn to live in. The longer he is incarcerated, the more ingrained prison values and mores become. As each year separates him from everyone and everything he cared about, the more he turns inward. He begins to internalize the negative messages about his worth that surround him each day, and he grows even angrier or is beaten down into neuroses or insanity.

There are effective programs scattered around the country that are designed to keep men in touch with their families. But they are only helpful if the husband or father has a short sentence and is housed within easy visiting distance. Continued years of absence extract a huge toll on relationships. If prison inevitably tears families apart and, by its nature, discourages continuing relationships, then those connections need to be replaced by other positive community interactions.

Not one of the men in my study was able to retain a relationship with his original wife or significant other over the years.[1] As years went by, the stresses on both sides became too overwhelming. Letters stopped, phone calls were refused, divorces happened. After ten years or a crucial setback, many of the men were truly alone. A large number admitted that I was the first person who had written or visited them in years. After twenty years, the men don't even mention the past relationships that used to come up frequently in conversation. They try not to think about the children they didn't see grow up, but they follow their progress at a distance if they can get information. The group of lonely men with no outside contacts are the ones who struggle the most and who buy into the prison mentality.

Clearly, all the men in this book have their private, ongoing struggles no matter how well they seem to be doing. But those who have continued to identify with people on the outside have benefited significantly from the contact. Wayne, Doug, and Cam have parents and siblings who have sacrificed much to visit regularly. The contact with their nuclear families brings inmates additional pain as they realize, with each visit and call, the burdens they have laid upon the shoulders of their loved ones. But the personal connections force the men outside themselves. The connections teach them empathy and help them learn to work through inevitable interpersonal difficulties. They teach the men to give of themselves.

Some of the men who are long separated from their families and friends have found substitutes that often serve the same rehabilitative purposes as the extended family. The correctional system would be wise to find appropriate avenues to encourage meaningful relationships and outlets for the incarcerated. Many men have benefited greatly from programs brought into the prison. The people from the larger community help the men stay connected to a more normal society.

All of the men in this study were initially involved in the prison college program. Professors from the community came into the facility each week to teach in their areas of expertise. This "normal" interaction and new knowledge of the world literally changed lives. A number of nationwide studies concluded that one of the most effective treatment programs in prisons is college classes, yet federal Pell Grant funds and most state funding were withdrawn years ago.[2] Some schools and states have found ways to continue this programming.

With post-secondary education, it is not the academic degree itself that is of the greatest value to the inmate. It is the increased awareness of the world within which we live and the interactions with people from outside prison. In the process of education, the men find hidden talents within themselves and a new sense of self-respect.

Other programs throughout the U.S. prison system, run by people from the community, are highly successful. Shakespeare Behind Bars helps men act out and face their crimes and human foibles through the works of Shakespeare. The men delve together into emotional depths, and support and care for one another as brothers. The recidivism rate for released inmates who participated in Shakespeare Behind Bars is near zero.

Many prisons have writing or drama groups sponsored by outside individuals or organizations. Author Wally Lamb brought fame to the women at York Correctional Institution with two best-selling books co-authored by the women.[3] The Alliance for Change program at San Quentin in California, recounted in Nancy Mullane's *Life After Murder*, is another successful effort sponsored by an outside group.[4]

The chapel programs discussed earlier also offer valuable outside contacts. It is true that a lot of chapel attendance is motivated by the desire to interact with people from the community, and there is criticism about that. But within reason, that motivation is not a bad thing. The men are hungry to talk to people from the outside, to interact with them in ways that are seldom found in the dormitories. The chapel allows personal conversations and discussions of emotions. It is one of the few places the men can talk with women, even though the subjects of discussion are limited. They practice polite and socially accepted behavior in these mixed settings. In turn, the inmates are treated with sincere respect.

Correctional officials would do well to find acceptable ways to incorporate community resources within their treatment framework. Even athletic competitions with visiting groups are valuable. It takes progressive administrators to do this, but the results are positive for both the free and incarcerated communities.

When stereotypes are broken down, when inmates are able to see themselves or their talents valued by people in the free community, when they feel a part of the larger society, everyone wins. That's not to say problems don't arise, but the extra supervision and occasional issues are well worth the trouble. The administrative support of these programs waxes and wanes as wardens come and go, much to the frustration and detriment of everyone.

Summary solutions: Programs and activities sponsored by approved and respected outside groups and individuals should be encouraged to come into the prisons. The inmates benefit in life-changing ways from this interaction. Additionally, community groups and individuals learn more about incarceration and become advocates for more funding of education and other rehabilitative measures.

3. The Crucial Need for Mental Health Care

Observation: Men generally do not enter prison if their lives and emotional states are in good order. They often bring with them a history of abuse, confused emotions, and dysfunctional relationships. Those personal problems need to be addressed if the men are to become whole, healthy individuals ready to reenter society.

Almost all of the men in this group have shared troubling personal issues that brought them to this point, and many are still struggling to deal with them. A number in the group are taking psychotropic medications for depression and anxiety. The medicine helps them function in the stressful prison environment but does little to move them forward to better futures.

It is in the area of mental health that the difference is the starkest between the group that has found positive direction for their lives within prison and those who have deteriorated as a result of their long stay.

The men who have changed and improved have mostly done it by looking carefully inward and, through a variety of other programs, basically treated themselves through introspection.

Those who have struggled most have more stories of serious childhood abuse and problems. Most have not received needed mental health care while incarcerated in order to come to grips with the damage their early lives caused on their psyches. They fully accept the responsibility of their crimes and behaviors, but they don't seem to have the same personal insights into their antisocial actions as the others.

Those men have deteriorated emotionally over the years. Their negative reactions vary but generally are not healthy. Some have become more enraged, more socially withdrawn, and probably more dangerous. Other men are more neurotic for lack of a better description. They have turned their focus inward, are increasingly suspicious, and have lost their earlier ability to appropriately interact with others. One man, a seemingly normal individual years ago, is now described by a fellow inmate as "crazier than a fruit bat." Several are so shut down emotionally that it is frightening to think what is buried inside, unknown even to them. A few are still on the cusp, fighting to decide what kind of men they will become but finding it hard to locate the needed internal guidance.

The male-dominated environment creates a barrier to building up needed mental health care programs within prison. The administrators usually acknowledge the need to provide help for the severely disturbed, but generally see little need for basic insightful counseling. With a more-than-average masculine, military-minded bent, many wardens mirror our society in thinking that men should learn to tough things out emotionally, that counseling and feelings are more in the feminine realm. As a result, personal insight and counseling are not priorities, and the mental health of the inmates suffers as a result.

It is doubtful that psychological care will ever be the level or quality that is needed within the prison setting. There are too many needs and too little money. Also, therapists themselves have a hard time dealing with the realities of long-term incarceration. There are several examples in our group of men who were encouraged by their therapists about their future releases, which the men grabbed onto as truth from an expert. The reality is, no one knows, and the therapists—often young and relatively naïve to prison life—must learn to deal with a situation new to them. Hope for a free life cannot be the centerpiece of the therapy.

Summary solutions: Mental health care and education are the two areas needing the largest increase in funding, I believe. If prison is to be rehabilitative, then men must understand what internal forces led them to this point. Their dark urges and doubts should be not buried and ignored. Men are reluctant to talk about childhood or adult abuse and do not seek out help. Skilled proactive, private counseling is the best avenue to effectively deal with those issues. In an ideal situation, every man placed in segregation should be visited by a counselor and options for treatment presented to him. Psychological counseling should be available at any point during a man's incarceration and not only during times of crisis.

4. The Importance of a Religious or Spiritual Foundation

Observation: Sincere religious or spiritual practices offer a stability, hope, and calmness that is not seen among those who do not engage in those activities. Spirituality seems to give the men an expanded view of their self-worth, and gives them tools to deal with the constant tensions and hot anger that eat at most prisoners.

The difference between religion and spirituality can be debated, but those men who have a grounding in one or both seem to do better. That does not mean that they necessarily carry the strictures of the teachings into their everyday lives on the yard. But those who at least work at finding inner peace, forgiveness, and patience adjust better than those who outright reject the possibility of a higher being or force larger than themselves.

The power and reality of religion can be debated, but having a sense of care and hope in a harsh and hostile environment is clearly a positive value among those I label as successful in their prison adjustments.

Religion and other spiritual practices help the men accept their current situation and encourage them to look for meaning in their lives. The Serenity Prayer does not apply only to alcohol or drug treatment programs. It is used in other prison settings, as well. The words—"God, grant me the serenity to accept the things I cannot change, the courage to change the things I can, and the wisdom to know the difference"—give the men needed directions for living in a situation where control is a central issue.[5]

Regardless of who or what they look to as a higher being, acceptance and serenity are the key traits that inmates need most to survive and thrive. Attention to spiritual matters leads the men in that direction.

Summary solutions: Prison administrators would be wise to allow a wide variety of programs into the institutions that would entice the men to approach their lives from a more spiritual perspective. Evangelical Christianity is the religion most practiced in prison, but it also brings some heavy baggage with it. Only a third of the men in prison attend chapel programs. There need to be additional avenues of programs or experiences with peace and serenity as a central focus. Yoga and meditation classes draw some in. One group established a spiritual labyrinth and provided classes on how to make use of it.

Obviously, such activities are not for everyone in a prison environment, but a warden with a streak of creativity and imagination could find a variety of ways to help men look inwardly. A place for solitary contemplation and quiet is needed—the walking track often seems to serve that function, according to the men in this study. Sometimes spiritual programs without a strong religious component are rejected by evangelical chaplains, but there should be room for any program that leads to self-contemplation and self-control. Related programs might be placed under recreation and thus attract more men to them.

5. The Redeeming Value of Work

Observation: There is a redeeming quality in regular, meaningful work and in the ability to be responsible for one's personal necessities.

Without exception, each of the men who are finding their way in a positive frame of mind have responsible, respected positions within their institutions. They work as legal aides, as clerks in the school, or have skilled jobs within prison industries. They stand in stark comparison to the others who are still mopping floors as janitors or doing other less fulfilling jobs that only take an hour or two a day.

Work is a universal activity. In working, individuals find a sense of responsibility and respect. Through working, people see how they fit into the larger picture of society. Their attendance and activities in the workplace affect their fellow workers as well as the people receiving their services. The intrinsic value of work can be realized behind bars as well as in free society.

A strong work ethic is something to be learned. The self-discipline of getting up and to a job on time each day is a practice to be learned. Responsibilities to others are learned. Plugging on regardless of how one feels is learned. These lessons, including the development of self-worth, normally are incorporated at an early age. They are lessons that are missed in many homes where children are raising themselves, where school attendance is erratic, and responsibilities to others is missing.

With all the lessons that work holds, it should be seen by prison officials as a major rehabilitative tool. But, like other programs, it is not successful if it is forced on inmates. Just like on the street, there have to be incentives to work. To maximize the benefits, the work needs to be meaningful.

In prison, that is easier said than done. Most of our prisons are operating far above the capacity for which they were originally built. Today there are twice as many men to mop the same floor or paint the same walls. Without increasing the jobs available, there is not enough work to go around.

There are plenty of tasks to be done within a complex institution that can be done with inmate labor. The men with their many talents are capable of handling just about anything that needs to be done within a facility. But they have to be carefully supervised. For example, there is much need for skilled labor in maintenance, but there is also much room there for serious mischief. Many knowledgeable, trustworthy supervisors are needed, and they come with a significant price.

There are positive examples where prisons have increased available work opportunities to the benefit of all. They have filled crucial needs within the institution while bringing valuable meaning to the inmate workers. An in-house emergency medical technicians unit, staffed by professionally trained inmates, handles medical emergencies in one facility. Another group is involved with suicide prevention activities in units housing the more troubled inmates. Many prisons have inmate-produced newspapers, cable channels, etc. Granted, the administration is often hog-tied by impossibly tight budgets. But it is important to provide creative work opportunities that help the institution while serving as an incentive and a treatment opportunity.

Most states have some version of Prison Industries (PI), where inmates work as contracted labor in such areas as data processing, printing, furniture making, and license plate production. This often causes big blowback from free enterprise and even the public. Business owners argue that PI is able to pay the inmates far less than labor on the street, thus giving PI an unfair advantage in the marketplace. This objection is addressed in some states by letting PI provide services only to nonprofits or governmental agencies.

The public does not understand the workplace process and is suspicious when they find prisoners are involved in the product or service they receive. People object if they find a call center is staffed by inmates or that a data processing center is located within prison walls. The public has little understanding about how security works and doesn't care to find out, no matter how efficient or how well supervised the inmates are.

Inmate workers in PI make more (ninety-five cents to two dollars an hour) than they make at other prison jobs. In contrast, state pay for a dorm janitor could be as little as seventy cents a day or twenty dollars a month.

Some states don't pay for any inmate jobs. The main incentive to work in those states is to beat the boredom of daily prison life. There are other reasons to work, of course—for example, larger food portions for people who work in the kitchen or access to a word processor for those with clerical positions. The non-paying states may be saving inmate wages, but they are paying higher costs in terms of illegal behavior. With no source of income, prisoners without money from their families are strongly tempted to resort to illegal activities as a way to raise needed funds. Even when they don't have an income, inmates in most states are still charged for items such as doctor's visits, medication, stamps, and hygiene. Their debts to the state pile up.

David served time in a state where they do not pay inmates for work. With no resources, he spent fifteen years as an indigent prisoner, breaking rules and constantly plotting how to get a radio, a watch, and batteries for both, as well as getting an occasional snack from the canteen. The lack of any income led him deeper into prison mores and away from the attitudes he would need when he became a free man. He recently left the system with a $732 debt on his back and not a penny in his pocket. While he had an opportunity to work off that debt in a transitional center, paying off the debt took away money he needed to get a new start.

Provided they could generate enough working positions for everyone, prisons could add incentives to work without significantly raising the pay.

By throwing in benefits for the workers such as preferred dormitory housing with more allowed activities and amenities, men could see the advantage of working a full day's job. A number of facilities are already doing this with good success.

Incentives could also be activated by further limiting the amount of funds allowed into the institutions by concerned families. Some men have a thousand dollars on their books with little need to do anything constructive with their days. That plan would never work, though, as the canteen where inmates spend their money generates millions of dollars for Corrections each year. The canteen money mostly comes from the inmates' families—many of them struggling themselves to make ends meet—who send money each month to their loved ones. In many states, the profits from the canteen go back to fund inmate programs. In other places, it goes into state or Corrections coffers.

Summary solutions: Meaningful work should be considered a major treatment tool. Prisons must be innovative in their attempts to make more jobs available to the inmates and to entice the inmates to hold those positions. There are a number of incentives that could be built into the work program that wouldn't break the bank, but which would pull, rather than push, the men into seeking prison employment.

6. The Need to Contribute and Reach Outward

Observation: The men who do the best are the ones who understand their ultimate moral responsibilities to the larger society. They are able to think beyond themselves and find personal redemption in meaningful giving to others.

Frequently, heartfelt conversations with inmates are laced with sadness and frustration about their inability to give back to society. The men want a chance to compensate for some of the damage they have done. They are frustrated that they are not allowed to donate blood or plasma. During community crises, those "behind the fence" in medium or maximum custody are not allowed out to help with the many physical needs that are spoken of on TV. They have limited ways to help or participate in activities that are needed by the community. I've seen them rise to the occasion and thrive when given a chance.

At Christmastime, inmate clubs raise money from the prison community, and large donations are made to buy toys for needy children. Inmates always have a soft spot for children.

Over the years, many service/learning projects were brought into the institutions, proving they can be successful. Thrilled with the opportunity, the men flocked to the activities and gained much, as did the recipients and community helpers. Blessed with cooperative wardens and vocational teachers who allowed their workplaces to be open on the weekends, outside groups worked side-by-side with the inmates, making wooden toys and games for needy children. The men prepared the basic forms before our arrival with scraps of wood, and together we talked, sanded, and painted. The men and vocational teachers got caught up in the activities and continued to produce items through the years to be sold in local charity silent auctions. They upholstered chairs, built children's furniture, and eagerly read brochures about the organizations and services they were helping. One man who had built an intricate dollhouse as part of his carpentry class, quietly retrieved it and put it in a volunteer's hand, asking that he find a needy child to play with it.

I brought college students from the community into the prison to meet with their counterparts to talk about social problems. We brought other groups to talk with the men about literature, and the discussions morphed into meaningful conversations about crime and punishment, helping everyone by expanding their understanding. Another person sponsored a prison art show in the community. The inmates reveled in the publicity, feeling their sense of self-worth.

For ten years, a local church sponsored Aunt Mary's Book Project, which is found in prisons around the United States. A group of women brought in boxes of children's books. The men came, picked out a book for each of their children, and spent a week practicing reading it aloud with expression.

"I am so tired of hearing those damned animal voices," one inmate humorously groused about his cellmate.

The next week, the women returned with tape recorders, and the men recorded the books. The books and tapes were sent to their children. The private tears that were shed during those times were heartbreaking to see, but the gratitude that the men had to be able to be involved in some way in their children's lives was palpable.

Even more valuable to the larger community is the rise of dog programs where inmates help train service dogs; braille programs where inmates translate books into braille for the blind community; and the rehabilitation of horses which occurs in prisons around the United States. Animals have much to teach lonely, hurting people. And the men have much to give.

Participation in those programs is considered an honor, and the inmates are crucially aware of the ways in which they are able to contribute. The programs give them a connection to the outside world, and the community facilitators offer another bridge to a meaningful life.

Methods by which the inmates can be made to feel useful and involved in the larger society, as well as in their own prison communities, are only limited by the willingness of administrators who have to make it happen and motivated people in the community to help get it started.

The move toward restorative justice programs also holds promise to bring the community and the prisoners together. Guided by trained workers, the victims and the inmates begin a conversation that leads towards positive actions on the part of the prisoners to give back to their victims and communities in a variety of innovative ways.[6]

In the cases I have recounted from personal experiences, there were many unexpected consequences. The more the church group (which was not involved in the chapel program at the time) came into the institution, the deeper they became involved in justice issues. They eventually established a successful reentry program for inmates leaving the prison. And from there, the involvement in criminal justice issues branched off into a number of areas.

Summary solutions: Helping men feel an empathy and responsibility to others should be a major rehabilitative goal of prisons. While it takes a good deal of innovation and creativity to establish the opportunities, there are innumerable ways that men physically separated from the community can still contribute to it. Prisons are full of bright, talented men who have much to give. If the proposed projects are presented correctly to the inmates, and the ways they will benefit others in need are clear, many will become eager participants.

7. Vision of the Future vs. Lack of Hope

Observation: When there is a total lack of hope, there are no incentives to lead to a better man or improved situation. It is the people without hope, those who are unable to see anything positive in their futures, who are the most dangerous in a correctional facility. They have very little to lose.

When an eighteen-year-old boy/man is told that he will spend the next eighty-five years in prison, even if he knows he will eventually be eligible to be considered for parole, he can't wrap his mind around the concept. If he gets a life sentence, even with the possibility of parole after twenty years, he feels his life is over.

If a man has young children he loves, he realizes they will be grown before he can be part of their lives again. He knows in spite of what he's told, that his wife or girlfriend cannot wait that long. He knows if he cares for them, he must let them move forward with their lives.

The increasingly long sentences being handed out these days breed hopelessness and desperation. If there is no hope, then there is no incentive to change one's situation.

Men with sentences of life without parole can be placed in tight, maximum-security settings or, in extreme cases, put in super-max institutions. There they can be housed securely underground where they will never see daylight again, but we can be certain they will become enraged or crazed. That may please the public, but it is not a situation we should strive to create.

Today throughout the country, there is an increasing number of men incarcerated with life-without-parole sentences. Three of the men in our group now fall in that category, having been served-out on their life sentences. A number more privately worry that they, too, are never going to see the outside world again. Hope grows dimmer each time they see the parole board.

Over a third of the men in our group have escaped from custody at least once during their long periods of incarceration. To those looking at the tight security in the institutions, it seems impossible to figure out how they got loose, but they were willing to take any chance they could find. With the exception of David, most are reluctant to talk about their run and the reasons for it. Today, it makes no more sense to them than it did for others at the time. Now they see those futile actions as embarrassing. They know they lengthened their prison stay by their attempts, but at the time, it seemed the only logical way to see a future. They had no hope, so they tried to find some.

Every warden and administrator I talked with mentioned their opposition to sentences that have no end.

"How do they expect us to have control if the man has nothing to lose?" asked one.

A number of our men mentioned they had attempted suicide. Others admitted they didn't have the nerve to do it themselves, but given the chance, they'd entice the police to shoot them.

However, the power of human determination continues to surprise me. Of the three men who have been told they will never be released, two of them still cling to some hope. Al says he still hopes that something will come up someday to change things. But if he has to serve another ten years, he wouldn't want out, because he'd not be able to care for himself. Stuart patiently waits for the Rapture or his progressing illness to release him. Lee, the third man, will not talk about it.

There is an interesting approach in a few institutions to long-sentenced offenders. There, a separate dorm area has been set up for the long-term residents, featuring some additional amenities and small but single-person rooms. Considered one of the most desirable honor dorms, it allows the long-time inmates some pleasantries that give them something to look forward to and an incentive to cut out dramatic behaviors. Working towards the better housing gives the long-term inmates the hope, however limited, to see that good behavior will pay off in the long run. The differences from regular honor dorms is subtle, but the extended-stay dorms allow the inmates who have settled in to the reality of their lives a setting that is more conducive to mental and behavioral health.

Summary solutions: The answer for the problems generated by those without hope does not lie primarily with the institutions that are required to hold volatile situations together. The best solutions lie with the courts who inexplicably increase sentencing lengths each year. They lie with the parole boards who increasingly refuse paroles. And they lie with the governors and legislators who allow, and even encourage, questionable processes to evolve within the prisons and the parole process. Those leaders need to develop an increased understanding of the correctional procedures that fall under their influence.

But the public holds the main key for solving the problems generated by hopelessness. For their own sakes, if nothing else, the public should become more aware of the intricacies of the criminal justice system. They should understand the processes of charging, sentencing, incarcerating. They should understand what prisons are like. They should insist their taxpayer money is spent to maximize the chances of rehabilitation. Those steps would be a much cheaper solution than incarcerating so many people for their entire lives.

8. The Correctional Motto: Fair, Firm, Consistent

Observation: If the justice system would actually practice its credo of "fair, firm, consistent," we would have a system that maximizes the safety of the public while helping men face the realities of their lives and strive to do better the next time around.

Being fair: The men in prison have broken laws established by our society. They were not fair to others when they stole, lied, or hurt. But they will not learn proper behavior unless they are treated the way we want them to act. In spite of the negative stereotype of grousing inmates refusing to take blame for things they have done, I did not find that true among the men I came to know. But they do burn with deep anger over unfair situations. Fairness is part of the old convict code and it is valued for a reason.

With one exception, every man in this study took ownership of his major crime. However, most of them have additional charges that they claimed they didn't do, and their resentment spills over. Many of the homicides were accompanied with a robbery charge that the men claim they are innocent of, but for which they may be serving up to twenty-five additional years. It seems to be a common practice in homicides, depending on the current state laws, to tack on an additional charge in order to make the case eligible to be considered for the death penalty.

Other men have charges stacked one on top of another, making it obvious that the police and prosecutors were trying to wring every last penalty out of the case. Doing time for something they know they did not do, or the creative building up of their charges, makes the men bitter and resentful and keeps them from focusing on the bare truth of their real crimes. If things were fair, they could more quickly come to the reality that no one is to blame for their situation other than themselves.

There is unfairness inherent in the whole justice system, from the arresting officers, to the availability and skill of attorneys, to the decision-making of the judge and jury, to the everyday operation of the correctional facility. The disparities between rural and urban courts are dramatic. The treatment of minorities, the poor, and other marginalized groups is strikingly different from the treatment afforded more privileged citizens. That is not to say that everyone is unfair, but justice is not always blind and scales are not always balanced.

Fairness is a troubling issue in free society, a popular expression being "life is not fair." But in prison situations, where there are so many forced inequalities between men and officers, and officers and administrators, trouble bubbles just below the surface. Calm prevails when rules reflect reasonable expectations and are applied equally and fairly.

Being firm: In dealing with a volatile, erratic population, steady firmness brings calm to troubled waters. If rules are fair and have a purpose, if they are carried out without malice, then the prison population knows what to expect. Firmness indicates steadiness. It does not mean ramping up the pressure on inmates. Firmness implies a lack of drama, of clear-cut and well-explained expectations.

Being consistent: Rules, procedures, and practices need to be the same throughout the correctional institutions. The inmates need to know what to expect. That does not mean that the officers walk the same route at the same time each day. It means that when they find infractions, the rules will apply the same to everyone, that the men can know what to expect from both good and bad behavior.

There obviously needs to be consistency among officers and their actions, but there should be more consistency between changing administrations. If one warden encourages contests for decorating cell doors during the holidays, and a year later, a new warden orders the institution stripped of any signs of Christmas decorations, there will be upheaval. If one warden spends his stay developing an educational-based program that permeates the whole institution and within months, the next warden dismisses the programs and incentives, there will be strong undercurrents.

Change and innovation are desirable and should not be considered as inconsistent. Consistency is born from a unified underlying philosophy of Corrections. Its practice rises from shared underpinnings held in place by responsible, professional leaders. Prisons do not have to be run identically to be consistent. Top administration in central offices should actively work to get everyone on the same philosophical page.

Summary solutions: Top correctional administrators need to know what is going on in the individual institutions, as well as among their own leadership. They need to carefully disseminate the appropriate and desired philosophies to their wardens and make sure the messages are passed onto staff. They need to insist that wardens spend time on the yard in their institutions and know firsthand what is going on. Tight administrative and staff friendship groups that impact job placements and performances need to be broken up. There cannot be consistency at any level if everyone—staff and inmates—is not treated equally in all situations.

Issues to Think About

1. Do you believe that the American prison system is more helpful or hurtful in changing people's long-term behaviors? In what ways?
2. The author identifies eight conditions that made a positive difference for the men in this long-term study. Which of those conditions seem the most important to you or surprised you?
3. The author contends that "the same community that isolated the men out of necessity holds the key to their salvation." How do you respond to that thought?

FOURTEEN

The Conversation Begins

Current Status
of Inmate Subjects

It's difficult to bring this story to a satisfactory end. The troubling problems within our society and the nation's criminal justice system cannot easily be fixed. The issues are too complex. There are too many players, social problems, personal agendas, and political involvements to find satisfactory resolutions. Money issues weave an insidious ribbon through any proposed solutions. Looking in depth at one area of crime and punishment only leads us to other caverns to explore.

But we cannot give up the conversation. We must peck away at social issues that lead people to crime and hurt. We must continue to examine our systems of justice and more clearly define what we want to accomplish when we lock people away. We need to make sure the financial hunger of the growing prison industrial complex does not devour good social policy and practices. We must learn to carefully consider the unintended consequences of our public demands for justice and punishment. We need to know what we are talking about and what we are asking for. We need to decide if we care at all.

The development of personal views and future conversations are the responsibility of individuals in our society. The questions to discuss and contemplate are endless. They involve politics, religion, social policy, and finances. No questions are easy. But the conversations need to occur.

This book was conceived to look at the effects of long-term imprisonment and to help the reader understand what being in prison is really like. It is appropriate to give the last words to the inmates who contributed to this effort and who have spent so much of their lives locked behind prison gates. They know well what those years have meant.

David

I've thrown away the biggest part of my life for nothing. I think about how *stupid* I've been. I'm a semi-intelligent man, and I've done some of the stupidest things. I realize some of the "why." It's impulse. I'm super impulsive. I think it, I do it. I'm not near as bad as I was, but I see that as the problem. I think belligerence and rebelliousness toward authority pretty much done me in. There's no excuse for throwing away so much of my life, and I know that I am completely at fault. No one to blame but myself. I'm proud that I realize that, because half of these guys blame all their problems on other people and things.

David has been released after twenty-six straight years of incarceration. He spent a total of thirty-nine years locked up in his fifty-nine-year life. He is living on his own and was able to earn some start-up money while living in a community-custody situation. He says he is on pins and needles. He worries about his finances, the security of his job, and how to operate in a completely changed environment. He struggles to change his prison mentality. He trusts some people too much and has been burned by them, while he is overly suspicious of others. "I used to be good at reading people, but I'm not as good at it out here," he says.

Al

The worst thing about being in prison is doing wasted time and watching your life pass before you, knowing that what you lose you can never get back. The most difficult time for me is knowing that every day of my life I have to accept that I may never get out of prison. So I would say my most difficult time is every day of my life.

After serving more than forty years in prison and receiving parole deferments of eighty-four months, then sixty-eight months, Al was stunned when the next time in front of the board, he was given a serve-out on a life sentence. They have told him he will never be released, but he still hopes.

Mel

Prison strangles the life and hope out of long-term inmates. It feels that I have literally been locked up and the key has been thrown away. It seems that life outside moves faster and faster, while each additional year in prison gets slower and slower.

In order to have a meaningful life, inside or outside of prison, one needs to have a feeling of belonging, being needed, being wanted, being appreciated. The longer I'm locked up, the farther I feel from ever having any of those things.

I had the idea that things would get easier as my years added up in prison. That staying out of trouble meant something. That participating in programming meant something. Instead, if you're in khaki, you're depersonalized, dehumanized, mistrusted. I am herded like cattle. I am no longer an individual. I become increasingly invisible by the day. I've disappeared from society and now I'm disappearing in prison.

Mel had never been in trouble with the law until he was arrested for the impulsive murder of his wife some years before—a murder over which he has agonized. He now has been incarcerated twenty-one years. He was deferred three times and hoped he would be released during his most recent parole hearing. Instead, he got a ten-year deferment, raising his fears that he will never be released from his life sentence. He questions how he would support himself as a senior citizen if he is eventually released. A former minister of music, Mel is now fifty-nine years old. His daughter and other family members actively oppose his release.

Steve

As a young boy, I never received the proper moral and ethical guidance a youngster needs to develop a healthy character. In my prison environment, I have been blessed with other wonderful people in the mental health area of my treatment programs. They have also inspired me through their examples of morals, ethics, and humane but firm treatment to become a better man. This is another factor which leads me to cling to hope for parole and to have the chance to give back in some way to society and my family.... All I ever hoped for was a chance to show that I was willing to live a moral, crime-free life; go to the VA hospital where I would not have to beg for proper medical treatment; and attempt to make amends to my precious sons and their precious mother.

Steve has always had a difficult time in the prison environment because of his close identification with his sexual offender treatment therapists and the lessons of honesty taught in the treatment program. The programs teach the participants to call out one another if they slip in their actions. Because Steve struggles to stay faithful to the morals and mores of free society, he often feels it is his duty to report the misbehavior of staff and inmates alike. This has put him in physical danger at times and keeps him in emotional turmoil. He is sixty-nine years old and in ill health, with heart problems and other issues. Everyone—prisoners and staff alike—agree he would not offend again. He has been incarcerated thirty years and will soon come up for his sixth parole hearing. If he is never granted parole, he is scheduled to remain in prison until 2129.

Billy

I've been locked up longer than I was born a free man. The twenty-six years I've been incarcerated was a waste of life that God blessed me with. I could have done so much and been the man my parents raised me to be. I have changed as a person for the good. I am still ambitious and driven. And I do have goals and dreams for a brighter future for myself before I leave the face of this earth.

Billy recently saw the parole board again and received another setback. His string of robberies, all committed within a few months' time, involved a gun, but no serious injuries. He has an unusually long and puzzling rap sheet— he claims additional crimes that he didn't do were piled on his head in order to clear the police books. But regardless, he has served more years than many people who have taken lives. He blames the color of his skin for his excessive time served.

Doug

No one deserves to be measured only by the worst thing they have ever done. You want to know how I feel? Read Psalm 142.

> With my voice I cry out to the LORD;
> with my voice I plead for mercy to the LORD.
> 2 I pour out my complaint before him;
> I tell my trouble before him.
> 3 When my spirit faints within me,
> you know my way!
> In the path where I walk
> they have hidden a trap for me.
> 4 Look to the right and see:
> there is none who takes notice of me;
> no refuge remains to me;
> no one cares for my soul.
> 5 I cry to you, O LORD;
> I say, "You are my refuge,
> my portion in the land of the living."
> 6 Attend to my cry,
> for I am brought very low!
> Deliver me from my persecutors,
> for they are too strong for me!
> 7 Bring me out of prison,
> that I may give thanks to your name!
> The righteous will surround me,
> for you will deal bountifully with me.[1]

Because Doug killed a police officer in a drug deal gone bad, there is enormous pressure from the police community to keep him behind bars for every day possible. In spite of support for his release from virtually everyone within the prison community, people in the administration say that the anticipated publicity will cause him to serve every day of his sentence. With his perfect behavior record, he will be released in 2028 when he is sixty-four years old, having served forty-two years behind bars.

Bob

Initially, when I didn't get paroled, I was both angry and shocked each time. Then I went through a process of trying to discern what I did or didn't do or needed to do. My biggest question was why. Eventually, I came to two conclusions: (1) My escape certainly did not enhance my parole chances, and (2) There was something God wanted me to learn, some change I needed to make in my life. These conclusions, especially the second one, led towards acceptance.

After thirty years in prison, Bob served out his sentence in 2015. He has moved out of state with his longtime girlfriend who has offered him much stability and support. They have weathered the initial adjustment period and seem to be in a permanent relationship. Bob is working on a master's degree.

Cal [written in 1994]

We go through stages in here. For myself, the first three years, I constantly thought about the robbery I committed and how wrong it was. For the next two years, I thought about the justice system and how it worked on me as well as others. The past year, I have spent trying to not be bitter toward the system which landed me where I am now. Now I am bitter and will, in all honesty, probably become more and more bitter as the years pass until I am released. If a maximum serve-out should occur in my case and I were then to be released, I expect to become transformed into a "sub-human." No longer would I care about my life or the lives of others around me. Laws will have no importance to me at all. The only thing that I would have is the instinct to survive—survival the only way I could.

Twenty years later, Cal chose not to discuss his feelings about his incarceration. His self-predictions were written after he had been incarcerated only five years. I am told now that each day he goes to work, returns to his cell, and talks to few people. He received a twenty-year deferment the only time he saw the parole board. His maximum serve-out ends in 2022, when he will reenter the community after being imprisoned for thirty-three years.

Grant

My hope for the future is helping other inmates and for Heaven. One day I will die and be free. Be grateful that you are not me. I have no one and with that, nothing really matters any more. I'm through trying.

Grant was finally released as a persistent felon after a stint of thirty-seven years in prison for assault charges. His fellow inmates wish him well and believe he should have been released long ago, but they are concerned about the level of anger that occasionally builds to an explosive level. Nine months into freedom, Grant seems to be thriving and is finding the peace he yearned for. Recently, while giving a talk at a local high school about drug abuse, he was asked some personal questions, which led to his realization that the inquisitive student was his grandson, whom he had never seen. There was not a dry eye in the room. Grant is starting over at age sixty-eight, aided by a significant but unexpected financial boost.

Cam

I don't see it being even remotely possible for me to fully and truly be happy, or even content, unless I am released. I've been through a 120-month setback and a mutual yet painful divorce, so I guess a certain amount of sadness and depression is warranted. But, as always, I'll wake up. I'll get up, and I'll continue to put one foot in front of the other. I've never been one for self-pity. These feelings, this personal agony, is a detrimental waste of time and energy. I'm still full of hope. I have much potential, many goals, and am very determined. I have such a drive. I just can't put it into "D" (drive). Not yet anyhow.

Cam has a life sentence and has been in prison for twenty-four years. He is forty-four years old and is not eligible again for parole for another six years. He struggles much to stay in touch with his better self and to stay on even footing, but it seems to be a continual internal fight.

Jack

Since becoming a convicted felon, it has changed my conception of who I am. Going through life (after prison) with the stigma of being an "ex-con" has, in my opinion, greatly reduced my prospect for the future. I no longer think of things I could be as endless. Now I know and have to accept that there are going to be limits on my future. I honestly feel that my future looks pretty bleak, but I also know I have to contend with it the best way I can without regressing back to a criminal mode.

I feel the public should see me for exactly what I am, a human being who has messed up, but also who is trying to build a new future while taking the punishment the courts have handed down. That is all I would ever expect from the general public. Not sympathy, not pity, not hatred, not resentment. Just understanding.

Jack's statement was written twenty years ago. In the interim, Jack was released after a number of years of imprisonment. But he reoffended and is back with extra time for being a persistent felon. He is not eligible for parole again until 2023. When contacted, Jack wrote a very friendly, reminiscing letter saying he would be "delighted" to help with the current book project. After I questioned him about his reoffense, he did not write again. In the past, he struggled with depression covered by a humorous demeanor.

Duane

Looking back, what do I say about the years I spent incarcerated? How have I changed and what has that meant to me? Looking back, I wouldn't give the thirty years I was incarcerated back. It has taken those thirty years to make me who I am today. Entering into the Department of Corrections I was uneducated, unlearned, and irresponsible. The Lord used DOC to give me the necessary tools that I needed to succeed in society. During my incarceration, I obtained a GED, an AA degree, an AS degree, most of a hotel-and-restaurant degree, a certification in network cabling, a certification in Microsoft Office, and [completed] numerous self-help programs. I am very thankful and grateful for my schooling and programming, but the change that made the real impact in my life came from within and worked its way out. That change came in the form of Jesus Christ and Him crucified. What has that meant to me? What has a person gained if they gained the whole world and lose their soul?

Once a well-known leader of criminal activity on the yard, Duane's personal changes and religious conversion shocked everyone. He has recently been released after thirty-one years of incarceration, and his twenty-year prison marriage seems to be holding strong. He has a good job and is thriving.

Michael

It does seem like I've spent my whole life in prison, and for the most part, I have. I don't really know what went wrong for me. As I look back at my life, it feels so wasted, and now as I approach my fifty-seventh birthday, the only word that comes to mind to describe me now is "insubstantial." I don't have anything and don't feel like I mean much to anyone. And although I am sad and lonely most of the time, that doesn't mean much either, because it doesn't change a thing. The wasted life is still there and I still can't figure out why things went so wrong. I picked up a saying somewhere that describes how I feel most days: "My heart is heavy with all the work it takes to keep on breathing."

Michael served out his sentence some months ago. But he is struggling to find his way. He has reconnected with some family members, but their dysfunctional lives disturb him. One of the last times we talked, he dissolved in tears. For the moment, he is hanging on.

Lee

In 1995, they took me back up for parole after doing the three-year flop from 1992 and served me out on the life sentence, stating past felony convictions and seriousness of the crime, plus [they] said I killed the guy during a robbery, which I tried explaining I did not. I'm served-out till I die for a robbery I didn't commit.

Then in December of 2010, they told me I was being called up again for parole in January 2011. I had to send some paperwork home to be filled out. My mom and dad was really excited and so was I. My mom died that month and my father the month after. Then they came and told me they made a mistake and I wasn't going up for parole. At least my parents both died thinking I might get out soon. Since then, I haven't really cared too much for correctional staff.

Lee is serving out his days in the state's maximum-security institution. He shares little of his feeling or activities, but his anger at the system comes through clearly. He is fifty-nine and has spent at least forty years behind bars. The parole board declares he will die in prison.

Wayne

For myself as with the others, I may not want to admit it, but yes, when I first got locked up, I did think about ending it all. And I did think about escape a number of times. In order to do that much time, you more or less block out the outside world. You have to prepare yourself, and for some unknown reason, we all keep going.

Wayne left prison a year ago, having served the full thirty-three years of his sentence. He went home to live with his parents. No one has heard from him since.

Stuart

I want to talk about my surrender to God and prison. God delivered me from all evil thoughts. What's left was the peace, which turned to joy. I was amazed at how many of Satan's acts I thought are normal. My job now is to keep the peace in my strife-filled world.

Stuart's rapidly progressing Huntington's disease affected both his body and mind and made communication and life in prison very difficult. This is from the last letter he was able to write. He was scheduled to see the parole board in 2023, but he knew he would not live that long. His request for medical release was denied. Stuart recently died alone in an area hospital in January, 2017. He is buired in Chicken Hill on prison property. He was sixty-six years old.

Wesley

I never expected to do this much time. I have served over twenty-three years since 1986, and it all started with a six-year sentence. I think I have served enough time and I am ready for a change. I can remember sitting in a cell when the reality hit me. I realized to what extent everybody really cared about me. I knew that if I died, that probably nobody would even come to claim my body, and I would be buried in a cardboard box at Chicken Hill. To realize that no one really cares about you, this is a feeling, well, it probably couldn't get much lower.

Wesley has been in and out of prison for years, mostly on drug-related charges. He has never managed to stay free longer than fifteen months. Once again released, he has just passed that milestone and seems on the right path. He is sober, has a cozy little apartment, and is receiving private counseling and partial disability. He says he is happier than he's ever been. Time will tell.

Issues to Think About

1. Do you agree with the author that the development of personal views and future conversations about correctional policies are the responsibility of individuals in our society? In what way are individual citizens responsible for today's correctional policies and those in the future?
2. Have your own views and positions changed since reading and thinking about the issue of imprisonment? In what way? Will you take any action as a consequence of reading this book?
3. Do you have further questions about long-term incarceration you would like to discuss?

Glossary of
Prison Terminology

accreditation—The American Correctional Association has established a standard of proper procedures and expectations at every level of function within the correctional community. Institutions choosing to participate are visited on a regular basis and administrations work hard to maintain the valued accreditation.

behind the fence—Refers to medium- or maximum-security institutions where inmates are not allowed unfettered physical access to areas outside the fence that encompasses the prison.

black box—A plastic or metal box placed over attached handcuffs, which is then anchored to the body with a chain, holding the prisoner's hands in an unmovable position. The black box is an additional line of security used when transporting prisoners to public places.

canteen—The store within the institution where inmates can purchase items from necessities to luxuries. Everything from stamps to hygiene items to snacks to shoes can be bought in a canteen. Items ordered from outside vendors often go through the canteen provider. Millions of dollars in canteen profits come into the institutions each year. Many of the items that the public objects to paying for with tax money are provided by the canteen profit. Cable TV, recreational supplies, and some educational programs are purchased from the canteen fund. In some states, the profits go into the general correctional fund.

classification—Upon entering the prison system, inmates are assigned a security level that determines the type of facility to which they will be assigned—maximum, medium, minimum, or community. While the seriousness of the crime is considered in the classification, more attention is given to the potential for escape and the risk the inmate presents to others in prison. See *security levels.*

community TV—In most prison dormitories, there is a central TV in the dayroom or other community area. It is often the source of conflict—even violence—when men disagree on what to watch.

contraband—Prohibited items brought into the prison compound. Contraband includes anything that is against the rules of the institution, such as cell phones, penknives, cigarettes, chewing gum, scissors and, of course, drugs.

dayroom—The part of the dormitory (cell block) that is designed as a common area. There men can sit outside their cells, visit with one another, and play board games, cards, or dominos. Often when prisons are overcrowded, the dayrooms are taken over and filled with lines of bunk beds; it is the most dreaded living assignment.

deferment—Informally referred to as a *flop* or *setback* by the inmates, a deferment is the amount of additional time the parole board determines the prisoner must serve before again being considered for parole. For example, "He got a sixty-month deferment."

double-bunked—Double-bunking usually means that the cell is holding twice the number of men it was originally designed for. The bottom bunk is preferred, and tensions can arise over bed assignments.

fish—The term given to new inmates and officers being introduced to prison for the first time. If there is a special area designated for newcomers, it may be referred to as the *fish tank*.

flop—See *deferment*.

good time—This is time taken off a sentence as an incentive for desired behavior. For example, depending on the state, a sentence might be reduced a day for every two days of good behavior. Ninety days of good time might be given for completing an educational degree. This is referred to as statutory, meritorious, or educational good time. Equivalent terms differ between states.

grievances—When inmates feel they are being treated unfairly or illegally, they can file a formal grievance. There are assigned trained inmate grievance counselors whose job it is to help them develop and present their case. The grievances are heard in front of a committee consisting of institutional employees. Examples of legitimate grievances include use of racial language by officers, personal harassment by staff, and employment of rules that are unequal or unfair.

hole—See *segregation*.

honor dorms—Dormitories or cell blocks that are reserved for the best-behaved inmates. Usually honor dorms allow extra amenities and are used to encourage good behavior and positive participation in work and school.

hooch—A homemade alcoholic beverage. In prison, it is made by fermenting fruit and sugar in hidden containers.

hygiene—The term inmates give to toiletry items such as soap, deodorant, shampoo, toothbrush, and toothpaste.

loan-sharking—Lending money or its prison equivalent at a very high rate of interest. When the inmate (usually young) cannot pay it back on time, he can be drawn into unwanted sexual activities, involvement in drug transfers, and other illegal activities on the yard. His family may receive threats that he will be harmed if they don't pay the debt with interest.

lockdown—A time when no free or unescorted movement from one place to another is allowed. Men are confined to their cells or bed spaces. Lockdowns occur for a variety of reasons, most often related to security.

medical—The medical facility's location as well as the system for medical and dental care of the inmates. For example, "I put in a request to go to medical" or "Medical said you don't need anything now."

on the street—Life outside of the prison environment.

parlay—An illegal betting business within prison. Bets can be taken on just about anything, but sports activities dominate. The inmate who runs parlay is equivalent to a bookie.

parole—In most states, inmates are eligible for release after serving a specified percentage of their sentence. The determination of their release at that time is usually up to a parole board and is decided at a parole hearing. The procedures can differ from state to state. If inmates are released before their sentences are completed, they are placed on parole—official supervision in the community. The federal system does not parole people early.

parole board—Although the procedures differ between states, most states have a parole board system. A group of individuals, usually appointed by the governor, control the decisions made in the state about each inmate's possible parole (release). In some states, the parole board is part of the Department of Corrections. In most cases, it is independent from Corrections and falls under the governor's office or a related cabinet. Board positions are usually paid, full-time positions, but not always.

PFO (persistent felony offender)—If an offender is arrested and has a prior felony conviction, extra prison time is added to his new offense because he is a PFO.

prison industrial complex—The complex interrelationships between government, industry, and politics as they relate to the increasing levels of incarceration in America. Some people believe that the burgeoning prison population is related more to economic and political benefits than it is to a need to control crime.

razor wire—The distinctive circles of barbed wire topping heavy chain-link fences or exterior walls, which are a distinguishing characteristic of a correctional facility. The barbs are large metal pieces, pointed at each end and sharpened to razor-fineness. With hundreds of razor-sharp barbs topping the perimeter wall, escape is greatly hindered.

reclassification—At any point in an inmate's incarceration, especially during times of misbehavior such as escape, drug dealing, or severe fights, his security level can be reevaluated. A reclassification can cause a move to a more secure institution. Conversely, depending on the nature of his original crime, the inmate may, with good behavior, receive a lower classification and be moved to a minimum-security institution. See *classification* and *security levels*.

R&D (Receiving and Delivery)—The area where inmates are transferred into and out of the institution. There is a sally port for vehicles at this entrance, adding another level of security.

risk assessment rating—In many states, inmates undergo an assessment process using objective criteria to determine their potential risk of offending again. Considerations include age, seriousness and type of crime, programs completed, institutional adjustment, educational level, etc. The assessment may be used in institutional placement and parole considerations.

sally port—A secure entryway separating the inmates from the outside world. It is usually composed of two moving doors or gates and is located well within the administrative area of the prison where employees and visitors have already gone through security measures. Similar to an elevator that opens front and back, a person walks through one gate or door that closes behind them. Only when it is securely closed does the second door open into the area of the yard.

security levels—The main security levels are *maximum, medium,* and *minimum.* Some states also have the equivalent of *community custody.* Inmates are assigned to a custody level depending on their perceived threat and ability to cooperate within the institution. The levels are not determined primarily by the crime, but by the adjustment of the inmate. However, most criminals with violent offenses are required to be kept in *medium-* or *maximum-*security institutions. Most *minimum-*security prisoners are not locked in a facility but must remain on the grounds unless escorted for work details. They remain at the correctional facility on their own volition although they are subject to regular head counts and prison restrictions. The nature of *community custody* differs between states, but at that level, the inmate is still incarcerated but has controlled freedom to leave the facility unescorted for work, school, and other approved activities.

segregation—*Segregation or the hole* is a prison within a prison. It is where inmates are sent for punishment for infractions, kept when they are out of control, or where some inmates request to be for protection when they feel threatened on the yard.

serve-out—Most states have the option of paroling a prisoner before the entire sentence is served, and having him or her supervised in the community. However, the parole board can decide that the entire sentence must be served out within the institution. When the inmate is released on a serve-out, he has no further obligation to the justice system. Serve-outs are controversial when they are applied to sentences of extreme length or to sentences of life with possibility of parole. In such cases, a serve-out decision essentially changes the court's sentence to life without parole, ensuring the inmate will never be released.

setback—See *deferment.*

shank—Homemade, illegal knife.

state pay—Most states pay inmates a very small stipend for their regular labor within the institution. It is minimal, around eighteen to twenty dollars a month. Inmates working in Prison or Correctional Industries may receive higher wages—approximately two dollars an hour. The wages differ between states.

store—As part of the underground prison economy, an inmate might establish his own store, selling items at greatly increased prices. Payment is made with stamps or other store items. With help of outside contacts, his profits are eventually turned into cash, which goes into the man's account in or out of the institution.

victim impact statement or hearing—In most states, the victims or their families and other interested parties are allowed to submit letters opposing the parole of the perpetrator. In most states, they are allowed to meet privately before the board hearing to personally recount the impact of the crime on their lives.

weight piles—The part of the recreational area that contains the weights for physical strength training. In many institutions, it is located outside under a covered pavilion.

write-ups—Discipline within the institution is managed through the system of write-ups, which are reports on the observed infraction of rules. Write-ups can be done on inmates by staff, and on staff by staff. The reports are taken to a committee, where they are handled in a formal manner during an administrative hearing. A variety of resolutions are possible, from segregation of the inmate to restrictions on visits, etc. In case of staff, write-ups can result in demotions, undesired assignments, termination, or other punishments.

yard—The yard is the entirety of the prison encompassed within the perimeter fences. It does not include the administration building. The yard includes all the areas accessible to the inmates where they live, work, study, and relax. The term encompasses buildings, as well as open spaces. The yard is entered through high-security gates, including sally ports, that ensure the complex can be closed down and the inmates secured.

Chapter Notes

Preface

1. In most states, the Department of Corrections is a large bureaucratic structure placed under the jurisdiction of the governor. The corrections' commissioner and other top administrators are located in the state's central office. Each individual prison is headed by a warden and various deputy wardens. Below them in each institution are multiple layers of officers—captains, lieutenants, etc., on down.

Introduction

1. Adam Liptak, "Inmate Count in U.S. Dwarfs Other Nations," *New York Times*, April 23, 2008, http://www.nytimes.com/2008/04/23/us/23prison.html.

2. Pamela Engel, "America is Sentencing Way Too Many People to Die in Prison," Business Insider website, September 19, 2013, http://www.businessinsider.com/more-prisoners-are-serving-life-sentences-despite-crime-decrease-2013-9.

3. American Civil Liberties Union, "End Juvenile Life without Parole," accessed May 24, 2016, https://www.aclu.org/end-juvenile-life-without-parole.

4. Melissa S. Kearney, Benjamin H. Harris, Elisa Jácome, and Lucie Parker, "Ten Economic Facts about Crime and Incarceration in the United States," Hamilton Project, Brookings Institution, May 1, 2014, http://www.brookings.edu/research/reports/2014/05/10-crime-facts.

Chapter One

1. Raca: A derogatory Aramaic word from Matthew 5:22 meaning vain, useless, empty.

Chapter Two

1. Norman Edwards is a pseudonym.

2. Most released sexual offenders are hindered by draconian limitations on their living and working conditions. In most states, regardless of the nature of their offense, they must live a certain distance from schools, day care centers, etc. In some places, they are forbidden to even drive by a school. The rules, which disregard the type of sexual offense, make successful reentry for sex offenders extraordinarily difficult.

3. "Stanford Prison Experiment: A Simulation Study on the Psychology of Imprisonment," Prison Experiment website, n.d., www.prisonexp.org.

Chapter Three

1. Wayne E. Wener, *The Environmental Psychology of Prisons and Jail: Creating Humane Spaces in Secure Settings* (Cambridge: Cambridge University Press, 2014).

Chapter Four

1. This warden was replaced before the printing of this book. Relative calm has settled back over the institution.

2. "Public Law 108–79: Prison Rape Elimination Act of 2003" (Washington, D.C.: U.S. Government Publishing Office, 2003).

3. The American Correctional Association offers an accreditation for correctional institutions, encouraging institutions to follow designated standards. Not all states choose to participate in the accreditation process,

which costs the states money. Someone on an accreditation committee explained that much help is given to the participating institutions to ensure they pass the inspection.

4. Lois M. Davis, Jennifer L. Steele, Robert Bozick, Malcolm Williams, Susan Turner, Jeremy N. V. Miles, Jessica Saunders, and Paul S. Steinberg, "How Effective Is Correctional Education, and Where Do We Go from Here? The Results of a Comprehensive Evaluation" (Santa Monica: RAND Corporation, 2014), http://www.rand.org/pubs/research_reports/RR564.html.

Chapter Seven

1. Catherine Wolf Harlow, "Prior Abuse Reported by Inmates and Probationers," NCJ 172879 (Washington, D.C: U.S. Department of Justice, Office of Justice Programs, April 1999), http://www.bjs.go.v/index.cfm?ty=pbdetail&iid=837.

2. R. Douglas Fields, "The Explosive Mix of Sex and Violence," *Psychology Today,* January 26, 2016, www.PsychologyToday.com/blog/the-new-brain/201601/the explosive-mix-sex-and-violence.

3. Tom Birch, "Justice Study: Prior Abuse Reported by Inmates," National CASA Association website, posted 1999, accessed May 27, 2016, http://www.casaforchildren.org/site/pp.aspx?c=mtJSJ7MPIsE&b=5525017&printmode=1.

Chapter Eight

1. David Patrick Connor and Wayne Tewksbury, "Prison Inmates and Their Visitors: An Examination of Inmate Characteristics and Visitor Types," *Prison Journal* 95 (June 2015): 159–177.

2. For a firsthand description of the black box, see Ray Ho, "What Does It Feel Like to be Handcuffed for a Full Day?" Quora website, November 17, 2013, https://www.quora.com/profile/Ray-Ho-8/Posts/The-Last-Mile-What-does-it-feel-like-to-be-handcuffed-for-a-full-day.

Chapter Nine

1. Stephanie Slifer, "Once a Criminal, Always a Criminal?" CBS News website, April

23, 2014, http://www.cbsnews.com/news/once-a-criminal-always-a-criminal/.

2. National Council on Alcoholism and Drug Dependence, Inc., "Alcohol, Drugs, and Crime," NCADD website, June 27, 2015, https://www.ncadd.org/about-addiction/alcohol-drugs-and-crime.

3. Rachelle Giguere and Kurt Bumby, "Female Sex Offenders," Center for Sex Offender Management: A Project of the Office of Justice Programs, U.S. Department of Justice, March 2007, http://www.csom.org/pubs/female_sex_offenders_brief.pdf.

Chapter Ten

1. Gaye Holman, excerpt from "From the Depths," which appeared in *Motif 4: Seeking Its Own Level,* ed. Denton Loving (Louisville: MotesBooks, 2014), 58. Minor edits have been made.

2. Byron R. Johnson, David B. Larson, and Timothy C. Pitts, "Religious Programs, Institutional Adjustment, and Recidivism among Former Inmates in Prison Fellowship Programs," *Justice Quarterly* 14, no. 1 (March 1997). An unpublished survey from Kentucky's largest prison, Kentucky State Reformatory, resulted in identical findings, 2015.

3. *Ibid.*

4. U.S. Department of Justice, *Inmate Religious Beliefs and Practices,* No. T5360.01 (Washington, D.C.: Federal Bureau of Prisons, 2002).

5. Pew Research Center, "Religion in Prisons: A 50-State Survey of Prison Chaplains," Pew Research Center website, March 22, 2012, www.pewforum.org/2912/03/22/prison-chaplains-exec/.

6. *Ibid.*

7. *Ibid.*

8. *Ibid.*

9. *Ibid.*

Chapter Eleven

1. This discussion is limited to those under state jurisdictions. The federal prison system does not offer parole.

2. SBB stands for Shakespeare Behind Bars, a Shakespeare-based treatment program that has been life changing for most of its participants. Doug received national recognition for his talents and insights when

an award-winning documentary was made of their program at Luther Luckett Correctional Complex.

3. Alexia Cooper, Matthew P. Durose, and Howard N. Snyder, "Recidivism of Prisoners Released in Thirty States in 2005: Patterns from 2005 to 2010," Bureau of Justice Statistics, April 22, 2014, http://www.bjs.gov/index.cfm?ty=pbdetail&iid=4986.

Chapter Twelve

1. Kevin Johnson, "Quashed Report Warned of Prison Health Crisis," *USA Today*, May 19, 2016.

2. National Academy of Public Administration, "Public Health and Corrections: An Intergovernmental Perspective and the Need for Connectivity" (Washington, D.C.: National Academy of Public Administration, January 2006).

3. The viewing of Internet child pornography is now more easily tracked and aggressively prosecuted, whereas it went undetected in the years when pornography was in print form. Also in recent years, there has been an increase in the reporting and conviction of child molestation.

4. Margaret E. Noonan and E. Ann Carson, "Prison and Jail Deaths in Custody, 2000–2009 Statistical Tables" (Washington, D.C.: U.S. Department of Justice, Bureau of Justice Statistics, December 2011), NCJ236219.

5. *Ibid.*

6. In this one instance, I did not change the inmate's name. There is no one alive who would read the piece and be damaged by it. The account serves as a eulogy for Jerry Lakes.

Chapter Thirteen

1. Bob may purport to be the one exception, but his significant other married another person during his incarcerated years, later divorced, and their relationship remained on and off for years. But still, he said she offered him hope and stability, especially in the latter part of his sentence.

2. Eric Westervelt, "Measuring the Power of a Prison Education," nprEd, July 31, 2015, http://www.npr.org/sections/ed/2015/07/31/427741914/measuring-the-power-of-a-prison-education.

3. Wally Lamb, *Couldn't Keep it to Myself: Wally Lamb and the Women of York Correctional Institution* (New York: Regan Books, 2003) and *I'll Fly Away: Further Testimonies from the Women of York Prison* (New York: Harper-Collins, 2009).

4. Nancy Mullane, *Life after Murder: Five Men in Search of Redemption* (New York: Public Affairs-Perseus Book Group, 2012).

5. The prayer was written by Reinhold Niebuhr for a sermon in the 1930s and was later adopted by Alcoholics Anonymous as the Serenity Prayer.

6. For further discussion, see the Center for Justice and Reconciliation website, http://restorativejustice.org/.

Conclusion

1. Psalms 142:1–7 (English Standard Version).

Bibliography

In this book, I wanted to let the men who were or still are incarcerated tell their own stories. I've frequently quoted their words, both from personal conversations and written correspondence. I also conducted interviews with many of the inmates, as well as prison staff and administrators. To ensure confidentiality, I am not listing the interviews in the bibliography.

I drew upon a number of other sources as well. Many of the following sources are cited in the notes. Others provided background or otherwise informed the writing of this book.

Adler, Jerry. "The Great Escape: Prison Reform Activist Max Kenner Champions the Transformative Power of College Degree Programs for Inmates Nationwide." *Smithsonian*, November 2014.

Alper, Mariel, Ebony Ruhland, and Edward Rhine. "Decreasing Organizational Autonomy of Paroling Authorities." University of Minnesota, Robina Institute of Criminal Law and Criminal Justice, December 7, 2015. http://robinainstitute.umn.edu/ publications/data-brief-decreasing-organizational-autonomy-paroling-authorities.

American Civil Liberties Union. "End Juvenile Life without Parole." ACLU website. Accessed May 24, 2016. https://www.aclu.org/end-juvenile-life-without-parole.

Austin, James, and Michael Jacobson. "How New York City Reduced Mass Incarceration: A Model for Change?" New York: Vera Institute of Justice, 2012. http://www. brennancenter.org/publication/how-new-york-city-reduced-mass-incarceration-model-change.

Beam, Adam. "Ky. Prison-food Contract Up for Bid." *Louisville Courier-Journal*, July 5, 2014.

Birch, Tom. "Justice Study: Prior Abuse Reported by Inmates." National CASA Association website. April 1999. http://www.casaforchildren.org/site/pp.aspx?c=mtJSJ7MPIsE&b= 5525017&printmode=1.

Bosworth, Mary, and Carolyn Hoyle, eds. *What Is Criminology?* Oxford: Oxford University Press, 2012.

Caumont, Andrea. "Chart of the Week: The Problem of Prison Overcrowding." Pew Research Center website. August 2, 2013. http://www.pewresearch.org/fact-tank/ 2013/08/02/chart-of-the-week-the-problem-of-prison-overcrowding/.

CBS News. "The Cost of a Nation of Incarceration." CBS News website. April 23, 2012. http://www.cbsnews.com/videos/the-incarceration-nation/.

Center for Justice and Reconciliation website, http://restorativejustice.org/.

_____. "Myths and Facts about Sex Offenders." Center for Sex Offender Management website. August 2000. http://www.csom.org/pubs/mythsfacts.html.

Clay, Nolan. "Oklahoma Parole Board Members Charged with Misdemeanors." *Oklahoma City Oklahoman*, March 13, 2013. http://newsok.com/article/3765466.

Connor, David Patrick, and Wayne Tewksbury. "Prison Inmates and Their Visitors: An Examination of Inmate Characteristics and Visitor Types." *Prison Journal* 95 (June 2015): 159–177.

Cooper, Alexia, Matthew P. Durose, and Howard N. Snyder. "Recidivism of Prisoners Released in Thirty States in 2005: Patterns from 2005 to 2010." Bureau of Justice Statistics website. April 22, 2014. http://www.bjs.gov/index.cfm?ty=pbdetail&iid=4986.

Dammer, Harry R. "Religion in Prison." In *Encyclopedia of Crime and Punishment*, edited by David Levinson. Thousand Oaks: Sage Publications, 2002.

Davis, Lois M., Jennifer L. Steele, Robert Bozick, Malcolm Williams, Susan Turner, Jeremy N. V. Miles, Jessica Saunders, and Paul S. Steinberg. "How Effective Is Correctional Education, and Where Do We Go from Here? The Results of a Comprehensive Evaluation." Santa Monica: RAND Corporation, 2014. http://www.rand.org/pubs/research_reports/RR564.html.

Desilver, Drew. "Feds May Be Rethinking the Drug War, but States Have Been Leading the Way." Pew Research Center website. April 2, 2014. http://www.pewresearch.org/fact-tank/2014/04/02/feds-may-be-rethinking-the-drug-war-but-states-have-been-leading-the-way/.

Drake, Bruce. "Incarceration Gap Widens Between Whites and Blacks." Pew Research Center website. September 6, 2013. http://www.pewresearch.org/fact-tank/2013/09/06/incarceration-gap-between-whites-and-blacks-widens/.

Engel, Pamela. "America is Sentencing Way Too Many People to Die in Prison." Business Insider website. September 19, 2013. http://www.businessinsider.com/more-prisoners-are-serving-life-sentences-despite-crime-decrease-2013–9.

Fields, R. Douglas. "The Explosive Mix of Sex and Violence." *Psychology Today*, January 26, 2016. www.PsychologyToday.com/blog/the-new-brain/201601/the explosive-mix-sex-and-violence.

First Amended Complaint Seeking Declaratory and Injunctive Relief. Inmates 1 through 23, in Their Individual Capacities and on Behalf of Others Similarly Situated v. the Kentucky Parole Board. Commonwealth of Kentucky, Franklin Circuit Court, 48th Judicial Circuit, Division 1, Civil Action No. 13-CI-021118.

Flatow, Nicole. "One in Nine US Prisoners Are Serving Life Sentences, Report Finds." *ThinkProgress* (blog). September 19, 2013. https://thinkprogress.org/one-in-nine-u-s-prisoners-are-serving-life-sentences-report-finds-56580fef5707#.gufmcimdv.

Giguere, Rachelle, and Kurt Bumby. "Female Sex Offenders." Center for Sex Offender Management: A Project of the Office of Justice Programs, US Department of Justice. March 2007. http://www.csom.org/pubs/female_sex_offenders_brief.pdf.

Goffman, Alice. *On the Run: Fugitive Life in an American City*. Chicago: University of Chicago Press, 2014.

Ho, Ray. "The Last Mile: What Does It Feel Like to be Handcuffed for a Full Day?" Quora website. November 17, 2013. https://www.quora.com/profile/Ray-Ho-8/Posts/The-Last-Mile-What-does-it-feel-like-to-be-handcuffed-for-a-full-day.

Holman, Gaye. Excerpt from "From the Depths." In *Motif 4: Seeking Its Own Level*, edited by Denton Loving. Louisville: MotesBooks, 2014.

Johnson, Alan. "Prison Health Care Costs on the Decline." *Columbus* (Ohio) *Dispatch*, July 26, 2014.

Johnson, Byron R., David B. Larson, and Timothy C. Pitts. "Religious Programs, Institutional Adjustment, and Recidivism among Former Inmates in Prison Fellowship Programs." *Justice Quarterly* 14, no. 1 (March 1997).

Johnson, Kevin. "Quashed Report Warned of Prison Health Crisis." *USA Today,* May 19, 2016.

Kearney, Melissa S., Benjamin H. Harris, Elisa Jácome, and Lucie Parker. "Ten Economic Facts about Crime and Incarceration in the United States." Hamilton Project, Brookings Institution. 2014. https://www.brookings.edu/research/ten-economic-facts-about-crime-and-incarceration-in-the-united-states/.

Kentucky Justice and Public Safety Cabinet, Criminal Justice Council. "2014 HB 463 Implementation Report." Kentucky Justice and Public Safety Cabinet website. October 2014. http://justice.ky.gov/Documents/Statistical%20Analysis/2014%20CJC%20Report.pdf.

Kentucky Parole Board. "Report FY 2013–14." Kentucky Justice and Public Safety Cabinet website, n.d. http://justice.ky.gov/Documents/Parole%20Board/Reports/FY13–14.pdf.

Kinnevy, Susan C., and Joel M. Caplan. "Findings from the APAI International Survey of Releasing Authorities." Center for Research on Youth and Social Policy. April 2008. http://www.apaintl.org/resources/documents/surveys/2008.pdf.

Lamb, Wally. *Couldn't Keep It to Myself: Wally Lamb and the Women of York Correctional Institution.* New York: Regan Books, 2003.

_____. *I'll Fly Away: Further Testimonies from the Women of York Prison.* New York: HarperCollins, 2009.

Larson, Jon. "Lawyer Outraged over Veteran's Harsh Treatment." *Louisville Courier-Journal,* February 12, 2015. http://www.courier-journal.com/story/opinion/2015/02/12/outraged-veterans-case/23309319/.

Libaw, Oliver Yates. "Incarceration Rate, Crime Drop Link Disputed." ABC News website. September 28 [no year]. http://abcnews.go.com/US/story?id=95580&page=1.

Liptak, Adam. "Inmate Count in US Dwarfs Other Nations." *New York Times,* April 23, 2008. http://www.nytimes.com/2008/04/23/us/23prison.html.

Mauer, Marc, and Tracy Huling. "Young Black Americans and the Criminal Justice System: Five Years Later." The Sentencing Project website. October 1995. http://www.sentencingproject.org/wp-content/uploads/2016/01/Young-Black-Americans-and-the-Criminal-Justice-System-Five-Years-Later.pdf.

Mullane, Nancy. *Life after Murder: Five Men in Search of Redemption.* New York: Public Affairs-Perseus Book Group, 2012.

National Academy of Public Administration. "Public Health and Corrections: An Intergovernmental Perspective and the Need for Connectivity." Washington, D.C.: National Academy of Public Administration, January 2006.

National Council on Alcoholism and Drug Dependence, Inc. "Alcohol, Drugs, and Crime." NCADD website. June 27, 2015. https://www.ncadd.org/about-addiction/alcohol-drugs-and-crime.

Noonan, Margaret E., and E. Ann Carson. "Prison and Jail Deaths in Custody, 2000–2009 Statistical Tables." US Department of Justice, Bureau of Justice Statistics. December 2011. NCJ236219.

Pew Charitable Trusts. "Kentucky: A Data-Driven Effort to Protect Public Safety and Control Corrections Spending." Pew Center on the States website. October 2010. http://www.pewtrusts.org/en/research-and-analysis/reports/0001/01/01/kentucky-a-datadriven-effort-to-protect-public-safety-and-control-corrections-spending.

_____. "Prison and Crime: A Complex Link." Pew Charitable Trusts website. September 2014. http://www.pewtrusts.org/en/multimedia/data-visualizations/2014/prison-and-crime.

_____. "Time Served in Kentucky, State Fact Sheet." Pew Charitable Trusts website. June 6, 2012. http://www.pewtrusts.org/en/research-and-analysis/fact-sheets/2012/06/06/time-served-in-kentucky.

_____. "Time Served: The High Cost, Low Return of Longer Prison Terms." Pew Charitable Trusts website. June 06, 2012. http://www.pewtrusts.org/en/research-and-analysis/reports/2012/06/06/time-served-the-high-cost-low-return-of-longer-prison-terms.

Pew Research Center. "Religion in Prisons: A 50-State Survey of Prison Chaplains." Pew Research Center website. March 22, 2012. www.pewforum.org/2912/03/22/prison-chaplains-exec/.

Pilkington, Ed. "More Than 3,000 US Prisoners Locked Up for Life without Parole for Non-Violent Crimes. *Guardian US*, November 13, 2013. http://www.alternet.org/civil-liberties/more-3000-us-prisoners-locked-life-without-parole-non-violent-crimes.

"Prison Incarceration and Religious Preference." Adherents website. Last modified April 2007. http://www.adherents.com/misc/adh_prison.html.

Project Censored. "Number of US Prison Inmates Serving Life Sentences Hits New Record." Project Censored website. October 1, 2014. http://projectcensored.org/23-number-us-prison-inmates-serving-life-sentences-hits-new-record/.

"Public Law 108–79: Prison Rape Elimination Act of 2003." Washington, D.C.: US Government Publishing Office, 2003. https://www.gpo.gov/fdsys/pkg/PLAW-108publ79/pdf/PLAW-108publ79.pdf.

Riley, Jason. "After 54 Years, Kentucky's Longest Serving Inmate Has Chance for Release." WDRB website. July 14, 2014. http://www.wdrb.com/story/25999947/sunday-edition-after-54-years-kentuckys-longest-serving-inmate-has-chance-for-release.

Robbins, Tom. "A Brutal Beating Wakes Attica's Ghosts." *New York Times*, March 1, 2015.

Saltzman, Jonathan. "Patrick Overhauls Parole: 5 on Board Depart as Report Faults Freeing of Criminal." *Boston Globe*, January 14, 2011. http://archive.boston.com/news/politics/articles/2011/01/14/five_out_as_governor_overhauls_parole_board/?page=2.

The Sentencing Project. "Facts about Prisons and People in Prison." The Sentencing Project website. January 2014. http://sentencingproject.org/wp-content/uploads/2015/12/Facts-About-Prisons.pdf.

_____. "Parents in Prison." The Sentencing Project website. September 2012. http://www.sentencingproject.org/wp-content/uploads/2016/01/Parents-in-Prison.pdf.

Slifer, Stephanie. "Once a Criminal, Always a Criminal?" CBS News website. April 23, 2014. http://www.cbsnews.com/news/once-a-criminal-always-a-criminal/.

"Stanford Prison Experiment: A Simulation Study on the Psychology of Imprisonment." Prison Experiment website, n.d. www.prisonexp.org.

U.S. Department of Justice. *Inmate Religious Beliefs and Practices*, No. T5360.01. Washington, D.C.: Federal Bureau of Prisons, 2002.

Watkins, Morgan. "Kentucky Ponders Use of Private Prisons." *Louisville Courier-Journal*, June 27, 2016. http://www.courier-journal.com/story/news/crime/2016/06/24/kentucky-ponders-use-private-prisons/86341304/.

Wener, Wayne E. *The Environmental Psychology of Prisons and Jail: Creating Humane Spaces in Secure Settings.* Cambridge: Cambridge University Press, 2014.

Westervelt, Eric. "Measuring the Power of a Prison Education" (interview with Lois Davis, senior policy researcher, RAND Corporation). Broadcast on nprEd, July 31, 2015. http://www.npr.org/sections/ed/2015/07/31/427741914/measuring-the-power-of-a-prison-education.

"Where We Were: Challenges Facing Kentucky. Public Safety and Offender Accountability Act (HB463) Justice Reinvestment Summary," n.d. http://www.ncsl.org/documents/nalfo/JusticeReinvestmentMikeMullins.pdf.

Wolf Harlow, Caroline. "Prior Abuse Reported by Inmates and Probationers." Bureau of Justice Statistics Selected Findings, NCJ 172879. April 1999. http://www.bjs.gov/index.cfm?ty=pbdetail&iid=837.

Wolfson, Andrew. "10 Years for 1 Pill." *Louisville Courier-Journal*, February 2, 2015.

Index